ROYAL HISTORICAL S

STUDIES IN HIST(

New Series

CREATING CAPITALISM

JOINT-STOCK ENTERPRISE
IN BRITISH POLITICS AND CULTURE
1800–1870

CREATING CAPITALISM

JOINT-STOCK ENTERPRISE
IN BRITISH POLITICS AND CULTURE
1800–1870

James Taylor

THE ROYAL HISTORICAL SOCIETY
THE BOYDELL PRESS

First published 2006
The Royal Historical Society, London
in association with
The Boydell Press, Woodbridge
Paperback edition 2014

ISBN 978 0 86193 284 9 hardback
ISBN 978 0 86193 323 5 paperback

ISSN 0269-2244

A catalogue record for this book is available
from the British Library

This publication is printed on acid-free paper

Contents

List of Illustrations

List of Tables

To my parents

Publication of this volume was aided by a generous grant from the Scouloudi Foundation, in association with the Institute of Historical Research.

Acknowledgements

This book grew out of my research as a graduate student at the University of Kent. The work would not have been possible without postgraduate studentships from first the British Academy, then the Arts and Humanities Research Board. I also wish to thank the Economic History Society for awarding me the Tawney Postdoctoral Research Fellowship for 2002–3, during which time I began to mould my doctoral thesis into this book. This process was completed after I became a Research Associate at the University of Hull. My research has also been aided by grants from the Colyer-Fergusson Fund at the University of Kent and the Scouloudi Foundation.

I would like to thank my doctoral supervisor, Hugh Cunningham, first for encouraging me to return to academia, then for his excellent supervision during my time at Kent. I must also thank Anna Gambles, for an all-too-brief time my co-supervisor. The comments of my examiners, Martin Daunton and Grayson Ditchfield, proved invaluable in shaping the form this book has taken. Miles Taylor read the entire manuscript and made many useful suggestions, and I am also grateful for Christine Linehan's guidance. I wish to thank Neal Garnham, Julian Hoppit, Donna Loftus, Dilwyn Porter, Julie Rugg and Frank Trentmann for sharing their unpublished work with me. In addition, I am grateful to Malcolm Andrews, Mark Connelly, Mark Freeman, John Gardiner, Paddy Ireland, Paul Johnson, Michael Lobban, Robin Pearson and Jeffrey Richards for help at various stages. The staff of the History Office at the University of Kent, led by Jackie Waller, proved unfailingly efficient and helpful, while Anna Miller, of the Templeman Library, was ever happy to help track down elusive books and journals. I located several of the illustrations reproduced here in the Centre for the Study of Cartoons and Caricature at Kent.

On a more personal level, I must express my gratitude to my parents, Colin and Sylvia, my sister Rachel, and her partner Deke, for the enormous encouragement and support of every kind they have given me over the years.

James Taylor

Abbreviations

AYR	*All the Year Round*
BEM	*Blackwood's Edinburgh Magazine*
BH	*Business History*
BM	British Museum
BT	Board of Trade papers
EcHR	*Economic History Review*
EdR	*Edinburgh Review*
EHR	*English Historical Review*
ER	English Reports
FM	*Fraser's Magazine*
HW	*Household Words*
PP	Parliamentary papers
PRO	Public Record Office
QR	*Quarterly Review*
TB	*Temple Bar*
TD	*The Dickensian*
TNA	The National Archive
TRHS	*Transactions of the Royal Historical Society*
VS	*Victorian Studies*
WR	*Westminster Review*

Introduction

'[T]he story of the joint-stock company is too well known to require or to suffer any further explanation': M. M. Postan, 'Recent trends in the accumulation of capital', *EcHR* vi (1935), 1–12 at p. 6.

It might be considered unwise to begin a history of the joint-stock company with Michael Postan's dismissive remark. But this book has been written in the belief that there is much still to say on attitudes to joint-stock companies and the development of company law in nineteenth-century Britain. For historians of Postan's generation, the emergence of the joint-stock company in this period was a straightforward case of economic necessity. As industry expanded, more capital was needed, and the joint-stock form, which permitted the capitals of hundreds, or thousands, of investors to be pooled, was adopted as the most efficient means of meeting these needs. For a while the prejudices of an earlier age, symbolised by the notorious 'Bubble Act' of 1720, hampered this process by restricting company formation, but common sense eventually prevailed, with legislators recognising the economic benefits companies brought and, by 1856, removing all restrictions on access to corporate privileges, chief among them limited liability. Yet any reading which accepts what it seeks to explain as inevitable is going to have its limitations, and such is the case with this explanation, which, albeit in less crude form, has continued to influence interpretations of the emergence of joint-stock enterprise to this day.

The fall of the Communist bloc at the close of the twentieth century encouraged a short-lived period of triumphalism, with free market capitalism buttressed by liberal democracy hailed in some quarters as the end-point of history.[1] But both the subsequent emergence of powerful 'anti-globalisation' and 'anti-capitalist' movements, and the challenge posed to western culture by fundamentalist Islam, have cast some doubt on such pronouncements. Historians, too, have proved sceptical, and recent years have seen the publication of a series of works rejecting teleological accounts of the emergence of capitalist society. The landmarks of many earlier works – the rejection of moral economy in favour of the cash-nexus, the inevitable rise to dominance of the free trade, *laissez-faire* consensus – are replaced by a fundamental re-evaluation of the construction of British economic culture in the nineteenth century. For example, G. R. Searle's *Morality and the market in Victorian Britain* has sought to uncover a lost debate on the parameters of the market

---

[1] F. Fukuyama, *The end of history and the last man*, London 1992.

and the ethics of capitalism.[2] Victorians did not shed their moral beliefs in a rush to embrace the logic of the market; instead, they greeted the development of capitalism with considerably mixed feelings. Margot Finn's recent study of credit and debt rejects simplistic notions that the 'cash-nexus' was the typical mode of market exchange in the nineteenth century, instead highlighting the persistence of moral economies of mutual obligation in the Victorian market.[3] Our understanding of the significance of the conflict between protectionism and free trade has been enhanced by much recent research, most notably by Anna Gambles and Frank Trentmann. Gambles's *Protection and politics* has argued that the rise of free trade ideology was not irresistible and that there were valid alternative systems of political economy. Conservative support for protection, she asserts, was motivated not by naked self-interest, but by a coherent ideology which saw tariffs as an integral element of a strategy to promote sustainable growth, contain political upheaval and reduce social unrest.[4] Trentmann's work has been equally useful in breaking down the artificial boundaries between politics and economics sometimes erected by historians, by exploring the complex and nuanced political culture that developed out of the movement for free trade.[5] Politics and economics also blend in imaginative ways in Martin Daunton's two-volume study of taxation, which explores the financial relationship between the state and its citizens. Here, Daunton demonstrates how a policy of 'fiscal containment' engendered sufficient trust among the public to legitimise the tax system in particular and the British state in general.[6]

The emergence of joint-stock enterprise on a large scale in the nineteenth century also had significant implications for Britain's political economy, and there have been two recent book-length studies on different aspects of this phenomenon. Timothy L. Alborn's *Conceiving companies* treats joint-stock companies as political, not merely economic, entities, thus providing a new perspective on relationships between directors, shareholders and consumers, and between companies and the state, while Ron Harris's *Industrializing English law* examines the legal changes of the nineteenth century in the context of economic developments before 1800.[7] Although both advance

2 G. R. Searle, *Morality and the market in Victorian Britain*, Oxford 1998.
3 M. C. Finn, *The character of credit: personal debt in English culture, 1740–1914*, Cambridge 2003.
4 A. Gambles, *Protection and politics: Conservative economic discourse, 1815–1852*, Woodbridge 1999, and 'Rethinking the politics of protection: conservatism and the corn laws, 1830–1852', *EHR* cxiii (1998), 928–52.
5 F. Trentmann, 'Political culture and political economy: interest, ideology and free trade', *Review of International Political Economy* v (1998), 217–51, and 'National identity and consumer politics: free trade and tariff reform', in P. O'Brien and D. Winch (eds), *The political economy of British historical experience, 1688–1914*, Oxford 2002, 187–214.
6 M. Daunton, *Trusting leviathan: the politics of taxation in Britain, 1799–1914*, Cambridge 2001, and *Just taxes: the politics of taxation in Britain, 1914–1979*, Cambridge 2002.
7 T. L. Alborn, *Conceiving companies: joint-stock politics in Victorian England*, London 1998;

our understanding of the development of the joint-stock company, neither has successfully challenged the fundamental assumptions of the story which Postan took for granted in 1935. Harris, though protesting originality, in fact accepts many of the assumptions of the earlier historiography, while Alborn's monograph takes the existence of joint-stock enterprise as a given. In contrast, this study reproblematises the emergence of the joint-stock economy by engaging with nineteenth-century attitudes to commerce, central to which was the assumption that individual rather than corporate enterprise was the normal form of entrepreneurial activity. As well as examining the views of regulators, it ventures outside parliament and the courtroom to explore popular conceptions of economic activity as expressed in works of the imagination such as novels, plays, cartoons and verse, as well as pamphlets and periodicals. This approach uncovers a persistent and pervasive fear of and hostility to joint-stock enterprise which was by no means the preserve of a reactionary or self-interested few. It enables us to jettison simplistic notions of the inevitable rise of the company, thus opening up a fresh perspective on the creation of an entirely new body of company law in the nineteenth century. This legislation was not a pragmatic attempt to maximise economic efficiency, but an ideological intervention whose political, social, as well as economic causes must be explored. It is hoped that this book goes some way towards achieving this aim.

A brief history of incorporation

Of course, companies were not an invention of the nineteenth century. Since medieval times, the state had delegated corporate powers to favoured subjects for public purposes, usually religious, educational or municipal. The resulting corporations had an existence distinct from their members: they could sue and be sued in the courts, own property, and lived on after their founders had died. From the sixteenth century, corporate powers began to be extended to profit-making concerns. These were mostly overseas trading companies, which in addition to the privileges of incorporation, were also granted monopoly trading rights over specified areas to counter the significant risks they faced. The first was the Russia Company, chartered in 1555, and this was followed by several other important incorporations, such as the Levant Company (1581), the East India Company (1600), the Hudson's Bay Company (1670), the Royal Africa Company (1672), the South Sea Company (1711) and a host of other shorter-lived or smaller concerns.[8] The

R. Harris, *Industrializing English law: entrepreneurship and business organization, 1720–1844*, Cambridge 2000.

[8] Strictly speaking, there were differences in organisation between these companies, most notably between 'regulated' companies (which bore some resemblance to gilds) and 'joint-stock' companies, but also within the latter category, between those with *ad hoc*

creation of profit-making corporations with monopolies attracted controversy at an early stage: were these institutions really serving the public interest, or were they the by-product of cash-strapped monarchs selling privileges to the highest bidders? Such ambiguity meant that corporations could be portrayed as corrupt, monopolistic monsters, exempt from the laws of the land, posing a significant threat to the public interest.[9] Despite this, the seventeenth and eighteenth centuries saw increasing numbers of companies for domestic purposes incorporated, most notably the Bank of England, but also a number of smaller schemes, less obviously linked to the government, such as water companies, river navigations and canals.[10]

In all cases, while private profit was served, what justified the delegation of state powers were the public benefits resulting from incorporation. Thus, to be incorporated, businessmen had to prove that their projects were in the public interest. Before the Glorious Revolution, this involved an application to the crown; afterwards, parliament became the chief dispenser of corporate privileges. But in either case, applications were expensive, and depended on high-level backing for success. So desirable were the attributes of incorporation, however, that from the 1690s entrepreneurs who had failed, or were not inclined to try, to secure parliamentary favour, began to form large partnerships, or 'unincorporated companies', which sought to exploit trust law in order to imitate the characteristics of incorporated companies. An unincorporated group of individuals could not own property as a group, but property could be held in trust for it. This was achieved by means of mutual covenants between the shareholders of the company and the trustees selected by them. These were set out in a company's deed of settlement, and the trustees undertook to observe the terms of the deed and to use the company's funds only for the purposes specified.[11] The company was therefore enabled to act through its trustees rather than as a mass of individuals, approximating the corporation's ability to sue and be sued in its own name. Lawyers who drew up the deeds also attempted to make the company's shares freely transferable, and in some cases attempted to limit the liability of shareholders.[12] Initially, the state did not take steps against those who were usurping state authority in this way. William Scott suggested that this was because its attention was distracted by its foreign wars; Harris, that enforcement would have associated

capitals raised on a voyage-to-voyage basis, and those with a permanent joint stock. Individual companies sometimes switched between different types of legal framework. For more on this see Harris, *Industrializing English law*, ch. ii.

9   For more on antipathy to corporate monopolies see W. R. Scott, *The constitution and finance of English, Scottish and Irish joint-stock companies to 1720*, New York 1951, i, ch. vi.

10 For the development of the corporate economy to 1720 see ibid. For a useful shorter summary see Harris, *Industrializing English law*, ch. ii. For the eighteenth century see A. B. DuBois, *The English business company after the Bubble Act, 1720–1800*, New York 1971, and Harris, *Industrializing English law*, chs iv–vii.

11 C. A. Cooke, *Corporation, trust and company*, Manchester 1950, 86–7.

12 P. L. Cottrell, *Industrial finance, 1830–1914*, London 1980, 39–40.

the new administration with the behaviour of the absolutist Stuarts.[13] In any case, the situation did not seem to be pressing, for many of the unincorporated companies were ephemeral affairs, swept away in the crisis of 1696.[14] But when another, larger, wave of promotions appeared in the late 1710s, the response was firmer: the famous Bubble Act of 1720, passed at the height of the boom, declared illegal those 'dangerous and mischievous Undertakings' which 'presumed to act as if they were Corporate Bodies' without legal authority.[15] The act reasserted the state's monopoly on corporate privileges and denied that individuals could achieve any degree of incorporation without state authority. Yet, as is well known, the act was rarely invoked in the eighteenth century, partly because there was no repeat of the bubble promotions of the 1710s. However, a small number of unincorporated companies, most notably in the insurance sector, did establish themselves in the course of the century, seemingly able to operate profitably without state sanction.[16]

Perhaps unsurprisingly, there was a degree of ambivalence about what these entrepreneurs were doing. Were unincorporated companies manifestations of the voluntarist, associational culture which had been growing in England since the seventeenth century?[17] Or were they sinister replicas of the corrupt, monopolistic monsters created by the state? The companies did their best to play up their local origins: company seals and letterheads employed the official emblems and colours of the town or county in which they operated; shareholder meetings were held in municipal or gild halls, or local taverns; local magistrates and other notables sat on company boards; imposing company offices were built in the high street, reinforcing local identities.[18] Company spokesmen contrasted the 'virtual representation' by a 'natural aristocracy' which held sway in the chartered corporations with the direct democracy their constitutions offered, and described themselves as the 'representatives of the people'.[19] Yet it was not so easy for companies to shake

---

[13] Scott, *Joint-stock companies*, i. 337; Harris, *Industrializing English law*, 53.

[14] Harris, *Industrializing English law*, 57.

[15] Geo. I c. 18, s. 18. The act's full title was 'An Act for better securing certain Powers and Privileges, intended to be granted by His Majesty by Two Charters, for Assurance of Ships and Merchandize at Sea, and for lending Money upon Bottomry; and for restraining several extravagant and unwarrantable Practices therein mentioned'. The term 'Bubble Act' only became commonly used in the early nineteenth century when narratives of the 'South Sea Bubble' were widely circulated. For an account of the act's passage see Harris, *Industrializing English law*, ch. iii.

[16] R. Pearson, *Insuring the industrial revolution: fire insurance in Great Britain, 1700–1850*, Aldershot 2004.

[17] For more on this culture see P. Clark, *British clubs and societies, 1580–1800: the origins of an associational world*, Oxford 2002.

[18] R. Pearson, 'Shareholder democracies? English stock companies and the politics of corporate governance during the industrial revolution', *EHR* cxvii (2002), 840–66 at pp. 847–8; Daunton, *Trusting leviathan*, 266–8.

[19] Alborn, *Conceiving companies*, chs i, iv.

off associations with their controversial predecessors. Adam Smith was representative of thought in the eighteenth century when he argued that all joint-stock companies were inherently monopolistic, and should be confined only to trades with capital requirements beyond the scope of individuals, or in which the returns were too uncertain or too long-term to appeal to private traders.[20] Smith was also representative of Scottish thought: although some historians have argued that unincorporated companies in Scotland enjoyed a much more favourable legal climate than their English counterparts, these claims are exaggerated. Scottish companies which had not received state sanction faced similar legal difficulties to English companies: doubts as to the benefits of joint-stock enterprise were shared on both sides of the border.[21]

But it was only in the nineteenth century that these issues began to attract sustained attention: before then, the joint-stock economy was very small. William Maitland's *The history of London* recorded just twenty-six companies in operation in 1739.[22] Such numbers could not support a national market in company shares: indeed, the trade in the shares of many of these companies was restricted, with most investment being local rather than national. Company shares contributed little to the expansion of the stock market in the eighteenth century, which was driven by government stock.[23] The number of joint-stock companies whose shares were listed in the *Course of the Exchange* fell from seven in 1753 to six in 1775, and five in 1800.[24] But this changed in the new century, with dramatic booms in the numbers of both incorporated and unincorporated companies, one result of which was the contentious revival of the Bubble Act. At no point in these years did joint-stock enterprise dominate the economy in the way that it was to in the twentieth century; it has been estimated that even by 1885, at least 90 per cent of 'important business organisations', excluding one-man firms and public utilities, were partnerships.[25] Nevertheless, the multiplication of new joint-stock companies dazzled contemporaries, for it was unlike anything that had been witnessed before. New technologies, first gas, then steam, then electricity, prompted booms in company promotions, and seemingly broad-

---

20 See chapter 1 below.

21 The exception was in banking: while the Bank of England was the only joint-stock bank permitted in England until 1826, Scottish joint-stock banking had a much longer history. For more on the Scottish context see chapter 3 below.

22 Harris, *Industrializing English law*, 170–1.

23 P. Mirowski, 'The rise (and retreat) of a market: English joint-stock shares in the eighteenth century', *Journal of Economic History* xli (1981), 559–77; S. J. Hudson, 'Attitudes to investment risk amongst West Midland canal and railway company investors, 1760–1850', unpubl. PhD diss. Warwick 2001, ch. iii.

24 P. Ireland, 'Capitalism without the capitalist: the joint stock company share and the emergence of the modern doctrine of separate corporate personality', *Legal History* xvii (1996), 41–73 at p. 62.

25 Though, of course, companies held more than a 10% share of the economy: J. B. Jefferys, 'Trends in business organisation in Great Britain since 1856', unpubl. PhD diss. London 1938, 105.

ened the scope of legitimate joint-stock enterprise. In the first year of Victoria's reign, the lawyer Charles Wordsworth was struck by 'the tendency of society to form combinations'. His response was to produce the first handbook of company law.[26] The phenomenon left many other traces. The extensive reporting from the 1820s of share lists in daily newspapers paid testimony to the growing importance of the corporate economy, while the 1830s and 1840s saw the birth of a specialist railway press, dedicated to reporting the latest company information to the investing public. Certainly, railways were the most visible embodiment of joint-stock power, revolutionising communications for all classes and in the process bringing about what has justly been described as 'the most dramatic infringement of private property rights in England since the Civil War'.[27] '[T]he age of Victoria is an age of iron', trumpeted the *Westminster Review* in 1853.[28] But the railways were just one aspect of joint-stock enterprise to leave an impact on people's daily lives. In 1846 J. W. Gilbart, managing director of the London and Westminster Bank, proclaimed 'This is the age of public companies':

> We receive our education in schools and colleges founded by public companies. We commence active life by opening an account with a banking company. We insure our lives and our property with an insurance company. We avail ourselves of docks, and harbours, and bridges, and canals, constructed by public companies. One company paves our streets, another supplies us with water, and a third enlightens us with gas . . . And if we wish to travel, there are railway companies, and steam boat companies, and navigation companies, ready to whirl us to every part of the earth. And when, after all this turmoil, we arrive at our journey's end, cemetery companies wait to receive our remains, and take charge of our bones.[29]

But the growing numbers of companies created fears that individual enterprise, on which the nation's industrial supremacy had been built, was being sidelined. The nation's economic pre-eminence was held to derive from its exacting commercial standards. The law of partnership embodied the natural order, upheld the principle of personal responsibility and allowed free play to economic forces: companies acting under different laws undermined this system and represented an unnecessary and destructive interference with the providential dispensation. The untrammelled expansion of joint-stock enterprise would prove deleterious to these standards, while limited liability was looked upon as a dangerous, 'un-English' doctrine. Corporate privileges were properly controlled by the state, but aggressive businessmen were acting as if

---

[26] C. F. F. Wordsworth, *The law relating to railway, bank, insurance, mining, and other joint-stock companies*, London 1837, p. ix. The *Law Times* (6 Oct. 1849) commented that 'The Law of Joint-Stock Companies is the growth of our own times'.

[27] R. W. Kostal, *Law and English railway capitalism, 1825–1875*, Oxford 1994, 144.

[28] Anon., 'Partnership with limited liability', *WR* lx (Oct. 1853), 375–416 at p. 396.

[29] J. W. Gilbart, *The moral and religious duties of public companies*, 2nd edn, London 1856, 3–4.

they had an inherent right to these powers. Their activities jeopardised the legitimate activities of individual traders, and enticed people away from honest labour and into stock market speculations. At a time when municipal, charitable and ecclesiastical corporations were becoming increasingly controversial, the spread of joint-stock companies looked to some to be part of this broader corruption.[30] The economic, legal, political and moral issues were impossible to separate, and so pervasive were the fears raised by the rapid increase in joint-stock activity that criticism of this form of enterprise was not confined to the fringes of political economic debate. Opposition to joint-stock enterprise was widely diffused throughout society and could be found in liberal circles as much as conservative, and in the counting house as much as in the Commons.

Siding against history

The vibrancy and complexity of the debate on joint-stock enterprise is not reflected in the existing literature on the subject. This literature itself has a long history. Though the late nineteenth and early twentieth centuries saw occasional surveys of the history of joint-stock companies, the subject first attracted sustained attention in the 1930s, the Great Depression perhaps prompting a degree of reflection about western society's economic arrangements.[31] Articles by H. A. Shannon and Geoffrey Todd were followed by monographs discussing company finance between 1775 and 1850 by George Heberton Evans, the development of company law in the nineteenth century by Bishop Carleton Hunt, joint-stock enterprise in the eighteenth century by Armand B. DuBois and a survey of business organisation from the mid-nineteenth century by James B. Jefferys.[32] These works, particularly those of Shannon and Hunt, provided evidence for what historians like Postan already assumed. They reinforced the notion that the Bubble Act, passed in response to the speculative boom and bust of 1719–20, frustrated economic development for over a century, until it was wisely repealed during another

---

30 On the perceived corruption of Trinity House, a non-profit body incorporated in 1514 see J. Taylor, 'Private property, public interest, and the role of the state in nineteenth-century Britain: the case of the lighthouses', *Historical Journal* xliv (2001), 749–71 at p. 765.
31 For a treatment from 1901 see T. B. Napier, 'The history of joint stock and limited liability companies', in *A century of law reform: twelve lectures on the changes in the law of England during the nineteenth century*, South Hackensack 1972, 379–415.
32 H. A. Shannon, 'The coming of general limited liability', *Economic History* ii (1931), 267–91, and 'The first five thousand limited companies and their duration', *Economic History* iii (1932), 396–424; G. Todd, 'Some aspects of joint stock companies, 1844–1900', *EcHR* iv (1932), 46–71; G. H. Evans, *British corporation finance, 1775–1850: a study of preference shares*, Baltimore 1936; B. C. Hunt, *The development of the business corporation in England, 1800–1867*, Cambridge, MA. 1936; DuBois, *English business company*; Jefferys, 'Trends in business organisation'.

boom in 1825. However, so this interpretation runs, prejudiced legislators and lawyers, demonstrating an extraordinary unresponsiveness to the needs of the business community, were slow to appreciate the necessity in a modern economy of removing all impediments to joint-stock enterprise. Some half-hearted and ineffectual measures by the Whigs in the 1830s notwithstanding, the country had to wait until the 1850s, when the tide of free trade had become irresistible, for legislation which removed all restrictions on access to corporate advantages.

A whiggish belief in the inevitability of the change in the law, and a tone of impatience with those who resisted it, are the chief characteristics of this version of events. Shannon gave no sense of the deep ideological conflict underlying debate in this period. For him, reform was inevitable simply because without it, 'full economic development was impossible'. The conservatism of the legal profession and of certain businessmen, and the indifference of the legislature conspired to stay 'the correction of an unsuitable body of law'. But the unquestionable superiority of the reformers' arguments eventually secured the necessary changes. We read, for example, that following Robert Lowe's speech in 1856 outlining his Joint-Stock Companies Bill, 'There was no debate – there could hardly be any after his speech – and the Bill passed easily.'[33] Hunt dished up a similar narrative. He was scornful of the nineteenth-century 'prejudice' against the company as a form of business organisation, and insisted that 'Hoary ideas of partnership' tended 'to confuse thinking with regard to corporate enterprise'. For Hunt, the history of the joint-stock company in England 'during the one hundred and fifty years following the statute of 1720 is the story of an economic necessity forcing its way slowly and painfully to legal recognition against strong commercial prejudice in favour of "individual" enterprise, and in the face of determined attempts of both the legislature and the courts to deny it'.[34]

In these accounts, the cause of joint-stock companies was closely associated with the principles of *laissez-faire* and free trade. Companies were the enemy of privilege, restriction and the corruption of the unreformed British state, and their victory, partial in 1844, and complete in 1855–6, was entirely consistent with contemporaneous measures such as the repeal of the Corn Laws, the Navigation Acts and the Usury Laws. Even left-wing historians agreed. John Saville found no reason to question the identification of limited liability with free trade, holding that, 'With the acceptance of limited liability in 1855 a free-trade Parliament had at last applied the principles of a laissez faire political economy to money and commercial dealings.' The reform had not come earlier because of 'the carryover of traditional ways of thinking and the confusions which resulted therefrom'.[35]

---

[33] Shannon, 'General limited liability', 274, 271, 289.
[34] Hunt, *Business corporation*, 129–31, 13.
[35] J. Saville, 'Sleeping partnership and limited liability, 1850–1856', *EcHR* viii (1956), 418–33 at p. 431.

These early views have coloured much of the subsequent literature on the subject to an unusual extent, and are frequently recycled without criticism. In 1979 P. S. Atiyah argued that the reforms of 1855–6 were a natural corollary of the rise of the principle of freedom of contract. He blamed the 'old-fashioned' views of senior legal authorities for the state's tardiness in granting companies full rights of incorporation: Lord Chancellor Eldon's judgements were 'irresponsible'; Chief Justice Best 'sided against history'. Atiyah, impatient with such obstructionism, declares, 'Clearly, this could not go on in the new age.' Writing on the controversy over limited liability, he states that 'the outcome of the debate appears today to have had an air of inevitability about it'.[36] In a similar vein, Henry N. Butler's account of the change in company law posits a straightforward struggle between the forces of 'liberalisation' and those of conservatism, which were aided by ignorance: 'the absence of a complete understanding of the important economic role of limited liability in the corporate firm may account for the tardiness of granting this final attribute of corporateness'. Thankfully, however, 'the political atmosphere of the time probably made it impossible to legislate against the freedom of contract'.[37]

Underlying these accounts to a greater or lesser extent is the assumption that joint-stock enterprise had become an economic necessity by the time of the period of accelerated industrialisation in the late eighteenth century, if not before, and that the unfriendly legal climate was a serious impediment to industrial and commercial progress. In these interpretations, the law is presented as unresponsive to, and autonomous from, the economy. This view has been challenged, most notably by P. L. Cottrell, who claims that the Bubble Act had little impact on industry because the individual proprietorship and the small partnership provided a framework 'within which nearly all concerns could raise the finance they required'. Cottrell points out that 'Extremely complex and capital intensive concerns involving multi-site operations and combining manufacturing, merchanting and even banking could and did operate as partnerships', and that partnership law continued to serve the needs of most businesses until late into the nineteenth century.[38] The implication was that far from responding to the needs of industry, the state, in allowing free incorporation between 1844 and 1862, was in fact acting in advance of economic developments.

If this is the case, we are left with the task of explaining why the state acted in the way that it did. An influential interpretation was advanced by

36 P. S. Atiyah, *The rise and fall of freedom of contract*, Oxford 1979, 564, 566.

37 H. N. Butler, 'General incorporation in nineteenth-century England: interaction of common law and legislative processes', *International Review of Law and Economics* vi (1986), 169–87 at pp. 181–2.

38 Cottrell, *Industrial finance*, 10. As Harris has pointed out, the belief that joint-stock companies were not important to economic development has led to their being wholly ignored by some economic historians: *Industrializing English law*, 5 n. 7.

Jefferys in the 1930s, to the effect that the main driver of reform was the growing demand of *rentier* investors in London and other commercial centres for new investment outlets. Pressure for reform became irresistible in the early 1850s, with the National Debt shrinking and the decline in demand for capital by railway companies. Frustrated investors, argued Jefferys, 'were the chief instigators of the Limited Liability legislation . . . their great eagerness to give their savings outran the demand for them by the industrialists'.[39] Cottrell disagrees with Jefferys, but seems at a loss to provide alternative explanations for the suddenness of the reforms of 1855–6, offering the somewhat inadequate comment that 'The reasons for this dramatic change in the basis of company law are still in some part unclear'. And despite the stress Cottrell lays on the tenacity of commercial hostility to joint-stock enterprise through the century, the ghosts of Hunt and Shannon haunt several passages of his book, such as his claim that 'reform of company law during the first half of the nineteenth century had been a slow and gradual process which had been checked by both the hostility of the courts and the inflexible attitude of the Board of Trade in interpreting legislation'.[40]

The most recent monograph to tackle the subject of joint-stock enterprise, Harris's *Industrializing English law*, claims to present a complex and radical new interpretation of the change in company law, declining to offer 'a simple and coherent thesis' and instead adopting 'a pragmatic and dialectic approach' to the subject.[41] Harris rightly questions earlier assumptions that the process of company law reform was 'linear and progressive', but in reality, as Paddy Ireland has commented, Harris's thesis is less original and a great deal simpler than he pretends.[42] It can be boiled down to the view that, before 1720, the law proved responsive to the demands of the business community, but that this was followed by a period of unresponsiveness, characterised by 'economic development' and 'legal stagnation'. The normal relationship of responsiveness was restored in the early nineteenth century, however, culminating in the legislation of 1844, principally due to the shock of stock market crashes and the healthy influx of middle-class members into parliament.[43] There is little to distinguish the substance of his argument from those of Hunt and Shannon: reform, retarded by prejudice and conservatism, was a pragmatic response to the demands of industry.

However, a couple of treatments of the subject have managed to operate outside the restrictive conceptual framework erected in the 1930s. Boyd Hilton's *The age of atonement* includes a valuable account of the way in which

[39] Jefferys, 'Trends in business organisation', 9–10.
[40] Cottrell, *Industrial finance*, 41, 45.
[41] Harris, *Industrializing English law*, 8–9.
[42] Idem, 'Industrialization without free incorporation: the legal framework of business organization in England, 1720–1844', unpubl. PhD diss. Columbia 1994, 9. See also idem, *Industrializing English law*, and P. W. Ireland, 'History, critical legal studies and the mysterious disappearance of capitalism', *Modern Law Review* lxv (2002), 120–40.
[43] Harris, *Industrializing English law*, 9.

joint-stock enterprise produced a profound moral and religious division of opinion in mid nineteenth-century Britain. Limited liability is presented not as the inevitable result of rational statesmanship, but as a policy chosen by a government driven by a particular set of ideological attitudes.[44] In *Conceiving companies*, Alborn eschews conventional narratives altogether in a novel account of 'joint-stock politics' in the nineteenth century. Here, the focus is on the political dimension of the activities of large joint-stock companies, which had to legitimise their authority with their 'constituents', composed of shareholders, customers and employees, in order to make a profit.[45]

Modern scholars writing on the joint-stock economy, Alborn claims, have been handicapped by assumptions of rigid divisions between public and private spheres not shared by the objects of their study.[46] But the difficulties go even further. Notions taken for granted today were entirely alien in the period covered by this book. That any collection of individuals associating in the form of a company should be able to sue in the courts as an autonomous entity, that individuals should be able to transfer into and out of the company at will, that they should bear only a limited responsibility for the actions of the company, that such responsibility should cease immediately on the sale of their shares and that such companies should continue to exist after all the original members had long since died, were alarming and unfamiliar concepts in the nineteenth century. While it was recognised that corporations sanctioned by the state for public purposes should possess these privileges, the idea that businessmen should have free access to these privileges for private purposes seemed absurd to many commentators. Writing today, when the term 'private enterprise' is synonymous with the company, it can be a difficult task to reconstruct how companies were perceived in an age whose commercial system was predicated on the assumption that economic activity was best conducted by individuals or small groups of entrepreneurs. In the twenty-first century, the legal fiction of the company which exists autonomously from its members seems a natural aspect of a capitalist economy. Long into the nineteenth century, however, joint-stock companies were conceived of as no more than collections of the individuals who made them up; a point reflected in the language contemporaries used to describe them. Companies, whether incorporated or not, were commonly referred to in the plural rather than the singular: the term 'company' was short for 'company of adventurers' or 'company of proprietors'. Significantly, this was true even in the courts, where precision of language was obviously vital: in one representative case in 1837, for example, it was judged that the company in question could 'do what *they* like' with their money, obtaining '*their* profit in any way *they* please from the

---

44 B. Hilton, *The age of atonement: the influence of evangelicalism on social and economic thought, 1795–1865*, Oxford 1988, 255–67.
45 Alborn, *Conceiving companies*.
46 Ibid. 257.

employment of *their* capital stock'.[47] This tendency caused one American observer to conclude that the English had a weakness when it came to 'corporation grammer'.[48] Even the preference for the term 'company' over 'corporation' (it was the latter which prevailed in America), used indiscriminately to describe incorporated and unincorporated companies, suggests a marked reluctance to embrace the concept of the autonomous firm. Long after the remodelling of company law in mid-century, these conceptualisations still had some influence, possibly helping to explain why the British state in the twentieth century was much slower than its American counterpart to treat companies as taxable entities in their own right and introduce a corporation tax.[49]

This book attempts to transcend traditional accounts of the development of the corporate economy by exploring the status of the joint-stock company in the nineteenth-century imagination. Parliamentary papers and law reports give a very incomplete picture of society's attitudes. Only by widening the survey to include cultural and literary sources do we gain a fuller understanding of the extent and nature of the social antipathy towards joint-stock enterprise and speculative activity. Consequently, the evidence provided by popular culture, in the form of novels, plays, cartoons and verse, is at the heart of this book's analysis of attitudes to commerce. While there is a substantial literature on popular representations of commerce and speculation, such works have often been produced by literary critics who are not primarily concerned with relating their conclusions to the historiography of company law.[50] The study of cultural sources has rarely been integrated with accounts of the development of company law. The surveys of the 1930s contain at most the occasional reference to a novel by Charles Dickens. More recent works, such as those by Cottrell and Harris, similarly neglect cultural sources, and detail processes of reform without reference to wider social attitudes. Cartoons, when reprinted, are typically employed for decorative purposes, rather than as historical evidence.[51] Yet an examination of such sources provides an invaluable insight into the role played by joint-stock companies in the imaginative world of the nineteenth century. The novel enjoyed enormous popularity in the nineteenth century. Serialisation, cheap editions, libraries and the availability of books in coffee houses ensured that novels were consumed in great numbers.[52] Book purchase was not an exclu-

---

[47] Ireland, 'Capitalism without the capitalist', 46. Emphasis added.
[48] Ibid. 47.
[49] Daunton, *Trusting leviathan*, 210–11.
[50] See, amongst others, J. McVeagh, *Tradefull merchants: the portrayal of the capitalist in literature*, London 1981; N. Russell, *The novelist and mammon: literary responses to the world of commerce in the nineteenth century*, Oxford 1986; and B. Weiss, *The hell of the English: bankruptcy and the Victorian novel*, Lewisburg 1986.
[51] See, for example, Kostal, *Railway capitalism*.
[52] On the peculiarly strong impact of serialised novels see L. K. Hughes and M. Lund, *The Victorian serial*, Charlottesville 1991, 4.

sively upper- and middle-class activity.[53] Popular novels enjoyed enormous sales: Dickens's *Nicholas Nickleby*, sold in parts in 1838–9, averaged 50,000 a part, while the first part of his *Our mutual friend* sold 30,000 within three days of its release in 1864.[54]

But fictive sources have frequently been used in an unsatisfactory manner. In several studies, novels are examined in order to garner 'facts' about the 'realities' of joint-stock enterprise and speculation. We are thus warned of the possibility of 'exaggeration', 'distortion' and 'misrepresentation' of business practice in works of fiction. J. A. Banks, for example, criticises Anthony Trollope for inaccuracies and exaggerations in *The way we live now*. For Banks, the novel 'lacks verisimilitude. It does not have the air of conforming to reality'.[55] Using similar criteria, Norman Russell praises Mrs Gore for her 'essentially practical and balanced view of Mammon', and holds that, 'Of all nineteenth-century novelists who turned their attention to the City and its doings, Mrs Gore was the most faithful to reality'. For Russell, Gore's works were a noble exception to the misrepresentations of business reality commonly peddled in Victorian literature, and he concludes that 'In seeking to gain some insights into nineteenth-century business life from the novels of the period, their readers need to tread a wary road.'[56]

What these critics do not acknowledge is that it is possible to ask a different set of questions of fictive sources. Novels and plays can be used as evidence not for the 'realities' of nineteenth-century business, but for 'prevailing social attitudes and preferred social values'.[57] And they did more than reflect: they also helped to shape how commerce and particularly the new phenomenon of joint-stock enterprise was understood. Victorian novels and plays constantly tackled the themes of speculation and bankruptcy. Of the 150 novels used in Richard Altick's extensive thematic survey of Victorian literature, one-fifth feature passages relating to bankruptcy, a frequency matched only by election scenes.[58] Many of these deal specifically with the misery caused by speculation in joint-stock company shares. The extent to which aspects of the corporate economy featured indicates a preoccupation on the part of novelists, and readers, with these new and unfamiliar aspects of Victorian commerce. A reading of these fictions with the aim of elucidating how joint-stock enterprise was popularly perceived in the nineteenth century is therefore valid.

53 L. James, *Fiction for the working man, 1830–50*, Harmondsworth 1974, 9.

54 R. D. Altick, *The English common reader*, Chicago 1963, 383–4.

55 J. A. Banks, 'The way they lived then: Anthony Trollope and the 1870s', VS xii (1968), 177–200 at p. 185.

56 Russell, *Novelist and mammon*, 203, 201, 24.

57 N. McKendrick, ' "Gentlemen and players" revisited: the gentlemanly ideal, the business ideal and the professional ideal in English literary culture', in N. McKendrick and R. B. Outhwaite (eds), *Business life and public policy*, Cambridge 1986, 98–136 at p. 102.

58 R. D. Altick, *The presence of the present: topics of the day in the Victorian novel*, Columbus 1991, 638.

It might be argued that novels and plays dealing with commerce tell us less about contemporary attitudes, and more about a literary tradition of antipathy to speculation. Russell traces this tradition back to 1692 and Thomas Shadwell's comedy *The stock jobbers*, continuing through the eighteenth century in the work of a variety of authors including Jonathan Swift, John Gay, Tobias Smollett and Oliver Goldsmith.[59] Yet the literary tradition was far from being uniformly 'anti-business'.[60] Furthermore, the sheer volume of novels and plays tackling this theme indicates that authors were doing more than merely rehashing old prejudices. Many of these novels and plays appeared after booms in company promotion or high-profile financial scandals, and dealt explicitly with issues raised by these phenomena. Authors and playwrights were responding in a spontaneous manner to the events they witnessed, and used fiction in order to try to interpret and make sense of the new economy, for themselves and for the public.

Winners and losers

Novels, plays and cartoons are particularly in evidence in part I of this monograph. Here, the aim is to use these materials in conjunction with the legal and political sources which have provided the raw materials for earlier studies in order to demonstrate how embedded suspicion of companies and speculation was in early to mid nineteenth-century society. Chapter 1 details perceptions of companies as economic actors, focusing on views on the role of character in commerce, and the perceived economic effects of an increase in joint-stock activity. Chapter 2 explores perceptions of speculation in company shares, the ways in which this activity was likened to gambling and the resultant conceptualisations of investors. Much of the historiographical distortion of the nineteenth-century debate on corporate privileges stems from the tendency historians have demonstrated, sometimes unconsciously, to privilege the arguments of the 'winners' of that debate. Part I attempts to provide a corrective by rehabilitating critics of joint-stock enterprise, the 'losers' who, by resisting the tide of economic progress, have been misrepresented and denigrated in so many accounts. Their opposition was based on more than a self-interested, backward-looking application of the lessons of 1720 to a radically altered situation. It was a legitimate opposition, based on a coherent political economy. In the same way that Gambles has rescued the Conservative discourse on protection and the role of the state from caricature, I am seeking to relocate the development of a corporate economy in Britain in its political and social context, and to provide a full account of the

---

[59] Russell, *Novelist and mammon*, 26.
[60] McVeagh, *Tradefull merchants*, chs ii–iii; McKendrick, ' "Gentlemen and players" '.

views of those who did not wholeheartedly support the changes they were witnessing.[61] In these chapters, I have not followed Harris's approach and arranged my material according to type of source. Harris has sections entitled, 'The attitudes of the business community', 'The joint-stock company in court' and 'The joint-stock company in parliament'. I have preferred to look for the continuities and overlaps in opinion across a range of institutions, individuals, parties and classes. It makes limited sense to consider sources in discrete categories, for when they were originally produced they entered into a dialogue with one another across genre boundaries. Legal decisions could spark pamphlets. Pamphlets were reviewed in periodicals. Periodicals serialised novels, as well as presenting satirical versions of plays, works of art and company advertisements. Attitudes relating to questions of responsibility and liability expressed in parliament were duplicated in popular novels. A cartoon might reiterate a point made by a chief justice, while select committees could present similar views of the careers of financial swindlers to those offered by comedies performed on the stage. By highlighting the broad interplay of ideas across the whole of society, it is argued that meaningful generalisations can be made regarding opinion in the first half of the nineteenth century. But these will not be made at the expense of the complexities and contradictions of contemporary belief: Hilton's claim that 'limited liability was essentially a Whig and Radical policy, and was opposed by most Tories, whether High or Liberal', does not do justice to the confusing ways in which issues of company law cut across traditional political lines.[62] Odd alliances and odder antagonisms were formed in the joint-stock debate, as Jefferys noted: 'Anti-Corn Law Leaguer found himself opposed to "brother Leaguers"'.[63] When these complexities are acknowledged, simple identifications between company law reform and political parties or movements become less tenable.

Part II switches from a thematic to a narrative approach, and aims to explain how the views explored in part I came to be increasingly challenged through the century by new ideas on the role of companies and speculation in Britain's political economy. Chapter 3 sets out these ideas as they were advanced in the first forty years of the century, and describes how this challenge was successfully contained. By 1840 the law on companies had changed very little, and orthodox opinion was still dominated by the assumption that access to corporate privileges needed to be carefully regulated by the state. The story after 1840, however, was very different, with measures promoted by the governments of Peel and Palmerston completely overhauling the law, giving companies a secure legal footing and allowing them easy access to all corporate privileges on registration. Chapter 4 contends that this legislation

---

61 Gambles, *Protection and politics*.
62 Hilton, *Age of atonement*, 256.
63 Jefferys, 'Trends in business organisation', 20.

should not be seen as the inevitable triumph of a pragmatic attitude to joint-stock enterprise, nor was it evidence that the state had entirely subscribed to a growth-orientated ideology in which limited companies, fuelled by the capital of small investors, were posited as the engine of the nation's economic advance. While it is argued that the reforms were implemented in part because the state's discretion over incorporation had become a troublesome responsibility which it was keen to shed, there were other motivations. Legislation in 1844 was intended to bring companies within the law, in part to protect them and their shareholders, but also to safeguard those with whom they dealt, and to stabilise what was seen as a chronically volatile sector of the economy. The reforms of 1855–6 which extended access to limited liability were, in part at least, a product of the growing belief that unlimited liability, by allowing companies to obtain credit too easily, was a destabilising force on the economy. Limited liability was therefore adopted as much to foster stability as to promote growth. This interpretation stresses the elements of continuity across these years. While the law changed dramatically, the aims of the state underwent a much less radical change: new methods were adopted to secure traditional objectives. Attitudes elsewhere in society were also changing more slowly than the pace of legislative change suggested. There was still an almost universal belief in the inherent superiority of private over corporate enterprise, which seemed to be borne out by the lack of a sudden dash to incorporate after 1856. The companies which did take advantage of the new law found that they had to imitate unlimited partnerships in some respects in order gain legitimacy: many companies continued to issue large denomination shares with large uncalled margins in order to provide security for creditors. In other words, these companies were only semi-limited, for if they collapsed, their shareholders would be obliged to pay up additional money on their shares in order to meet company debts.

This practice, along with the whole legal framework erected between 1844 and 1856 was challenged by the commercial crisis of 1866, which is the subject of chapter 5. Yet this threat, far from undermining the limited liability laws, actually strengthened them, for the consensus at Westminster was that the crisis and the resulting depression had not been caused by limited liability, but by the fact that liability was not limited enough. Companies were therefore encouraged to reduce their capitals and their share denominations. Opinion elsewhere was rather more critical of the principle of limited liability, but the government's rejection of regulatory measures was legitimised by the pervasive view that shareholders could and should regulate the companies they invested in, and that government intervention would only relieve shareholders of this responsibility, allowing them to gamble in company shares with impunity. At the same time, there was no appetite to return to any system of government discretion over incorporation, indicating that the joint-stock company, which had started life as a tool of the state to carry out enterprises in the public interest, had become conceptually privatised.[64] The epilogue suggests that governmental attitudes to companies evolved very little in the years after 1866, despite a glut of conversions and new promotions from the 1880s, providing the basis for a relatively stable body of company law into the twentieth century. Serious doubt was cast upon the ability of shareholders to exercise an adequate regulatory check on their boards of directors, prompting calls for the state to fill the vacuum and adopt a more interventionist role. In 1900 it responded with a new companies act, but this disappointed reformers: incorporation remained a freely available right, and although shareholders were given some new powers, directors remained fully in control. By the end of the nineteenth century, the idea that the state should restrict free access to corporate privileges seemed as absurd as it would today.

---

64 For an excellent study of this process in America see W. G. Roy, *Socializing capital: the rise of the large industrial corporation in America*, Princeton 1997.

PART I
ATTITUDES TO JOINT-STOCK ENTERPRISE

1

Companies, Character and Competition

In 1845 the financial journalist David Morier Evans produced an account of the City of London, subtitled *The physiology of London business*. At one point, Evans reflects on the varied effects that the emergence of joint-stock companies was having on business practice:

> It is generally remarked that a wide difference exists between the class of people employed in Joint Stock banks and those employed in private banks. Instead of meeting in the former, as you do in the latter, cashiers and clerks peering through spectacles with a steady and staid appearance, whose only inquiries are respecting the weather and the prospects of business, you find yourself in the company of sprightly young gentlemen, who talk about new operas and the other amusements of the town with all the ease of connoisseurs in high life; and whose chief study is to give effect to chequered neckerchiefs, showy chains, and mogul pins. This no doubt is the march of improvement, but to the quiet man of business, the times, in this respect, are scarcely so acceptable as the old days of white ties, venerable faces, and tranquil attention to the wants of customers. The modern improvements do not facilitate the counting or weighing of sovereigns, crossing cheques, or balancing ledgers.[1]

This light-hearted passage neatly conveys how, for Evans and his contemporaries, business organisation was much more than an abstract question of economics. The legal structure of a firm affected every aspect of its identity, and the service it offered the public, down to the character of the clerks sitting behind the counter. Evans casts doubt on the assumption that the spread of joint-stock companies represented any form of progress by focusing on the 'sprightly young gentlemen' who worked for the new banks. His description of them gently evokes the connotations of dissipation and excess which joint-stock companies had for many in early to mid nineteenth-century Britain. They are flashy, insubstantial and, ultimately, not as good at their job as the 'steady and staid' cashiers of the private banks; in short, they share all the faults of the institutions which employed them. While it would not do to take Evans's words too seriously, they provide just one among many examples of the apprehension with which the phenomenon of joint-stock enterprise was regarded in these years. The preference for private over joint-stock enterprise was widespread and in some cases instinc-

---

[1] [D. M. Evans], *The City; or, the physiology of London business*, London 1845, 14–15.

tive; it was a commonplace that individuals and small partnerships were better at business than companies.

Why was this? Long before the start of the nineteenth century, a set of attitudes had evolved towards joint-stock companies, based primarily on perceptions of how the large chartered trading corporations operated. Although new companies, particularly unincorporated ones, played up their local, associational roots, all companies tended to be viewed through the prism of the large state-favoured corporations, and thus were indelibly associated with privilege, monopoly, inefficiency and 'Old Corruption'. Harris has recently described this legacy as a 'mercantilist burden' leading to 'confused' thinking which the British eventually managed to 'escape' in the middle of the nineteenth century. Yet inherited attitudes to companies deserve to be studied without the *a priori* assumption that they were a distortion of reality.[2] Furthermore, these perceptions did not gradually dissolve in the face of economic progress and modernisation in the late eighteenth century; in fact, they solidified as Britain's economic prosperity seemed to rest on the dynamism and integrity of the private partnership. While the canals which had contributed so much to the spurt in industrial activity from the late eighteenth century were mostly dug by joint-stock companies, it was taken for granted that the uses of this form of business organisation were strictly limited. Both the manufacturing enterprises of the north and the merchant firms of the metropolis were private, not joint-stock, concerns. Such feelings were reinforced by the evangelical revival developing in the late eighteenth century, with its emphasis on economy, personal responsibility and financial rectitude.[3] At the same time, the events of 1719–20 coalesced into an accepted narrative of the 'South Sea Bubble', emblematic of the follies of over-speculation.[4] Consequently, an array of contemporaries believed that whereas the partnership system of commerce was predicated on notions of character, trust and credit, companies marginalised these qualities and encouraged their members to behave immorally. Such views were not easily attributable to distinct groups or parties, but were culturally diffuse, ranging across such divides. And while they began to be undermined by mid-century, they were by no means entirely supplanted: as will be argued in chapter 4, a belief in the superiority of private enterprise was not incompatible with support for limited liability legislation. In this chapter, the focus is on Britain in early to mid-century, but later examples of anti-company views are also included in order to give a sense of the persistence of such ways of thinking.

It will be argued that notions of character underpinned the partnership system of commerce, and that central to the case against companies was the charge that they undermined the importance of character in business. They were associations of capital rather than individuals, and could not therefore

---

2 Hunt, *Business corporation*, 16; Harris, *Industrializing English law*, 59, 209.
3 Hilton, *Age of atonement*.
4 J. Hoppit, 'The myths of the South Sea Bubble', *TRHS* xii (2002), 141–65 at pp. 163–5.

be expected to behave morally. Nor would they trade thriftily or efficiently, for the divided responsibility which characterised the joint-stock form of management was thought to lead inevitably to extravagance and waste. While companies tried to defend themselves by claiming that they were promoting ethical commerce, and bringing benefits to the population by means of technological innovation, such assertions were met with considerable scepticism. Similarly, ideas that companies promoted competition were widely disbelieved: the fear was that untrammelled joint-stock enterprise would have disastrous economic effects, primarily by subjecting private traders to unfair competition, but also by acting as a monopolistic burden on consumers in the provision of public services. To permit joint-stock enterprise on a large scale would be to invite monopoly and economic dislocation, and to undermine the foundations of British greatness.

Character

Samuel Smiles, that famed apostle of what later became known as 'Victorian values', believed character to be 'the highest embodiment of the human being, the noblest heraldry of Man'. It dignified and elevated the individual, and formed the 'motive power' of society.[5] This was more than mere Victorian humbug: such views were the product of a longstanding national emphasis on character, credit and trust in commerce which can be traced back to the sixteenth century. Craig Muldrew has demonstrated how credit expanded enormously in England after 1530 as the limited volume of gold and silver circulating in the economy could not keep pace with the growing scale of commercial transactions. Long chains of credit developed, often based on informal arrangements; defaults were common, leading to economic insecurity. As a result of this growing insecurity, a new stress was laid on trust as the only way to support an increasingly complex economy. Muldrew argues that 'credit as a currency of reputation' enabled trade to expand 'beyond local face-to-face dealing between people who knew each other'.[6] Business success therefore depended upon commercial reputation: credit was the key to profit. As Daniel Defoe argued, high social status was not enough: 'A private shop-keeper shall borrow money much easier than a prince, if the credit of the tradesman has the reputation of being an honest man. Not the crown itself can give credit to the head that wears it, if once he that wears it comes but to mortgage his honour in the matter of payment of money.'[7] In the economic world of the small partnership and the sole trader, notions of character were crucial; a tradition which persisted into the nineteenth century. Margot Finn

[5] S. Smiles, *Character*, London 1882, pp. v–vi.
[6] C. Muldrew, *The economy of obligation: the culture of credit and social relations in early modern England*, New York 1998, 7.
[7] Cited ibid. 154.

has recently rejected the idea of an impersonal Victorian market in which cash payment ruled supreme, instead pointing to the 'myriad moral economies' which continued to mould market relations. Consumer credit was still 'shaped most decisively by notions of personal character', she concludes.[8] This remained a market regulated by morality, argues Stefan Collini. A reputation for moral rectitude was crucial to success in business: 'to be known as a man of character was to possess the moral collateral which would reassure potential business associates'.[9] Trade depended on trust: bank notes issued by private banks, trade tokens issued by local shops, bills of exchange and promissory notes all 'rested on assumptions of others' creditworthiness'.[10] This was not an age of mobile capital, divorced from its owners, seeking the highest rates of profit regardless of all other considerations. Rather, as Michael Postan justly observed, capital was 'intimately bound up with human personality'.[11] Leonore Davidoff and Catherine Hall have argued that 'the personality of the entrepreneur, or partners, *was* the firm'.[12] Indeed, the individual's business was an outgrowth of his personality; the same rules regulated the individual's activity in the market as regulated his behaviour at home. And the business and the home were not so rigorously separated either conceptually or physically as they came to be. The businessman often lived in his place of work; business and domestic accounts were kept together.

Notions of character underpinned partnership law. A partnership was based on trust and knowledge; it was a voluntary alliance of businessmen, personally known to one another, who had sufficient trust in each other's character and abilities to want to trade together. This step was not to be taken lightly, for as John George, a solicitor writing in 1825, averred, 'persons entering into partnership for carrying on any trade or business place themselves in the eye of the law in a peculiar relation with regard to each other . . . The law regards partners as having placed a peculiar degree of confidence in each other'.[13] Indeed, the arrangement implied such closeness between members that partners could be likened to brothers.[14] All partners had equal rights over the partnership property, and the law of agency meant that one partner could bind the others by his actions. Contracts made by one partner were binding on all other members, crucial in order to give third parties the security of knowing that they could recover against the property of the whole

---

8   Finn, *Character of credit*, 67, 19.
9   S. Collini, *Public moralists: political thought and intellectual life in Britain, 1850–1930*, Oxford 1993, 106. See also his 'The idea of "character" in Victorian political thought', *TRHS* 5th ser. xxxv (1985), 29–50.
10 L. Davidoff and C. Hall, *Family fortunes: men and women of the English middle class, 1780–1850*, London 1992, 208.
11 Postan, 'Recent trends', 5.
12 Davidoff and Hall, *Family fortunes*, 200.
13 J. George, *A view of the existing law affecting unincorporated joint stock companies*, London 1825, 5, 9.
14 Davidoff and Hall, *Family fortunes*, 200.

partnership. The implications of the law of agency were significant. Any partner could rescind a debt due to the partnership, payment to one partner was payment to all and any partner could do what he liked with the partnership property without consulting his fellow partners.[15] As the *Edinburgh Reviewer* W. R. Greg wrote in 1852, 'The law assumes that the property of the partnership is the property of each member of it; – and accordingly any individual may march off with goods or money belonging to the body, with perfect impunity.'[16] Furthermore, debts incurred by the partnership were regarded by the law as debts incurred by the partners: each partner was liable for these debts, in Lord Eldon's famous phrase, 'to his last shilling and acre'. This was a major ethical, as well as economic, consideration. It was an established legal principle that those who speculated for gain, must be fully liable for loss: 'if a partner shares in advantages, he also shares in all disadvantages', as Lord Loughborough ruled in 1788.[17] 'Sleeping partners', those not active in management, still had to be held fully liable for the firm's debts, for if they were exempted, they would be receiving usurious interest for their capital, without this gain being attended with any risk.[18] Unlimited liability guaranteed that all partners had a direct interest in ensuring the responsible and honest behaviour of their colleagues, thus guarding the public who dealt with the firm from harm.

To form a partnership with individuals of whose character one was not certain was obviously therefore an act of great folly. This was even more true when one considered that disagreements between partners could not be resolved in courts of law. The law did not see the partnership as an entity distinct from its members, but merely as an aggregate of individuals. In any legal action, all the partners had to be party to the suit. A partner could not therefore sue his fellow partners, as this would involve an action against himself. Deprived of any remedy in law against his colleagues, a disgruntled partner's only recourse was an action in Equity, an expensive and lengthy process.[19] Furthermore, partnerships were easily formed, but once established, could be difficult to leave. The lawyer George Henry Lewis explained in 1845 that, 'The circumstance of one trade being carried on under the names of A, B, and C, is sufficient to create a partnership between those individuals, with all its liabilities as regards the world . . . the bare permission of an individual, that his name shall be used . . . makes him responsible as a partner.'[20] A

---

[15] George, *View of the existing law*, 5–12; G. H. Lewis, *The liabilities incurred by the projectors, managers and shareholders of railway and other joint-stock companies considered: and also the rights and liabilities arising from transfers of shares*, London 1845, 3–5.

[16] [W. R. Greg], 'Investments for the working classes', *EdR* xcv (Apr. 1852), 405–53 at p. 440.

[17] *Coope v. Eyre* (1788), 1 H. Blackstone 37, 126 ER 24.

[18] See the judgement of Lord Mansfield in *Hoare v. Dawes* (1780), 1 Douglas 371, 99 ER 239.

[19] Harris, *Industrializing English law*, 163–5.

[20] Lewis, *Liabilities incurred*, 3; N. Gow, *A practical treatise on the law of partnership*, London 1823, 6.

partner could only leave the partnership by circulating notice of his retirement 'in the most extensive manner'.[21] In addition, personal responsibility for the actions of a partnership could not be ended at the whim of a partner. A partner leaving a partnership remained fully responsible for all contracts made by the partnership with third parties while he was a member, so could be implicated in lawsuits years after ceasing his connection with the firm: he was exonerated 'from liability for the future, though not for the past'.[22] Moreover, it was considered impossible for a partner to leave a concern with contracts between partners unfulfilled: 'A, B, and C contract between themselves mutually to use their endeavours, and to bear the expenses in case of failure, to obtain a certain desired end. It would certainly be wrong that any one of the three should be at liberty to retire from the agreement and leave the weight of it on the remaining two, or cause its abandonment' without the consent of the others.[23]

These aspects of partnership law were all products of the fact that the law saw partnerships as collections of individuals, not as entities existing separately from the partners who formed them. Corporate law, however, was different. Incorporated bodies were recognised in law as distinct from their members. The difference has been summarised by Paddy Ireland: partnerships are 'mere collections or aggregations of individuals – in which the members *are* the association', whereas corporations are 'objects in themselves whose members stand in an essentially external relationship to them', entities 'effectively cleansed' of their members.[24] This distinction had many important implications for shareholders of profit-orientated corporations. They could not act on behalf of the company; rather, the company itself contracted, bought, sold, sued and was sued, in its own name. Therefore, members could not act independently and without the knowledge of the others, but they were able to sue the company. The company's finances were distinct from those of its members, so a member could not be asked to contribute more than his investment in the company to satisfy the company's creditors. Thus, liability was not only limited but also easily transferable: people could transfer into and out of the company at will with the purchase and sale of shares; existing members did not 'vet' entry into the company, while, on transfer, all personal responsibility for a company's contracts ceased.

Corporate law therefore made for a more casual and less rigorous relationship between the members of a firm. As shareholders could not bind their fellows by their actions, as they bore only limited responsibility for the debts of the company, and as they could join and leave the company at their pleasure, the moral standing of an individual shareholder was of no interest to the

21 Lewis, *Liabilities incurred*, 4; J. Collyer, *A practical treatise on the law of partnership*, London 1832, 310–11.
22 Collyer, *Practical treatise*, 311.
23 Lewis, *Liabilities incurred*, 17.
24 Ireland, 'Capitalism without the capitalist', 41.

group. The presence of a person of low character among the body of share-holders posed no threat to the others. Shareholders were not expected to contribute talent, ideas or character to the enterprise, simply money. *The Times* was voicing conventional wisdom on the subject when it argued in 1840 that the principal effect of joint-stock companies was 'that persons engage in them who are ignorant of business, who may be also without ability and character, who may even be without money or means beyond the partic-ular value of their shares'. They were, the newspaper continued, 'societies in which friendship, ability, knowledge, education, character, credit, even monied worth is in a great measure disregarded, and money, the mere amount and value of the shares standing in the name of each, is the sole bond of connexion between the proprietors'. The joint-stock system was an attempt to 'substitute money for mind'. Such an endeavour would stultify the creative capacity of industry by removing the individual from the equation: 'money cannot make money of itself . . . what board of a company would ever have invented a spinning jenny!'[25] Some years later, Karl Marx made the same point more pithily in one of his many newspaper articles, stating that 'in joint-stock companies it is not the individuals that are associated, but the capitals'.[26]

This implied a significant breakdown in personal relations in business, mirroring the way in which Thomas Carlyle feared that 'Cash-payment' was becoming 'the sole relation of human beings', replacing more substantial links of friendship and obligation between employers and workers.[27] In companies, the individuals were effaced: the character of the members was of little importance; what mattered was the corporate personality. This was all the more disturbing since the capacity of companies to behave in a moral manner was in doubt. As they were autonomous entities, they were not 'moralised' by the people who held shares in them, unlike partnerships whose character was wholly determined by the partners. In the individualist nine-teenth century, there was a great deal of mistrust of the manner in which corporate bodies operated. Those who managed these organisations felt less bound by ethical standards than individuals acting for themselves. Angered by the libel suit filed by Maynooth College against the *Courier*, the *Morning Chronicle* wrote in 1825 that

> A public body is without principle, because it is without fear. All public bodies are unprincipled, from committees of the House of Commons down to the lowest Corporations, because where the responsibility is shared with many, there is no dread of censure, and consequently no principle on which any dependence can be placed. In bodies of men, impulse rather than reason may be said to prevail, for all public assemblies partake, more or less, of the nature

---

[25] *The Times*, 9, 21 Oct., 9 Nov. 1840.
[26] K. Marx, 'The French Credit Mobilier', *New York Daily Tribune*, 11 July 1856, repr. in K. Marx and F. Engels, *Collected works*, London 1986, xiv. 21.
[27] T. Carlyle, *Past and present*, London 1895, 114.

of mobs, and any man who knows any thing of mobs, is aware that men are often led to participate in measures from which they would shrink with apprehension, if not kept in countenance by others.[28]

Joint-stock companies were no exception, and also engaged in unjust litigation. In 1838, for example, the *Circular to Bankers* was disturbed by a case just decided by the judges of appeal between the British Iron Company and John Attwood, in which the company had resorted to a variety of 'unscrupulous methods' to defeat Attwood's claims. The *Circular* was moved to comment, 'If a great Joint-Stock Company, composed in part of men of high commercial station and great influence in society, and backed by a million sterling of paid-up capital, could act in this manner towards an individual, what safety, it was natural to ask, can there be in dealing with such associations?' The decision was ultimately in Attwood's favour, but the case had taken twelve years to reach a resolution, and the *Circular* feared 'for the safety of individuals against powerful combinations of men acting in a corporate capacity'.[29]

Merchants, brokers and clergy all agreed that the absence of responsibility felt by men associated together in a corporate capacity acted as a powerful incentive to immoral behaviour.[30] This phenomenon also attracted the attention of satirists. Captain Barabbas Whitefeather, the hero of Douglas Jerrold's *The handbook of swindling*, published in 1839, offers this advice:

> let every man with all possible speed enrol himself as one of a body corporate . . . What the superficial world denominates and brands as swindling in the individual it applauds as spirited speculation, wisdom, foresight, a fine knowledge of business in a number. Hence, if a man would swindle safely, steadily, and above all, respectably, let him become one of a public company, and his dearest wish is straight fulfilled. What a profound liar he may be on the Stock Exchange, and yet what an oracle of truth at his own fireside! . . . what a relief it is for the individual man, compelled to walk half his time through the world in tight moral lacing, to be allowed to sit at his ease at the Board![31]

But few Victorians were amused. Herbert Spencer had his interest awakened in the subject of corporate morality by his employment as a railway engineer in the 1840s. During this time he gained a first-hand knowledge of the joint-stock company at work. In his autobiography he recalled a drive with a party of the directors of the company he was working for. This gave him the opportunity of judging those whose names were about to be put before the

---

28 *Morning Chronicle*, 4 Jan. 1825.

29 *Circular to Bankers*, 30 Mar. 1838.

30 Anon. ['A Merchant'], *Letter to John Taylor, Esq respecting the conduct of the directors of the Real del Monte Company relative to the mines of Tlalpuxahua*, London 1825, 5, 18; H. English, *A complete view of the joint stock companies formed during the years 1824 and 1825*, London 1827, 32; Revd R. Bickersteth, 'Introduction', in H. A. Boardman, *The Bible in the counting-house: a course of lectures to merchants*, London 1854, p. v.

31 W. Jerrold (ed.), *The handbook of swindling, and other papers*, London n.d., 13, 66–7.

public as sponsors. 'Neither intellectually nor morally did they commend themselves to me. In some, the eager grasping at pecuniary advantage was very conspicuous; and one I more especially remember – a London barrister – left on me an impression of greed such as we hear of in those round a Monte Carlo gaming table.'[32] But in his 1854 article in the *Edinburgh Review*, 'Railway morals and railway policy', Spencer made it clear that he did not believe those involved in joint-stock enterprise 'to be on the average morally lower than the community at large'. Rather the problem was what he described as 'the familiar fact that the corporate conscience is ever inferior to the individual conscience – that a body of men will commit as a joint act, that which every individual of them would shrink from, did he feel personally responsible'. Spencer also argued that this decline in standards was a two-way process. Employees and customers of a company found it much easier in conscience to defraud the company than they would an individual, due to the 'indirectness and remoteness of the evils produced' and the perception that 'a broad-backed company scarcely feels what would be ruinous to a private person'.[33] Spencer did not argue that the moral tone of society was higher in previous ages when governments regularly debased the coinage and the slave trade was thought justifiable; but although 'great and direct' frauds were diminishing, 'small and indirect' frauds were increasing, in part due to the spread of the corporation. Realisation of the pain inflicted was the crucial moral restraint to the aggression of man on man, and this, while 'sufficiently acute to prevent a man from doing that which will entail immediate injury on a given person', was not 'sufficiently acute to prevent him from doing that which will entail remote injuries on unknown persons'.[34] With its diminution of personal responsibility and its substitution of impersonal for personal business relations, corporate enterprise facilitated these kinds of frauds, and thus contributed to the low morals of trade.

In a related manner, J. W. Gilbart explored the religious dimension to the question of corporate morality in his essay, *The moral and religious duties of public companies*. As manager of the London and Westminster Bank, Gilbart had first-hand experience of the realities of joint-stock business, and it was clear that he was far from impressed by the morality of the practices he observed. His essay was an attempt to inspire companies to behave in a more ethical manner, by setting out the place of companies in the moral framework of society. He was eager to impress on his readers his belief that companies, as much as individuals, were moral agents with duties and responsibilities, and were answerable to God. But companies, as collectives, could not go to

---

[32] H. Spencer, *An autobiography*, London 1904, i. 285.
[33] Idem, 'Railway morals and railway policy', *EdR* c (Oct. 1854), repr. in his *Essays: scientific, political, and speculative*, London 1878–83, ii. 251–311 at pp. 260–1.
[34] Idem, 'The morals of trade', *WR* lxxi (Apr. 1859), repr. in his *Essays*, ii. 107–48 at p. 139.

heaven: such an idea Gilbart thought 'too wild to need refutation'.[35] As a result they could only receive punishments or rewards in this world, unlike individuals who might receive their desserts in the next. Because the sole object of a public company was to make money, it could only be rewarded by an increase of its wealth, and punished by a reduction of its wealth. Gilbart could therefore prove that immoral behaviour by companies was self-defeating, as it would be met by divinely-inspired commercial failure, while upright behaviour, even if not immediately profitable, would eventually reap divine dividends.

To this end, a considerable portion of his essay was given over to spelling out the duties facing companies, and exhorting companies to behave in a moral way. For example, directors were told:

> Insert no erroneous statements in your prospectus; make no incorrect calcula-
> tions in order to deceive a parliamentary committee; circulate no unfounded
> rumours for the purpose of affecting the market value of your shares; and let
> your annual reports contain nothing but the truth . . . Do not go to law with a
> man merely because he is poor, and therefore unable to contend against your
> large capital; nor trespass on any man's rights because he cannot afford the
> expense of obtaining legal redress.[36]

Yet it can be inferred from the promulgation of such detailed and specific commercial commandments that Gilbart thought that in practice most companies did the opposite. Indeed, it is significant that the pamphlet was very specifically targeted: the first edition of the work, in 1846, was 'for private distribution, among such of the writer's friends as were in a position to influence the conduct of public companies'.[37] The fact that he republished the work in 1856 for general sale and with an unchanged text suggests that he did not feel the moral conduct of companies had improved over the inter-vening period, and felt that the exhortation to more moral behaviour needed a wider audience.

Immoral corporate behaviour was made possible by the absence of the individual responsibility of directors for their actions in their corporate capacity. While the members of unincorporated associations were liable to an unlimited extent for the actions of the business, members of a corporation enjoyed limited liability. If a business corporation failed, the personal wealth of the directors (and the shareholders) of the corporation could not be reached by the firm's creditors; only the corporation's assets were at stake. It therefore seemed that limited liability extended an artificial and unfair protection to directors which made them all the more likely to exploit the divided responsibility of the corporate form. The inequity of limited liability was presented in emotive terms. One MP, seeking to block a marine insur-

---

35 Gilbart, *Moral and religious duties*, 43.
36 Ibid. 16, 21.
37 Ibid. 2.

ance company's parliamentary application for incorporation in 1810, argued that the company would prove a failure. 'But,' he stated, 'the proprietors, sheltered under that limited responsibility which is the great object of their present application to Parliament, would still have continued men of opulence: their carriages would still have rolled along the streets, and have splashed with mire the unfortunate individuals, who had been ruined by their insolvency as a company.'[38] For political economists like J. R. McCulloch, unlimited liability was the only guarantee to the public that the names involved with a company would behave conscientiously and honestly: because they faced unlimited losses, they would almost certainly behave fairly and honourably. Limited liability, on the other hand, created 'a fortress whence speculators of all sorts may sally forth to prey upon the public, and to which they may safely retreat if their forays fail of success'.[39]

Limited liability was rejected because it was unfair – an unjustifiable redistribution of rights from creditors to shareholders – but also because it would prevent businessmen from learning from their mistakes – a crucial element in dominant, evangelical notions of a sound economy. The prospect of failure was a salutary check on unsound business adventures but, just as important, the actual experience of bankruptcy had a positive influence on character.[40] Such views were not confined to the realms of abstract economic debate but were deeply ingrained in nineteenth-century attitudes. Listen, for example, to the popular novelist Mrs Riddell on the subject of entrepreneurship: 'a man never makes a good rider till he has been thrown . . . the management of the business steed is rarely understood by those who have not, some time or other, licked the dust'. Once thrown, a man will learn the value of caution and 'will attend to his business, he will eschew marshy ground . . . He will remember that misfortune is usually another name for folly; that being deceived, implies having been over-confident; and so goes on safely to the end'.[41] These lessons could only be learned when responsibility was unlimited and a man could lose everything. Limited liability tampered with the divinely-ordained way of things, with grave implications for the nation. It was 'by the competition of individual exertions, that Great Britain has risen to her present unexampled height of commercial prosperity; and in proportion as that system is exchanged for a system of monopolizing combination, that prosperity will again decline'.[42] McCulloch thundered that it was not by 'shirking responsibility and evading the risks inseparable from all undertakings, that we attained to [sic] our pre-eminence in character, in wealth, and in manufacturing and commercial industry'. The adoption of a contrary system

---

[38] J. Marryat, *Hansard*, 1st ser. xv. 410 (14 Feb. 1810).
[39] J. R. McCulloch, *Considerations on partnerships with limited liability*, London 1856, 13.
[40] Hilton, *Age of atonement*, 131–47.
[41] F. G. Trafford, *George Geith of Fen Court*, London 1865, 81. F. G. Trafford was a pseudonym.
[42] Marryat, *Hansard*, 1st ser. xv. 419 (14 Feb. 1810).

threatened to 'mark the era of our decline'.[43] If other nations made corporate privileges more freely available, this was a sign of their economic weakness, indicating that capital in these countries required artificial protection and encouragement, which was not the case in Britain.

Negligence and profusion

In 1803, George Peter Moore, the member of parliament for Queenborough, stood to oppose the Marine Society Fishery Bill. He gave a humorous account of what would happen should the bill pass into law.

> no doubt but the plan would be speedily extended by subscriptions; that very speedily a board of 24 directors would be found necessary, who would not like to act without ample salaries; that a house like the India House, or the South Sea House, would be found necessary for their operations, with appropriate officers, secretaries, and clerks; and, in a little time, so far from reducing the price of fish would their scheme be found, that they must sell every sprat they could catch at the price of a turbot, in order to defray their expences.[44]

Moore had obviously read his Adam Smith. The Scottish political economist had been unequivocal when it came to companies: 'To establish a joint stock company', he wrote, 'for any undertaking, merely because such a company might be capable of managing it successfully; or to exempt a particular set of dealers from some of the general laws which take place with regard to all their neighbours . . . would certainly not be reasonable.' The establishment of such companies, he continued, could 'scarce ever fail to do more harm than good'. The fundamental reason for this lay in the constitution of these companies. Directors

> being the managers rather of other people's money than of their own, it cannot well be expected, that they should watch over it with the same anxious vigilance with which the partners in a private copartnery frequently watch over their own . . . Negligence and profusion, therefore, must always prevail, more or less, in the management of the affairs of such a company.[45]

Smith's views were representative of late eighteenth- and early nineteenth-century commentators. In their *Annals of commerce*, for example, David Macpherson and Adam Anderson asserted that the joint-stock company 'is never so frugally managed as private adventurers manage their own money'.[46] Later, the political economist Thomas Tooke confidently asserted that

---

43 McCulloch, *Considerations on partnerships*, 26.
44 *Hansard*, 1st ser. i. 1053 (27 Mar. 1803).
45 A. Smith, *An inquiry into the nature and causes of the wealth of nations*, Indianapolis 1981, ii. 757–8, 741.
46 D. Macpherson, *Annals of commerce, manufactures, fisheries, and navigation*, London

'according to all recorded observation, public companies are rarely, if ever, so carefully, economically and skilfully conducted as private establishments'.[47] These views had a tenacious hold on thought throughout nineteenth-century society, rehearsed not only by political economists, but also by barristers, newspaper correspondents, merchants and manufacturers. The reasoning was simple: the interests of directors and their shareholders were not identical; directors had control of vast sums of money, only a fraction of which was their own; they would therefore manage the business of the company with negligence or extravagance, while seeking to secure as much of the company's money to themselves as payment for their services as they could.[48] In small partnerships, each partner was alive to his responsibility, and did his best to obviate extravagance or mismanagement. But this attentiveness did not characterise great associations in which individual members felt that their efforts were likely to have little influence or effect, and carelessness shaded into recklessness and foolhardiness when the business was carried on with limited liability and therefore limited risk.[49]

In likening the humble Marine Society to the East India and South Sea Companies, Moore was doing more than striving for comic effect. Moore, and many of his contemporaries, were convinced that the division between ownership and control which allowed these large corporations to behave corruptly and wastefully applied just as much to more modest associations. Notions of middle-class virtue and aristocratic vice were important here. In an age when character was becoming ever more central to middle-class identity, joint-stock companies occupied precarious ground. 'The increased circulation of the language of character', notes Collini, 'represented part of a wider reaction against the alleged vices and indulgences of the territorial aristocracy, especially in their metropolitan form.'[50] These vices included luxury and waste, and were contrasted to middle-class virtues of prudence and austerity. The middle classes were able to display these virtues in their business dealings, as partners or sole traders. Joint-stock companies occupied a more ambiguous position, however. Though they arguably had their roots in liberal associational culture, rather than sharing the middle-class virtues, they were thought to share the vices of the ruling elite. Constituted by the authority of the state, and with constitutions that looked like those of the chartered companies, they were easily viewed as part of the edifice of 'Old Corruption'. Such feelings were reinforced by associations between companies and corruption made in popular fiction. In W. M. Thackeray's *The great*

1805, iii. 87. This series of volumes was assembled by Macpherson from earlier work by Adam Anderson, who had died in 1765.

[47] *Report on the law of partnership*, PP 1837 xliv. 33.

[48] Letter from 'an old-fashioned fellow', *Morning Chronicle*, 9 Nov. 1807; George, *View of the existing law*, 62–3.

[49] McCulloch, *Considerations on partnerships*, 5–6.

[50] Collini, *Public moralists*, 106.

Hoggarty diamond, for example, John Brough, chairman of the Independent West Diddlesex Fire and Life Insurance Company, and allegedly engaged in 500 companies, is MP for Rottenborough.[51] In Victorian novels, company boards invariably ate on an aldermanic scale. In Dickens's *Martin Chuzzlewit*, we see the directors of the Anglo-Bengalee Disinterested Loan and Life Assurance Company at lunch. The cloth is thrown back from the tray, revealing 'a pair of cold roast fowls, flanked by some potted meats and a cool salad'. Following this, a 'bottle of excellent madeira, and another of champagne' were then brought on: 'eating and drinking on a showy scale formed no unimportant item in the business of the Anglo-Bengalee Directorship'.[52] When the chairman returns home, he has a remarkably full dinner, consisting of choice dishes, wines and fruits.[53]

Of course, companies were supposed to operate an internal check against directorial corruption and extravagance. While the shareholders did not take an active part in management, they did possess significant supervisory powers. Most company constitutions enabled them to appoint directors, fix their salaries, examine the company accounts and call special general meetings to discuss pressing issues, and many gave them additional rights such as the power to hire and dismiss managers, to remove errant directors and to dissolve the company if it was losing money. But recent research has questioned the extent to which shareholders were able (or willing) to use these powers effectively, especially when companies became larger as the nineteenth century progressed. Shareholders found it difficult to summon the necessary voting power at general meetings to defy the wishes of the board, as directors were able to marshal proxy votes to get their way. Flashes of shareholder activism usually receded in the face of steady dividends.[54] It therefore became increasingly difficult for the proponents of joint-stock enterprise to point to their companies as manifestations of democratic principles rejected by the British state. While liberals like Herbert Spencer admitted that company constitutions were based on the representative principle, company behaviour offered proof that 'governmental arrangements in advance of the time will inevitably lapse into congruity with the time'. Using the railways as evidence, Spencer believed that joint-stock enterprise had by mid-century descended into little more than despotism. Instead of using their franchise, shareholders allowed it to become a dead letter: directors reaching the end of their term were invariably re-elected, so that boards became closed shops. Where elections were contested, canvassing was accompanied by corruption. Directors did not regard themselves as servants of their constituents, the

51 W. M. Thackeray, *The history of Samuel Titmarsh and the great Hoggarty diamond*, in his *The Yellowplush correspondence*, London 1903, 278, 313.
52 C. Dickens, *Martin Chuzzlewit*, Oxford 1994, 377.
53 Ibid. 389. For another description of directors' diets see [S. Sidney], 'Ruined by railways', *HW* xi (1855), 114–19 at p. 117.
54 Pearson, 'Shareholder democracies'.

shareholders; indeed, they rejected all interference from them, and interpreted shareholder amendments to their proposals as votes of confidence. The vices of the political state were reproduced, therefore, in the governments of railway companies, and indeed, Spencer argued, in a number of respects, the companies were even less democratic: whereas proceedings in parliament were directed by an impartial member chosen by the House, general meetings were led by the company chairman, a director chosen by his fellows, and hardly an impartial arbiter. Directors did not scruple to break the company's laws to ensure they got their way against recalcitrant shareholders. And, as Spencer reminded us, 'in railway government there is no "second reading," much less a third'.[55]

Directors were thus free to conduct their companies' affairs as wastefully as they liked. But some argued that companies were inherently extravagant for another reason. For private firms, extravagance spelt ruin, yet with joint-stock enterprise, the rules were reversed. Rather than prudence and economy, show and display were necessary for the success of a joint-stock company because it was by these means that it won the trust and confidence of the public. Iain Black has illustrated how this worked in practice by comparing the architecture of private and joint-stock banks. Private banking houses were modest structures which aimed to reflect the personal qualities of their private banker owners, especially discretion and integrity, on which the success of their businesses was founded. The bank's parlour, where private business was transacted, was often modelled on a Georgian drawing room, while the banker and his family would in many cases live above the bank. The bank was therefore in several ways expressive of the personality of the banker. Joint-stock banks had a different set of priorities, and had to project different ideas. They dealt with a larger clientele, and there could not be the personal contact between clients and bankers on which the private bank system was based. Consequently, Black has argued, for these new banks' customers, 'trust in the fidelity of the joint-stock banker relied more on the scale and richness of the bank's architecture to compensate for the loss of personal contact'.[56] Thus, in 1838, the public would see the head office in Lothbury of the London and Westminster, 'brashly towering above its next-door neighbour the private bank Jones Loyd'.[57] Banks were not the only institutions to act in this way. From 1836 to 1843 a series of insurance companies erected new central offices in 'the grand Italian manner'. The Atlas in Cheapside, the Globe, the Alliance and the Sun, were all, David Kynaston argues, 'testimony to a belief in the reassuring properties of uncompromising physical solidity'.[58] 1849 saw the construction of the Imperial Assurance

---

[55] Spencer, 'Railway morals', 251–3, 276–80.
[56] I. S. Black, 'Spaces of capital: bank office building in the City of London, 1830–1870', *Journal of Historical Geography* xxvi (2000), 351–75 at pp. 355–7, 371.
[57] D. Kynaston, *The City of London: a world of its own, 1815–1890*, London 1995, 139.
[58] Ibid.

Office at the junction of Old Broad Street and Threadneedle Street. The building was considered the equal of Tite's recently-completed Royal Exchange.[59] Railway companies were engaged in a similar pursuit: 1838 saw the opening of Euston station, with its Doric portico, conveying to the public the grandeur and importance of the London and Birmingham Railway, and other companies followed suit with similarly ambitious architectural feats, sometimes to the dismay of shareholders.[60] By these means did joint-stock companies seek to evoke feelings of solidity and permanence, to try to dispel fears that companies were transitory, unstable and untrustworthy.

The extravagance went beyond architecture. In Marx's view, abstention and prudence no longer characterised the behaviour of the speculating trader, for his very extravagance 'becomes a means of credit'. In the joint-stock system, men did not trade with their own capitals. 'The actual capital that someone possesses, or is taken to possess by public opinion, now becomes simply the basis for a superstructure of credit.' It was now absurd to say that the origin of capital was saving, 'since what this speculator demands is precisely that *others* should save for him'.[61] The speculator himself did not have to be frugal; indeed, parsimony would be fatal to the aim of building credit. These views were so ubiquitous that they even found their way onto the stage. Edward Howard's 1870 play *True forgiveness* concerns the fraudulent Land Company of Algiers, a bogus scheme whose main purpose is to purchase vast tracts of land in Algiers from one of the company's promoters at a vastly inflated price. The schemers behind the company have learned that

> The more we spend on offices and fees;
> Lawyers, Surveyor's bills, a mile in length;
> Acres and acres of advertisements;
> The more we pay contractors, and delay
> Closing accounts, the richer we shall be.

This was because 'The faster we can spend the more we're trusted.'[62]

Paradoxically, however, while business conducted on a grand scale encouraged public trust, it rendered profit-making more difficult. It was axiomatic that it was more difficult to make a profit from a large stock than from a small one: large capitals encouraged complacency and inefficiency. Successful businessmen, argued *The Times*, 'must be able to condescend to little details of business, to little sums, and to little things . . . Great amounts of profit are made up of little sums . . . But the capital of a company being so magnificent a sum, and the directors being such gentlemen, and used to look at such large

---

59 Ibid.
60 J. Simmons and G. Biddle (eds), *The Oxford companion to British railway history*, Oxford 1997, 16–18; Letter from 'a "poor debtor"', *The Times*, 24 Aug. 1852.
61 K. Marx, *Capital*, Harmondsworth 1981, iii. 570.
62 Dr E. Howard, *True forgiveness: a drama in three acts (illustrating the commercial crisis of 1866)*, London 1870, 21.

figures, they cannot give attention to the little things'. Companies could 'no more be conducted with the economy of private concerns than can those of a Government'. The joint-stock system was 'applying the machinery which is suited only to new, and simple, and large operations, to old, and puny, and to intricate ones – what is practicable only with a kingly and equestrian monopoly, to the pedestrian competition of every day trade'.[63] A young Benjamin Disraeli thought along the same lines: the grandeur of companies meant that they 'cannot sell, or work, cheaper or better than an individual'.[64]

Benevolent traders

In the face of these criticisms, companies did their best to legitimise their existence by claiming the moral high ground for themselves. But the ostentatious and insincere public-spiritedness of companies attracted much criticism. Writing at the height of a boom in company promotions in the early nineteenth century, a correspondent of the *Morning Chronicle*, calling himself 'A Plain Dealer', complained, 'They are all for the public good – all to reduce the price of the commodity – all to give you that *genuine* which is now *adulterated* – all to destroy monopoly, combination, forestalling, regrating, and other monstrous mischiefs, to which the poor deluded people of London are now subject.'[65] During the later boom of 1824–5, Francis Burdett stated in the Commons that he 'looked with extreme suspicion at those companies where there was a pretence of benevolence mixed up with them. There was a kind of benevolent trading about them which he did not like'.[66] Likewise, an 'Old Merchant' grumbled that companies trumpeted their concern for the public good 'in many a well-turned paragraph', and portrayed their opponents as greedy, selfish and opposed to the public interest. He held that these arguments were a cover for the promoters' own self-interest, and doubted that it was 'the pure love of their country' that prompted their industry.[67]

Edward Bulwer-Lytton's popular novel *The Caxtons*, originally serialised in *Blackwood's Edinburgh Magazine* in the 1840s, satirises the altruistic claims of joint-stock enterprise in the character of Uncle Jack. Jack is the ultimate benevolent trader, who had 'spent three small fortunes in trying to make a large one'. We are told that 'in all his speculations he never affected to think of himself, – it was always the good of his fellow-creatures that he had at heart'. In this spirit he established successively the 'Grand National Benevolent Clothing Company', using steam power 'to supply the public with

---

[63] *The Times*, 21 Oct., 9 Nov., 21 Oct. [sic] 1840.

[64] [B. Disraeli], *Lawyers and legislators: or notes on the American mining companies*, London 1825, 27–8.

[65] *Morning Chronicle*, 16 Nov. 1807.

[66] *Hansard*, n.s. x. 857 (25 May 1824).

[67] Anon., *Remarks on joint stock companies by an old merchant*, London 1825, 53–4.

inexpressibles of the best Saxon cloth', the 'New, Grand, National, Benevolent Insurance Company, for the Industrious Classes', which would 'rais[e] the moral tone of society' while paying 24½ per cent, and the 'Grand National anti-Monopoly Coal Company', to destroy the monopoly of the London Coal Wharfs and to yield dividends of 48 per cent. He argues that 'England could not get on' without 'a little philanthropy and speculation'.[68] The early chapters of Dickens's *Nicholas Nickleby* present a similar satire. We see a public meeting held by the promoters of a new joint-stock concern, the United Metropolitan Improved Hot Muffin and Crumpet Baking and Punctual Delivery Company. The directors of the company attack the existing combination between private traders to keep up the price of muffins. The company had been formed in the public interest in order to break this combination. At the meeting, one of the directors made a speech

> which drew tears from the eyes of the ladies, and awakened the liveliest emotions in every individual present. He had visited the houses of the poor in the various districts of London, and had found them destitute of the slightest vestige of a muffin . . . He had found that among muffin-sellers there existed drunkenness, debauchery, and profligacy, which he attributed to the debasing nature of their employment as at present exercised; he had found the same vices among the poorer class of people who ought to be muffin consumers; and this he attributed to the despair engendered by their being placed beyond the reach of that nutritious article, which drove them to seek a false stimulant in intoxicating liquors.[69]

Companies paraded their benevolence, and also their use of new and exciting technologies. It was by harnessing these new technologies that companies would out-perform existing traders and thus benefit mankind, but such claims engendered much scepticism. One merchant was dismissive of the 'vague, indefinite, and feverish expectation of magnificent results to be produced by the advance of science . . . we gaze at the bright vista which we fondly believe is opening before our eyes, of interminable prosperity and unimagined greatness, until we grow giddy with its brilliance'.[70] Joint-stock companies pandered to these delusions, and the boasts made by company promoters on behalf of the new, often unproven, technologies they were employing were easily and regularly satirised. The fecundity of ambitious railways schemes in the 1840s was the backdrop to Edward Stirling's 1845 farce *The railway king!* which concerns the speculator Bob Shirk and his efforts to promote a 'magnificent national undertaking, that must benefit all mankind! The Great Universal Chinese North Pole and New York – making Europe, Asia, and America into one snug family'.[71] George Henry Lewes's 1851 play *The game of*

68 E. Bulwer-Lytton, *The Caxtons: a family picture*, London n.d., 24–6, 34.
69 C. Dickens, *The life and adventures of Nicholas Nickleby*, Ware 1995, 20–1.
70 Anon., *Remarks on joint stock companies*, 45.
71 E. Stirling, *The railway king! A laughable farce*, in one act, London 1845.

speculation, starring the swindler Affable Hawk, targeted the same fantastical promotions. One of Hawk's schemes is the 'Conservative Pavement' – 'a pavement upon which and with which barricades are impossible!' It is 'the most brilliant invention – a speculation so grand . . . which was certain to realize gigantic profits'. He enthusiastically outlines his project to a potential investor:

> You see, all the Governments interested in the maintenance of order become at once our shareholders. Kings, princes, ministers, form our committee, supported by the banker lords, the cotton lords, and all the commercial world. Even the very Republicans themselves, finding their chance ruined, will be forced to take my shares, in order to live![72]

And in Tom Taylor's 1850s play, *Still waters run deep*, the fraudulent promoter Captain Hawksley tries to interest the sceptical John Mildmay in his latest venture, the Galvanic Navigation Company. Galvanism, Mildmay is informed, will 'strangle steam in the cradle'. The Company's ships, leaving from the west coast of Ireland, will outperform their steam-powered rivals, and Liverpool, Bristol, and Hull will all be destroyed.[73]

Such grand claims were also satirised in cartoons. George Cruikshank's 'A scene in the farce of "lofty projects" ' (*see* plate 1), published in July 1825, offers a sceptical view of the promotions of that year. They are depicted as balloons, filling the skies over London like bubbles jostling for our attention. This is an age where traditional means of transport have been eliminated and man's genius enables companies to convey passengers cheaply around the capital in balloons. These include the 'Patent Safe High Flyer To Halifax', and 'The Sky Rocket Pleasure Balloon'. We also see a row of company offices, and these include the 'Office of the Honorable Company of Moon Rakers'. But this is not a celebration of technological advance: the wonders are on the verge of collapse. One of the cab balloons in the foreground is deflating, while one of the airborne balloons is sinking rapidly, its passengers tumbling to the ground. Furthermore, the row of company offices is propped up by struts and seems liable to crumble at any minute. The beneficiaries of this new age are not the customers or investors in these 'lofty projects', but the rescue balloons, one of which is marked 'Royal Humane Society For Catching Falling Persons', and another balloon which supports a large box marked 'New Lunatic Asylum'.[74]

A similar view of modern schemes was offered by William Heath's 1829 cartoon, 'March of intellect', subtitled, 'Lord how this world improves as we grow older' (*see* plate 2). Here, the scene is dominated by a huge tube marked 'Grand Vacuum Tube Company Direct to Bengal'. In the distance, a huge

---

[72] G. H. Lewes, *The game of speculation*, repr. in M. Booth (ed.), *'The lights o' London' and other Victorian plays*, Oxford 1995, 65.
[73] T. Taylor, *Still waters run deep*, London n.d., 35–7.
[74] M. D. George, *Catalogue of political and personal satires*, London 1978, x. 479–81.

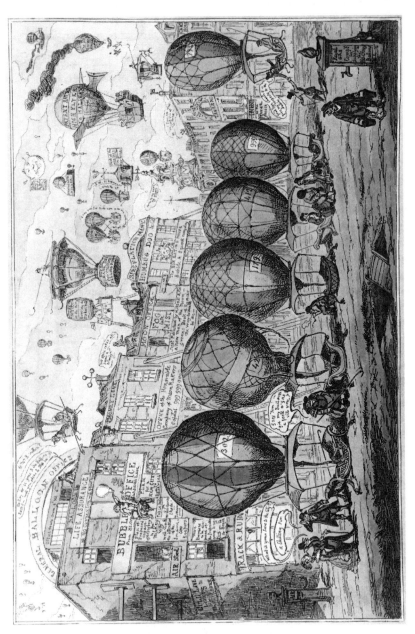

Plate 1. 'A scene in the farce of "lofty projects" as performed with great success for the benefit and amusement of John Bull'. Source: BM 14787, *English cartoons and satirical prints, 1320–1832.*
© The Trustees of the British Museum.

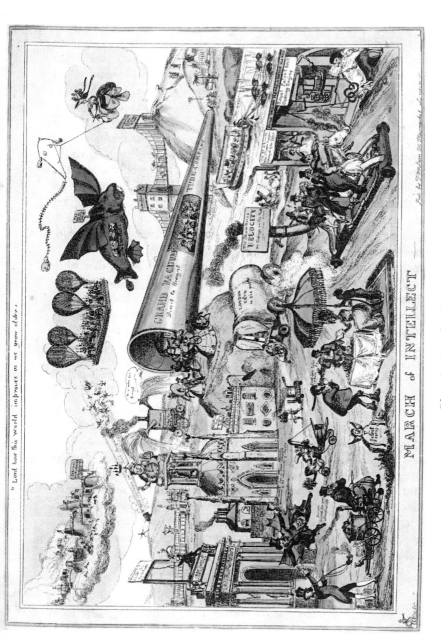

Plate 2. 'March of intellect'.
Source: BM 15779, *English cartoons and satirical prints, 1320–1832*.
© The Trustees of the British Museum.

suspension bridge connects Bengal to Cape Town. The rest of the scene is taken up with similarly outlandish inventions, such as a steam-powered boot polisher, a steam razor and various flying machines.[75] As with Cruikshank's cartoon, we are left in some doubt, to say the least, as to the viability of these schemes. In both, the sheer number of inventions means that they have to vie with one another for space and for our attention. The density of schemes is such that it requires some time for the viewer to take them all in: the effect is initially bewildering. This mode of presentation suggests the apprehension with which many contemporaries regarded the profusion of joint-stock projects which were formed in the periodic waves of company promotions in the first half of the century, during which company adverts competed for space in the columns of daily newspapers, and the share lists swelled. A similar impression was conveyed by McCulloch, who surveyed the range of companies promoted in 1836 with some incredulity: 'There are companies for every sort of undertaking . . . for the manufacture of cottons, for tanning, for the manufacture of glass, pins, needles, soap, turpentine, &c., for dealing in coals, for raising sugar from the beet root, for making railways in Hindustan, for the prosecution of the whale fishery, and so forth!'[76]

Despite the ridicule of Grand Vacuum Tube Companies and the like, what contemporaries of McCulloch found most absurd was the application of the complex machinery of the joint-stock association to minor domestic trades. During the boom of the 1820s Disraeli mocked the phenomenon of respectable gentlemen entering trades which hitherto had 'scarcely repaid a few harmless and hardworking individuals in the lowest class of life'. He mercilessly ridiculed those 'noble bakers . . . right honourable milkmen . . . people who require a million sterling for the construction of a french roll, and dare not approach the cow's heels without the advice of a solicitor'.[77] Similarly, the European Magazine thought the idea of a joint-stock association 'selling fish or measuring out a pint of milk' in competition with private traders was 'an absurdity which could not have gained admission into the head of the most unreflecting, had not the rage for speculation overpowered the dictates of common sense'.[78] Such views persisted through the first half of the century. A merchant testifying before a select committee established to investigate the joint-stock company frauds of the 1830s deemed that 'no joint stock company ought to be allowed to be established for a comparatively trumpery undertaking, such as a bakers' company, a shoemakers' company, a watchmakers' company, or a bitumen company, of which there have been so many

75 Ibid. xi. 150–2.
76 [J. R. McCulloch], 'Joint-stock banks and companies', EdR lxiii (July 1836), 419–41 at p. 422.
77 [Disraeli], Lawyers and legislators, 27, 31.
78 Cited in W. Smart, Economic annals of the nineteenth century, New York 1964, ii. 296.

specimens which have been some of the most swindling concerns in London'.[79]

Unwholesome competition

The prevalence of such beliefs was likely to inform government policy, but the conclusions to be drawn were ambiguous. Should the state tolerate the formation of unincorporated companies where private enterprise was adequate on the grounds that their inherent inferiorities were bound to bring them down? Disraeli, writing in 1825, thought so. While confident in the ultimate profitability of the foreign mining companies in which he had invested heavily, he was scathing of the prospects of domestic companies: 'Such things should be treated with a sneer, and they would soon wither.'[80] But others were not so sanguine, believing that such companies, though bound to fail, would cause untold mischief before they eventually collapsed. As *The Times* saw it, 'private trade and enterprise are the life and support of a country, its strength and riches; and joint-stock companies are but occasional remedies, powerful and efficacious in certain disorders and contingencies, but destructive, debilitating, and disorganizing, when used as food, and applied habitually'.[81] When economic orthodoxy urged the primacy of stability over growth, sound rules of political economy dictated that the partnership system operating under unlimited liability was the best way to regulate demand and supply, and to guarantee sufficient competition to ensure a cheap product to the consumer. Where profits were high, more traders would be attracted, resulting in more competition, and therefore, lower prices. Where profits were low, traders would look elsewhere, and there would be no overproduction. All traders were exposed to the same risks, all had the same prospect of gain, none had favours from the state. But joint-stock companies, especially those with limited liability, upset this natural order by giving an artificial encouragement to trade. That the prospect of unlimited gain should be balanced by the possibility of unlimited loss was of more than moral interest: if risk were lessened, and responsibility curtailed, the natural check in the system to overtrading and speculation would be removed, to the detriment of producers and consumers alike.

This is what led Marx to argue that capitalism was tending towards overproduction and excessive speculation. Those in control of other people's capital 'proceed quite unlike owners who, when they function themselves, anxiously weigh the limits of their private capital'. The 'swindling and cheating with respect to the promotion of companies, issue of shares and share dealings' which ensued was the result of a system of 'private production

---

[79] 'CD', a merchant, *Select committee on joint stock companies*, PP 1844 vii. 117.
[80] [Disraeli], *Lawyers and legislators*, 28.
[81] *The Times*, 9 Nov. 1840.

unchecked by private ownership'.[82] Marx here was merely voicing what had long been conventional commercial wisdom. Years earlier, one merchant had argued:

> The fear of injuring his fortune, the whole of which may be involved by an indiscreet engagement, causes the merchant, the manufacturer, or the agriculturalist, to exercise a caution, before he orders an additional bale of goods to be imported, a new engine to be raised, or a fresh spade to be put into the ground, most salutary for the public weal; but where, I would ask, in the whole constitution of these Joint Stock Companies is such a motive for caution to be found?

In all joint-stock schemes, there was 'scarcely to be found a man amongst their promoters, who cares a straw for their ultimate success, or who had not some object to serve independent of it'. As a result, these men showed a 'total want of responsibility' and plunged on, 'with an absolute recklessness of consequences'.[83] If limited liability were made more freely available, argued another merchant, trades which were currently conducted to the healthy profit of individual businessmen would be invaded by companies established by speculators jealous of these profits, who hoped they would be able to earn similar returns, and knew that their losses should they fail would be restricted. The prospect of unlimited gain with limited risk would be sufficient to tempt large amounts of capital into channels already naturally full. 'Stoke would have a dozen new potteries; Nottingham and Leicester would double their preparations for lace and stockings'. Boards would be constituted, subscriptions opened, works constructed, all in expectation of, rather than in response to, demand. Such companies would eventually fail, but only after they had caused severe damage to existing traders by exposing them to artificial and 'unwholesome' competition and glutted the market, as 'the farce of supply before demand [was] turned into a tragedy'.[84] *The Times* underscored this view. Companies could not outperform individual enterprises fairly, so they would use their large capitals to undercut their rivals. Their influence was destructive: they lowered profits 'below a remunerating amount', thus ruining their competitors 'by their miscalculated competition'.[85]

---

82 Marx, *Capital*, iii. 572, 569.

83 Anon., *Remarks on joint stock companies*, 64.

84 E. Potter, *Practical opinions against partnership with limited liability, in a letter to a friend*, London 1855, 26–7.

85 *The Times*, 9 Nov. 1840. For similar views on the deleterious effects of companies on trade see letter from 'an old-fashioned fellow', *Morning Chronicle*, 9 Nov. 1807, and Sir W. Rawson, *The present operations and future prospects of the Mexican mine associations analysed by the evidence of official documents, English and Mexican, and the national advantages expected from joint stock companies considered; in a letter to the right hon. George Canning*, 2nd edn, London 1825, 65–6.

Granting special privileges was therefore thought to end in monopoly and unemployment. The latter was a potent prospect in the early nineteenth century, particularly in the post-1815 depression when the state was expending large sums annually by means of the Exchequer Bill Loan Commissioners to provide employment.[86] While limited liability was especially controversial, many objected even to the grant of lesser privileges, such as the power of suing and being sued, for the same reasons. Writing in 1825, the legal expert John George opposed these grants to any company engaged in a domestic trade in competition with individuals, regarding the legal inconveniences faced by companies as a natural protection for individual enterprise. George thought applications for privileges by such companies utterly unjustifiable:

> The Joint Stock Company is, in substance, saying – 'We, by means of our great capital, shall be able to supply you with milk, or garden stuff, or fish, at a lower price than the ordinary milkman, market gardener, or fishmonger can afford them to you for. But from our very numbers we are exposed to some natural and necessary inconveniences in the bringing of actions, which we will thank you to remove, in order that we, who are a giant, may the more successfully oppose and drive out of the market the common tradesman, the little isolated dealer, who is working to support himself and his family by his individual exertions.'[87]

One broker agreed that the establishment of companies in trades able to be conducted by individuals could only 'be attributed to some sinister motive of the projector'.[88] In a similar vein, the *Weekly Dispatch* argued that 'it should be a leading principle with Parliament, never to give its sanction to any plan, by which numerous bodies of men propose to carry on any trade or business, which it is in the power of individuals to carry on; because every plan of that kind operates as a direct injury to the little traders, and leads to monopoly and extortion'.[89]

Parliament's actual response to applications for privileges varied. Where a company successfully enlisted sufficient political support, and where the scheme threatened few existing interests, bills could pass parliament quite easily. But MPs were sensitive to the interests of individual traders (particularly when they shared these interests), and would oppose bills they believed jeopardised the interests of producers and consumers, making the passage of a bill much more difficult, and sometimes impossible. The fear of creating monopolies permeated parliamentary debates. In 1803, for example, the Marine Society Fishery Bill was prevented from going into committee

---

[86] J. Taylor, 'Transport, *laissez-faire*, and government policy in Britain in the first half of the nineteenth century', unpubl. MA diss. Kent 1999, 26–31.
[87] George, *View of the existing law*, 73.
[88] English, *Complete view*, 32.
[89] *Weekly Dispatch*, 20 Mar. 1825.

because of parliamentary sensitivity to the rights of Billingsgate fishmongers. John Calcraft did not want to deprive 'one of the most laborious and useful classes of men in society, their wives and children, of their means of livelihood' simply to promote the interests of 'any monopolizing company'.[90] He compared the company to the recent London Flour Company, which also promised to lower prices, but which failed. This was because competing traders already ensured low prices to consumers.[91] The Equitable Loan Society Bill was opposed on the grounds of the threat the company would pose to pawnbrokers. William Whitbread 'looked with great jealousy at the combination of gentlemen to destroy the trade of individuals'.[92] John Monck contended that 'the object of the speculators was, to monopolize the profits which the Jews at present enjoyed'.[93] Applications for bills by marine insurance companies were opposed in order to defend Lloyd's insurance brokers. Joseph Marryat, independent MP for Horsham, and himself a Lloyd's underwriter, led the successful opposition to the Marine Insurance Company's bill for incorporation in 1810 because he feared 'this great leviathan will swallow up all the small fry . . . it will deprive the insurance brokers and underwriters of those avocations to which they have devoted their time, in which they have embarked their fortunes, and by which they have maintained themselves and their families'.[94]

The interests of these small traders were inextricably linked with the public interest, for driving such traders out of business would leave consumers at the mercy of combinations of capitalists. John George was by no means sure that once a company had ruined all competing traders, 'forcing them to become your journeymen or to apply to the parish for relief or to starve', the company would 'continue to supply us with your commodities at the same prices as before you got rid of your competitors'.[95] Protection of the consumer was a central tenet of free-trade ideology and, unsurprisingly, radicals were particularly vocal in defending this constituency against companies.[96] The

---

90 *Hansard*, 1st ser. i. 1048–9 (27 Mar. 1803).

91 Several years later the Metropolitan Fish Company Bill was opposed on identical grounds, with Calcraft arguing that the 'effect of this and every similar company was, to take the bread out of the mouths of industrious individuals'. He was backed by Sir Joseph Yorke, Tory vice-admiral in the Royal Navy, who held that 'it was extremely iniquitous to interfere with the hard earnings of a class of persons whose calling was honourable': ibid. n.s. xii. 1021 (15 Mar. 1825).

92 Ibid. x. 960 (1 June 1824).

93 Ibid. 1st ser. i. 1048–9 (27 Mar. 1803).

94 Ibid. xv. 415–16 (14 Feb. 1810). An anonymous pamphleteer agreed: Anon., *Observations on the manner of conducting marine insurances in Great Britain; and on the report of the select committee of the House of Commons*, London 1810, 20. The Marine Insurance Bill of 1824 was (unsuccessfully) opposed on similar grounds, with William Thompson arguing that the measure 'would produce severe injury to 3,500 brokers and underwriters': ibid. n.s. x. 929 (28 May 1824).

95 George, *View of the existing law*, 74.

96 Trentmann, 'Political culture and political economy'.

third reading of the St George's Steam Packet Company's Bill in 1833, which would grant extra privileges to the company, including that of increasing its capital, was opposed by the prominent radical, Feargus O'Connor. For O'Connor, the measure was inconsistent with the Whig government's commendable battle against corporations. Steam packet monopolies on other lines kept freight charges artificially high, and legislators ought not to be encouraging similar monopolies, especially now, 'just at the time when the House was doing away with other corporations. This Bill did, in fact, go to establish a corporation on the high seas'. Lord Sandon interjected, saying, 'It is a Joint Stock Company.' O'Connor retorted, 'Whatever it might be called, it was in effect a corporation.'[97] Radicals identified the grant of such privileges with the policy of corrupt governments through the ages: they were 'of the same character of the *monopolies* and *exclusive privileges* which were granted, or rather sold by the Stuarts in the latter part of their dynasty', and were 'baneful to the community at large'.[98]

Public burdens

The issue of competition with private traders was a major obstacle to the grant of corporate powers. But this did not mean that the creation of corporations in fields where they would not compete with small traders was entirely unproblematic. Here, the public interest was equally threatened, but in different ways. Normal rules of competition did not apply in the provision of services to a small captive market. This became clear during the first intensive period of gas and water company formation: fifteen acts establishing water companies were passed between 1801 and 1820, while the number of gas promotions was greater still.[99] But competition was not working, even in the metropolis. William Thompson asked the House to consider the effects of competition between such companies:

> Had any good resulted in the numerous establishments of Water and Gas Companies? They became so numerous as to risque [sic] their ability to continue. And what was the expedient? They had portioned the metropolis into different districts, under a positive engagement not to interfere with

[97] *Hansard*, 3rd ser. xviii. 995 (19 June 1833). O'Connor was supported by fellow radicals Major Aubrey William Beauclerk, and John Jervis: ibid. 996–7. Radicals were also prominent in opposing the Dublin Steam Packet Company's Bill of 1836: ibid. xxxii. 206–7, 1187.

[98] Letter from 'a plain dealer', *Morning Chronicle*, 5 Nov. 1807.

[99] J. A. Hassan, 'The growth and impact of the British water industry in the nineteenth century', *EcHR* xxxviii (1985), 531–47 at p. 534; M. E. Falkus, 'The British gas industry before 1850', *EcHR* xx (1967), 494–508 at p. 496.

each other; so that in the end the public were obliged to pay at a much higher rate than when the nominal competition was less.[100]

Likewise, an anonymous author contended that, 'Up to a certain point such establishments will compete with each other to reduce prices. Beyond it, and if so many competitors are introduced that ruin impends over all, they will coalesce, and raise their rates.'[101] The problem persisted, and in 1836 James Morrison, a Reformer, argued that even if two companies did enter into competition, they would soon work out an 'understanding' on prices. Echoing Thompson, he cited the example of the metropolitan water companies: the public was 'served not merely with a dear, but also with a bad article; and the probability of relief is perhaps more distant than it would have been had some of the companies not been established'.[102] He argued that the public needed legislative protection from these entrenched monopolies which were acting against the public interest: some power should be retained in the hands of the Legislature 'when creating associations to which the ordinary principles of competition do not apply'.[103]

These issues were brought into sharp focus by the expansion of the railway infrastructure in the 1830s. The earliest railway acts had merely intended the recipient companies to build and maintain roads usable by all who were willing to pay a toll, much like the system of turnpike trusts in use since the 1660s. But this situation changed with the development of the locomotive engine and the railway companies became the sole carriers. Thus it came to be argued as early as 1831 that railway companies had become 'a sort of combination against the public'. Railway projects often ran disastrously over budget, and, in an effort to reduce their debts, directors would seek extra favours from parliament such as the power of charging their customers higher tolls. Thus, schemes which were intended as public benefits, were 'converted into public burthens'.[104] But the critique of railway companies became much sharper once their monopolistic nature became clear. 'A colossal monopoly, never contemplated by parliament, nor even foreseen by the companies themselves, had come into being', argued Dionysius Lardner in the *Edinburgh Review* in 1846.[105] This railway monopoly roused strong feelings. The *Illustrated London News* complained that the directors of the leading companies acted towards the public as they liked: 'They make their own terms because they know the public have no remedy.' Companies were bent on securing more than the ordinary rate of interest for their money, and the public were at

---

100 *Hansard*, n.s. xi. 929 (28 May 1824).
101 Anon., *Remarks on joint stock companies*, 82.
102 *Hansard*, 3rd ser. xxxiii. 980 (17 May 1836).
103 Ibid. xxxiii. 986–7.
104 Anon. ['Investigator'], *Beware the bubbles!!! Remarks on proposed railways, more particularly on that between Birmingham and London*, London 1831, 13–14.
105 [D. Lardner], 'Railways at home and abroad', *EdR* lxxxiv (Oct. 1846), 479–531 at p. 525.

their mercy. As middle-class indignation grew, demands for greater legislative control of railways increased. As extravagant prices resulting from monopolies in corn were everywhere denounced, exorbitant rail fares should not be considered any differently, the journal argued.[106] Lardner thought that, 'to suppose the indefinite continuance of an arbitrary power over the personal and commercial communications of the country, exempt alike from the operation of competition and legislative control, is an absurdity too palpable to be, by any one, seriously asserted'.[107] The fact that the state had granted this power meant that the state had a right to step in and adjust these privileges if such an action appeared to be in the public interest.[108] Railway companies were public bodies, and how they exercised their powers was a public issue.[109] This distinction between companies which enjoyed monopolies and those which did not influenced policy: as R. H. Parker has pointed out, the former were subjected to a greater degree of regulation through the nineteenth century than the latter.[110] But the gas, water and railway companies of the nineteenth century did not create the relationship in the public mind between joint-stock companies and monopoly, for, as argued above, all companies were viewed as potentially monopolistic.

Freedom and restriction

The historiography on joint-stock companies has tended to present government policy as restrictive: by 'withholding' corporate privileges, the state was 'interfering' in trade. Yet this is simply to repeat the arguments of the proponents of companies who were eventually successful in rewriting the law in the 1840s and 1850s, and to ignore the substantial body of opinion which thought along very different lines. Partnership law was the natural, providential system governing business activity, rooted in notions of personal responsibility and reinforcing the primacy of character in commerce. The law of partnership did not 'restrict' trade: under its terms, according to one contemporary authority, 'every person may lawfully carry on any trade, or manual occupation for gaining his livelihood, in any place he choose, and either alone, or in partnership with others, and with as many others, as he pleases'.[111] Interference came when the state granted privileges exempting particular firms from the operation of the law of partnership. By adhering to

---

106 *Illustrated London News*, 24 Feb. 1844.
107 Lardner, 'Railways at home and abroad', 529.
108 A. Smith, *The bubble of the age; or, the fallacies of railway investments, railway accounts, and railway dividends*, 3rd edn, London 1848, 8.
109 For a general discussion of the 'public' status of corporate property see [W. Empson], 'English corporations and endowments', *EdR* lxviii (Jan. 1834), 469–98.
110 R. H. Parker, 'Regulating British corporate financial reporting in the late nineteenth century', *Accounting, Business and Financial History* i (1990), 51–71.
111 George, *View of the existing law*, 5.

the principles, the state was upholding the providential order, and enforcing the highest standards of commercial dealing between individuals. Political economists upheld this line because the state's role did not deny natural rights to individuals or groups. McCulloch, for example, did not accept that anyone had a natural right to corporate privileges such as limited liability: 'we are told with much emphasis and pomp of diction that it is manifestly *unjust* to interfere to hinder A, B, and C, from engaging in a partnership under such conditions as they may please to specify; that this is a liberty to which they are naturally entitled'. But he rejected such arguments as 'transparent sophistry'. Society was 'founded on the principle that every man and set of men shall be responsible, in the widest sense of the term, for his or their proceedings'. Governments were obliged to enforce this rule rigidly 'unless in cases where it is clearly shown that the public interests will be promoted by its suspension'.[112]

This view of the question was not a national idiosyncrasy. The differences between British law and systems in other industrialising nations were less pronounced than was claimed by some contemporaries who painted British law as backward. Other nations made the same legal distinction between corporations and partnerships, and were unwilling to distribute the privileges of incorporation too freely. In France, the law as codified by the *Code de Commerce* of 1807 stated that to form a *société anonyme*, the equivalent of the corporation, application had to be made to the *Conseil d'Etat*, which was cautious in making grants of such privileges.[113] Partnerships, however, did have access to limited liability: the *société en commandite* was a partnership where the liability of sleeping partners was limited, but the liability of active partners remained unlimited. Intended as a privilege for small firms only, in practice French capitalists exploited the law to form limited companies free from government control, though not free from controversy.[114] Nor did the New England states allow free incorporation. Applications for incorporation had to be made to the state legislatures, and applications could be refused, on the grounds that the company had insufficient capital to warrant incorporation, or that the company was operating in a sector where incorporation was unnecessary. But the legitimate sphere of joint-stock enterprise was considered wider in New England than in Britain, including as it did manufacturing, and the cost of applications was small. As in France, limited

---

112 McCulloch, *Observations on partnerships*, 13–14. Thomas Tooke also dismissed the 'vague notion that something like a right exists, on the part of individuals, to circumscribe their liability': *Report on the law of partnership*, PP 1837, 34.
113 A. L. Jules Lechevalier, *Select committee on investments for the savings of the middle and working classes*, PP 1850 xix. 73–4; M. Lobban, 'Corporate identity and limited liability in France and England, 1825–67', *Anglo-American Law Review* xxv (1996), 397–440 at pp. 406–9.
114 C. E. Freedeman, *Joint-stock enterprise in France, 1807–1867*, Chapel Hill 1979, ch. iii; Lobban, 'Corporate identity', 412.

partnerships could be formed, though not in the banking and insurance sectors, and these tended to be small concerns, with up to five partners.[115]

The British state, like other states, therefore faced a difficulty which would only grow as the century progressed. It had not set its face against all joint-stock activity: in some ways, this would have caused it less trouble. Instead, it had to decide which applications for incorporation were in the public interest, and which were not. For Smith, incorporation was justified in trades which could be reduced to a routine, which required great capitals and which were of undoubted public utility. In 1776 only four areas of the economy met these criteria: banking, insurance, canals and waterworks.[116] In the early nineteenth century, these assumptions continued to dominate: politicians of all stripes agreed that the state had a duty to incorporate legitimate enterprises, but to reject unsuitable applications. The views of Eldon, sometimes portrayed as the reactionary arch-enemy of joint-stock enterprise in the 1820s, were not so extreme. He told the Lords that 'He was no foe to joint-stock companies if they were for proper purposes, and under due provisions. There were many great national objects which could be accomplished by no other means, and which were fairly entitled to the privileges of a charter, or of an act of parliament.'[117] On the opposite wing of the Tory Party, William Huskisson could strike a cautious note:

> To authorize an unlimited number of trading companies in such a manner, would be to do a material mischief to the country . . . He would not object to giving bodies who might be about to do business on a large scale, the power of suing and being sued collectively; but he certainly should oppose the taking every wild and idle speculation that might offer itself, out of the general operation of the laws of the country.[118]

Politicians were aware of the constitutional dangers of placing too many firms above the ordinary laws of the land. In 1824 Lord Redesdale expressed considerable alarm at the number of companies being formed, and argued that the Lords needed to 'be careful how they allowed so many companies with large capitals to be formed, as they might have a dangerous influence on the constitution and government of the country'. The earl of Westmorland agreed: 'The creation of so many companies might be dangerous to the state'.[119]

---

[115] J. Davis, Secretary to the American Legation, *Select committee on the law of partnership*, PP 1851 xviii. 117–27.

[116] Smith, *Wealth of nations*, ii. 756–8. As late as 1856 McCulloch held very similar views: *Considerations on partnerships*, 4.

[117] *Hansard*, n.s. xiii. 901–2 (27 May 1825).

[118] Ibid. xi. 609 (10 May 1824).

[119] Ibid. xi. 1340 (15 June 1824).

While these views were to come under increasing assault from those who argued that joint-stock companies should be free of government 'interference', in the early nineteenth century there was a broad political consensus that the state needed to retain its discretionary powers over joint-stock enterprise. Without this control, the public would be at the mercy of a plethora of companies competing unfairly with individual entrepreneurs, destabilising trade, establishing monopolies and dragging commercial habits into the gutter. These were not the only reasons for retaining this control, however. It was widely feared that the existence of a great number of companies would encourage wild speculation in the shares of these companies by the public. This, it was believed, would draw capital away from legitimate and necessary trades, as well as undermining the social hierarchy. These fears are the subject of the next chapter.

2

The Sins of Speculation

Anthony Trollope's 1857 novel *The three clerks* is a story of the degrading effects of greed and ambition on moral standards. It concerns the rise of the ambitious young civil servant Alaric Tudor, who falls in with Undy Scott, a corrupt MP, and abuses his position to make large profits speculating in Cornish tin mines. Early in the novel we see how Scott seduces Tudor with the prospect of wealth, and salves his conscience by reassuring him that everyone speculates. Tudor is persuaded, and his moral fall is externalised by the grim description Trollope gives us of the mine site:

> It was an ugly uninviting place to look at, with but few visible signs of wealth. The earth, which had been burrowed out by these human rabbits in their search after tin, lay around in huge ungainly heaps; the overground buildings of the establishment consisted of a few ill-arranged sheds, already apparently in a state of decadence; dirt and slush, and pools of water confined by muddy dams, abounded on every side; muddy men, with muddy carts and muddy horses, slowly crawled hither and thither, apparently with no object, and evidently indifferent as to whom they might overset in their course . . . On the ground around was no vegetation; nothing green met the eye, some few stunted bushes appeared here and there, nearly smothered by heaped-up mud, but they had about them none of the attractiveness of foliage. The whole scene, though consisting of earth alone, was unearthly, and looked as though the devil had walked over the place with hot hoofs, and then raked it with a huge rake.[1]

Indeed, the devil was usually to the fore of nineteenth-century discussions of speculation in joint-stock companies. But fictional accounts such as this from Trollope did not merely reflect dominant perceptions of stock market activity, they also helped to shape them. As Andrew H. Miller has noted, Victorian political discourse on the joint-stock economy 'drew on novelistic vignettes, emblematic stories of individual characters ruined by their investments in failed joint-stock concerns'.[2] Actual incidents of fraud and crash

---

[1] A. Trollope, *The three clerks*, Oxford 1989, 108–9.
[2] A. H. Miller, 'Subjectivity Ltd: the discourse of liability in the Joint Stock Companies Act of 1856 and Gaskell's *Cranford*', *English Literary History* lxi (1994), 139–57 at p. 139. Similarly, in her study of credit and debt, Finn argues that 'fiction and melodrama . . . were the very stuff of debt and credit obligations in England, rather than simply literary means by which social and economic experience was represented in signs, symbols and texts': *Character of credit*, 320.

were presented in conformity with the familiar narratives of the rise and fall of wicked company promoters and of the ruin of hapless speculators. Thus in 1844, as the taste for new company promotions was rapidly turning into another 'mania', *The Times* presented an extended account of how bubble companies were 'got up' which borrowed heavily from novelistic convention. Lists of directors were invented 'by a stroke of a pen'. The promoter 'must simply lie; lie positively, negatively and collusively – lie by statement, lie by implication, lie by shrug, sign, wink or nod; but always lie'. Doubting investors were won over by 'good dinners . . . The soup dissolves the frost of suspicion; the salmon provokes the first nod of approbation; the champagne unlocks the wariest tongue, and the moselle completes what the champagne has begun . . . caution is entombed in *pâté de foie gras*, and inquisitiveness choked with *crème Italienne*'.[3] Ten years later, the boundaries between fact and fiction were further blurred in an account of the recent fad for foreign mining companies, purportedly written by a ruined shareholder in one of these concerns, but bearing many of the hallmarks of the comic fictional account. The recipient of the investor's fortune, for example, is 'The Great Doo and Diddle Gold, Silver, Copper, and Brass, Smash, Dash, and Crash Company', with a capital of £10,000,000 divided into 10,000,000 £1 shares. A trip to the company's offices reveals 'chairs and tables, as polished as glass; a carpet into which the feet sank as if it has been grass'.[4]

Mary Poovey urges us to view all kinds of writings on finance, fictional ones included, as 'part of a discursive system in which Britons constructed ideas about finance and money alongside the system of finance itself'.[5] Novelists, as well as journalists, pillaged select committees and royal commissions for ideas, while witnesses before these enquiries clothed their evidence in novelistic garb. Indeed, Robert Lowe admitted as much when he said of the evidence gathered before the 1844 select committee on joint-stock companies that 'a hurried glance at the contents might make a man fancy he was reading a novel instead of a blue-book'.[6] At the point of consumption, scarcity of reliable information on how the financial system actually operated meant that the public had to piece its understanding together from a variety of disparate sources, many of which were fictional.[7] The infiltration of novels into political discussions of joint-stock enterprise helped to shape attitudes long into the second half of the nineteenth century. Directors of companies which failed were cheap fraudsters and conmen who resorted to the crudest forms of deception to turn a fast profit; those who were caught up in their schemes were driven by stupidity and greed for quick gains, and deserved their fate. The career of George Hudson, the infamous railway promoter,

---

3   *The Times*, 22 Mar. 1844.
4   Anon. ['A Shareholder'], *Mining & miners and diggers & priggers*, London 1854, 19–20.
5   M. Poovey (ed.), *The financial system in nineteenth-century Britain*, Oxford 2003, 5.
6   *Hansard*, 3rd ser. cxl. 117 (1 Feb. 1856).
7   Poovey, *Financial system*, 4.

became such an exemplary story for the Victorians because it fit, or could be made to fit, so neatly the novelistic convention of the rise and fall of the terrible villain.[8] Hudson's fall was a moral lesson in the dangers inherent in the lust for wealth, and a reassuring reminder that the guilty would be punished in the end, for all their short-lived success. The activities of directors of other unfortunate companies were also viewed through the lens of the morality tale. The directors of the Royal British Bank, which collapsed in 1856 after several board members had 'borrowed' company money, were widely pilloried as common thieves who had 'taken from the till'. In the columns of the press, their behaviour was explicitly equated to the speculators in Dickens's novels such as Montague Tigg and Mr Merdle, and their claims to clemency therefore dismissed.[9]

The complex ways in which fictive representations of joint-stock business practice were influenced by, and in turn influenced, other representations make it difficult to agree with Neil McKendrick, who dismisses Victorian novelists' treatment of business themes as 'literary Luddism'. For McKendrick, this treatment was primarily an emotional rather than an intellectual reaction to the problems thrown up by industrialisation and urbanisation, and an extreme rejection of the commercial society which had grown up in the nineteenth century.[10] But to imply that a questioning of commercial morality only came from a handful of embittered and out-of-touch novelists is to ignore the much broader cultural resonance of this critique. Furthermore, these representations were more sophisticated than is sometimes suggested. Contemporaries distinguished between different types of entrepreneurial activity. While it is true that diatribes against 'Mammonism' were sometimes indiscriminate in scope, it was just as common, perhaps more so, for commentators to seek to draw a contrast between honest and dishonest business practice: not all commerce was corrupt. Thus it is difficult to accept Martin Wiener's argument that the work of these novelists is evidence of a straightforward rejection of commercial society and a preference for gentry values.[11] Many Victorian condemnations of joint-stock enterprise contain representatives of ideal commercial behaviour. Dickens was particularly adept at this. His *Nicholas Nickleby* features the Cheeryble brothers, benevolent German-merchants, to balance the evil Ralph Nickleby, while *Little Dorrit* juxtaposes the honest partners Daniel Doyce and

[8] For the latest study of Hudson see A. J. Arnold and S. McCartney, *George Hudson: the rise and fall of the railway king*, London 2004.
[9] See J. Taylor, 'Commercial fraud and public men in Victorian Britain', *Historical Research* lxxvii (2005), 230–52.
[10] N. McKendrick, 'Literary luddism and the businessman', in P. N. Davies, *Sir Alfred Jones, shipping entrepreneur par excellence*, London 1978, pp. ix–lvi at pp. xii, xxix.
[11] M. J. Wiener, *English culture and the decline of the industrial spirit, 1850–1980*, Cambridge 1981, esp. pp. 27–40.

Arthur Clennam with the corrupt banker Merdle.[12] Similarly, in Robert Bell's *The ladder of gold*, Richard Rawlings, the railway promoter, is contrasted to the honest City merchant Sir Peter Jinks.[13] The two types of enterprise are explicitly contrasted in Bell's description of Jinks: 'the habits of a counting-house, where business was conducted on the strictest principles, had rendered him distrustful of all speculations and speculators'.[14] Jinks spends considerable time and effort accumulating evidence to prove Rawlings's frauds, and his efforts culminate in an exhaustive denunciation of Rawlings in the Commons.[15] Like Bell, Mrs Riddell may have been intolerant of the immorality of the joint-stock system, but proselytised the virtues of honest commerce. Trade, she wrote in *George Geith*, had yet to find a writer worthy of it: it was 'the back-bone of England'.[16]

This chapter explores representations of speculation in novels alongside a range of other sources in order to explore how and why stock market activity was stigmatised. Riddell celebrated the virtues of thrift, self-denial and hard work, but speculation came to be associated with idleness, corruption and greed, and was perceived as a sin committed in the ungodly pursuit of wealth, a temptation to which many succumbed as the opportunities for idle investment grew. Contemporaries frequently made the contrast between honest labour and dishonest speculation. Speculation, particularly speculation beyond one's means, was perceived as a godless activity which undermined habits of hard work and thrift. Speculation was identical in nature to common gambling, except that its effects on the economy were far more deranging. The Stock Exchange came to be synonymous with greed and immorality, and was symbolic of the new morality based on shares, which robbed men and women of the simple pleasures of life and threatened the family and the home. To convey the cataclysmic effects of speculation, a recurring imagery of disease and madness was deployed in descriptions of this form of market activity. Perhaps unsurprisingly, therefore, representations of speculators were unflattering, and stressed their perceived ignorance, greed and blind worship of success and wealth. Yet the prospect of easy gain was thought to act as a potent lure to people of all ranks, and the social instability precipitated by investment booms was reprehended as vigorously as the economic dislocation they caused.

---

12 'If I have a prejudice connected with money and money figures', Doyce says, 'it is against speculating': C. Dickens, *Little Dorrit*, London 1992.
13 McKendrick admits that positive literary representations of businessmen, though often ignored today, are easy to find. But because he does not distinguish between representations of different varieties of business activity, he fails to detect the hostility to specifically joint-stock enterprise, and consequently accuses novelists of ambivalence or inconsistency: ' "Gentlemen and players" ', 113.
14 R. Bell, *The ladder of gold, an English story*, London 1850, ii. 88.
15 Ibid. iii. 35–7.
16 Trafford, *George Geith*, 106.

Idleness and industry

For much of the nineteenth century, buying and selling shares in joint-stock companies was an activity commonly perceived to be fraught with dangers for the morality of the individual. Primarily this was because it was seen to sever the crucial connection between hard work and its just reward, profit. Evangelical notions of retribution were central here. As Boyd Hilton has noted, evangelicals had a conception of society 'in which men are governed by rewards and punishments'.[17] Honest, virtuous labour would be rewarded, and idleness punished. These values solidified into dogma in the early nineteenth century, feeding into the Victorian 'gospel of work'. Thomas Carlyle believed that there was 'a perennial nobleness, and even sacredness, in Work . . . in Idleness alone is there perpetual despair'.[18] Wealth acquired through work might be slow to accumulate, but it would be honestly acquired. For Samuel Smiles, the apostle of self-help, work was ennobling. 'Labour may be a burden and a chastisement, but it is also an honour and a glory', he wrote.[19] The moral elevation provided by labour was open to all, irrespective of means: 'Industry enables the poorest man to achieve honour, if not distinction.'[20] With justice has Stefan Collini argued that, for the respectable classes, 'work was the chief sphere in which moral worth was developed and displayed'.[21]

Joint-stock enterprise, reliant on passive investment rather than active involvement by shareholders, challenged these tenets by holding out the prospect of profit without work. For *The Times* in 1840, the joint-stock company was 'a means of making money in idleness', without any attention or exertion. The newspaper accused investors of wanting to 'enjoy the profits of trade consistently with the luxury of being a sleeping partner'.[22] The fear was that speculation, by appealing to people's worst instincts, would encourage the population to abandon their trades, to the detriment of the nation's economic position. Soon after the boom and bust of 1825, the anti-capitalist political economist Thomas Hodgskin opined that 'Industry loses all its charms when affluence may be acquired by a lucky hit. At present the order of nature is reversed, and opulence, instead of being the result only of pains-taking labour, is the reward of some chance speculation.'[23] Conservatives were equally concerned that by promising large returns without effort, speculation paralysed the natural instinct to labour. The Tory *Fraser's Magazine* feared that 'those who had seen 50 per cent depend upon the turn of the moment, could no longer toil for months to obtain the certain 10'. Many had

---

[17] Hilton, *Age of atonement*, 259.
[18] Carlyle, *Past and present*, 148.
[19] Smiles, *Character*, 88.
[20] Idem, *Thrift*, London 1882, 7.
[21] Collini, *Public moralists*, 106.
[22] *The Times*, 9 Oct., 9 Nov. 1840.
[23] T. Hodgskin, *Popular political economy*, London 1827, 177.

found temptation impossible to resist during the speculative boom of 1825, with disastrous results for the economy: 'million upon million was drawn from the activity of trade . . . The farmer abandoned his plough-shares to possess shares in the new companies – the merchant gave up his packages to join in *baleing* water from the golden cavities of Peru or Chili . . . the shoe-maker staked his all on the new doctrine of chances'.[24] Tories were particu-larly disturbed by foreign schemes which encouraged a drain of capital from the nation. John Barrow, writing in the Tory *Quarterly Review*, would support any domestic project over these foreign schemes as he was

> convinced that, as a national benefit, it would be preferable that the surplus wealth of the country should be expended at home, upon the most unpromis-ing and unprofitable projects that the perverted ingenuity of man can devise, than be sunk in loans and speculations, which benefit only needy foreigners and domestic sharpers, at the expense of British folly and British capital.[25]

Speculation was perceived to be a godless activity. As Hilton has noted, the term 'implied not merely economic irresponsibility but even philosophic doubt and atheism'.[26] For the Revd J. B. Owen, addressing the Manchester Young Men's Christian Association, speculation betrayed 'an insubordina-tion to the will of God' and 'impatience of present allotments'.[27] Such ideas were worked out in more detail in the Anglican novel *Speculation*. The novel concerns Edward Hughes, a successful merchant and Independent Dissenter, who is lured into speculation in company shares, to which he dedicates himself wholeheartedly. Speculation is presented as an outgrowth of his reli-gion, which was 'the means of gratifying his self-confidence, his impatience of control, his selfishness'. Soon, he is 'in a whirl of gains, living on hopes, and had small care for the present, and none for the past'. His neighbour Ramely, an old Tory and Churchman, warns him that speculators are prone to 'a forgetfulness of God'. They know that they are doing wrong, so enter into dangerous undertakings without consulting God, and may enter a great crisis without his help. If they fail, they are in Satan's clutches; if they succeed, they develop dangerous sentiments of independence from God. Hughes retorts that 'all business is speculation'. But Ramely makes a distinction. Legitimate businessmen did not go out of their way to take risks, whereas speculators courted these risks. His advice is 'for a man to keep to his own business, honestly to shrink from great risks, to follow the course which God seems to have marked out for him, and to be content with sure bread in God's path and God's time'.[28]

24 Anon., 'The Stock Exchange, no. I', FM iv (Dec. 1831), 577–85 at pp. 583, 579–81.
25 [J. Barrow], 'Canals and rail-roads', QR xxxi (Mar. 1825), 349–78 at p. 355.
26 Hilton, *Age of atonement*, 123.
27 Revd J. B. Owen, *Business without Christianity*, London 1856, 6.
28 Anon., *Speculation*, Oxford 1850, 9, 75, 90–1, 93.

These distinctions were not new. Thomas Chalmers, the prominent 'Christian economist', distinguished between 'solid commerce', divinely sanctioned, and 'excrescent trade', 'the blotch and distemper of our nation'.[29] As Boyd Hilton has noted, such distinctions were in some respects vague and imprecise. Furthermore, they provided 'cover for some socially conservative attitudes': speculation was in part condemned as it was practised by those who wanted to get rich too quickly, upsetting the natural order of society.[30] But the illegitimacy of speculation also stemmed from the nature of the commercial transaction it implied. Legitimate business was characterised by the mutual benefit incurred by the parties involved, unlike speculation, where there had to be winners and losers. Those who attacked speculation advocated 'pure commerce', commerce which did not take from one and give to another, but which met the needs of both parties engaging in it, so that 'there shall be gain and advantage on both sides'.[31] While legitimate trade added to national wealth, illegitimate trade was a form of plunder which only redistributed existing resources from the gullible to stock market fraudsters. 'The merchant and manufacturer add to the general stock of the community every pound their operations gain; the speculator in shares can only gain by another's loss.'[32] Speculation was therefore not only unproductive, it also encouraged immoral behaviour. One fictional tale of the railway mania described the degrading effects of the lust for speculation on a neophytic dealer, who learns that some railway securities he sold the day before have just fallen a pound a share: 'Andrew, the benevolent, the amiable, the well-meaning Andrew, actually chuckled when he heard of this fall. His eye looked really Jewish; it flashed so at that moment.'[33]

Commentators of various shades equated speculation with gambling, which was another means of illustrating the chasm between company investment and 'pure commerce'. For William Cobbett, joint-stock companies appealed to those who wanted to gain wealth by 'dexterity and trick' rather than 'patient industry'. 'Men, and particularly young men, generally dislike a *slow* operation in getting rich, especially as it must be accompanied with labour, or restraint, or both.' Consequently they turned to 'fraudulent gambling' to get rich quick.[34] The 'spirit of gambling and speculation', claimed one merchant, was 'altogether foreign to those habits of patient and well-directed industry which can alone really advance individual or national prosperity'. A country which had abolished lotteries and aspired to put down

---

[29] T. Chalmers, *On political economy*, 229–32, cited in Hilton, *Age of atonement*, 122.

[30] Hilton, *Age of atonement*, 122. For more on this see pp. 80–9 below.

[31] G. Fisk, 'The moral influence of the commercial spirit of the day', in *Lectures delivered before the Young Men's Christian Association, 1847–8*, London 1848, 261–84 at p. 265.

[32] Anon., *Remarks on joint stock companies*, 55.

[33] A. MacFarlane, *Railway scrip; or, the evils of speculation: a tale of the railway mania*, London 1856, 32. MacFarlane condemned as 'absurd and false' the principle that the profit of one must result from the loss of another: ibid. 109.

[34] *Cobbett's Weekly Register*, 12 Feb. 1825.

gambling houses should turn its attention to 'this infinitely more extensive and more pernicious gambling'.[35] Company investment came to seem even more like gambling with the railway mania of the 1840s, which was likened to 'one great game of hazard'.[36] Walter Bagehot believed that gambling in the guise of speculation was becoming part of the national character: 'John Bull can stand a great deal, but he cannot stand Two per cent . . . Instead of that dreadful event, they invest their careful savings in something impossible – a canal to Kamchatka, a railway to Watchet, a plan for animating the Dead Sea, a corporation for shipping skates to the Torrid Zone.'[37] Such ridiculous schemes would of course fail, but Edward Cox, editor of the *Law Times*, argued that under a system of limited liability, the largest speculation was 'the most prudent course'. As the speculator did not pay for his failures, it made sense for him to speculate in as many schemes as possible, 'for the greater the number of his speculations, the more his chances of gain upon the whole venture'. Limited liability 'enables a man "to hedge" in trade as a gambler does with his bets on the racecourse'.[38]

While such gambling might have made sense for the individual protected by limited liability, the implications for the economy as a whole were cata-strophic. Speculation drew men and women away from their legitimate pursuits and wasted their energies in gambling. In contemporary imagery, legitimate commerce was solid and real; speculation was shadowy and ethe-real, typically represented as a bubble. As soon as man left the solidity and safety of ordinary work, he was doomed: 'The filmy bubble rises above the surface, looks down upon the waters, and thinks itself all safe; but it finds, in no long space of time, that it lost its safety when it forsook the stream, and ceased to have any reality when it separated from the solid flood.'[39] Joint-stock enterprise was built on nothing more substantial than air. Take Robert Bell's view of the railway crash of 1845: 'The crash was as instanta-neous as the collapse of a balloon, when, after ascending gaily into the clouds, to the admiration of gaping multitudes, it suddenly discovers a rent – the gas escapes, and the gaudy structure comes tumbling to the earth.'[40] Fictional speculators understood perfectly well the nature of the joint-stock system in

---

35 Anon., *Remarks on joint stock companies*, 55. Such views were often echoed in parlia-ment. See, for example, W. Huskisson, *Hansard*, 2nd ser. xii. 717 (28 Feb. 1825), and W. Clay, 3rd ser. xxxii. 203 (11 Mar. 1836).

36 M. D. Lowndes, *The Liverpool Stock Exchange considered; with suggestions for its re-constitution on a safe footing*, Liverpool 1845, 3. See also *The Times*, 13 Nov. 1845, for a sustained linkage of speculation and gambling.

37 W. Bagehot, 'Investments', *Inquirer*, 31 July 1852, repr. in N. St John-Stevas (ed.), *The collected works of Walter Bagehot*, London 1965–86, ix. 273.

38 E. W. Cox, *The Joint Stock Companies Act 1856, for the regulation of companies with or without limited liability*, London 1856, p. ix. For other examples of contemporary linkages between speculation and gambling see Searle, *Morality and the market*, 81–3.

39 MacFarlane, *Railway scrip*, 52.

40 Bell, *Ladder of gold*, iii. 9. For a similar description of the bursting of a bubble, see [E. Robinson], *The gold-worshippers; or, the days we live in*, London 1858, 303.

which they operated: the swindling 'hero' of Dion Boucicault's play, *The school for scheming*, claims that 'Facts exist no more – they have dwindled into names – things have shrunk into words – words into air – cash into figures – reputation into nothing. This is the reign of NOTHING; to possess it, is the surest foundation of fortune in every walk of life.'[41] In Anthony Trollope's *The way we live now*, Augustus Melmotte, the corrupt financier, explains that the joint-stock system was based on confidence and credit, and explains the nature of credit thus: 'how strong it is – as the air – to buoy you up; how slight it is – as a mere vapour – when roughly touched'.[42] The hopes which fuelled speculation were as unsubstantial as smoke, and were liable to vanish at any moment. One amateur speculator sits by himself late at night, contemplating his investments. 'As the fumes rose from his indulgent pipe, castles of wondrous size and description rose up in mid air.' But, 'Uneasy twitchings of conscience now and then – they disturbed him. Fear rose up at times – it swept over his castles with a howling tempest; they vanished.'[43]

In nineteenth-century novels, impressive-seeming companies are in fact built on no foundations whatsoever. Charles Dickens's Anglo-Bengalee Disinterested Loan and Life Assurance Company is a sham. David Crimple, the secretary, asks Tigg Montague, the chairman, what the paid-up capital of the company will be according to the next prospectus. Montague replies, 'A figure of two, and as many oughts after it as the printer can get into the same line.' This figure bears no relation to the actual property of the company. Indeed, the company had been designed to deceive from the very beginning. Montague reminds Crimple of the original idea behind the company: 'provided we did it on a sufficiently large scale, we could furnish an office and make a show, without any money at all'.[44] In *The great Hoggarty diamond*, John Brough's Muff and Tippet Company falls, 'after swallowing a capital of £300,000, as some said, and nothing to show for it except a treaty with some Indians, who had afterwards tomahawked the agent of the Company. Some people said there were no Indians, and no agent to be tomahawked at all; but that the whole had been invented in a house in Crutched Friars'.[45] Appearances were not to be trusted. Mr Merdle, the 'commercial colossus' of Dickens's *Little Dorrit*, was in fact worth nothing. The public 'wondered how much money he had in the wonderful Bank. But, if they had known that respectable Nemesis better, they would not have wondered about it, and might have stated the amount with the utmost precision'.[46]

Investments which seemed as safe as the Bank of England could prove to be fraudulent enterprises with no sound basis at all. Old realities, old certain-

---

[41] D. Boucicault, *The school for scheming*, London 1847, 8.
[42] A. Trollope, *The way we live now*, Harmondsworth 1994, 312.
[43] MacFarlane, *Railway scrip*, 28.
[44] Dickens, *Martin Chuzzlewit*, 370–2.
[45] Thackeray, *Great Hoggarty diamond*, 322.
[46] Dickens, *Little Dorrit*, 570.

ties, could no longer be taken for granted. Contemporaries were especially worried because money which should have been pumped into legitimate trades was being drained away into these hot air schemes. The fear was that this was having terrible effects on the economy. An anonymous pamphleteer of 1831 argued that while a 'strong tendency to speculate' was 'the principle which has given to England so many mechanical and commercial advantages over all the nations in the world', this urge could also do much harm. The 'uncontrolled exercise of the spirit of speculation' in 1825 brought ruin to many and placed millions in the hands of 'mere projectors, and their attorneys', money which, 'had the public mind been in a state of sober watchfulness, might have quietly been applied to an extension of the productive industry of the country'.[47] Speculative manias led to crashes. Investors, encouraged to over-commit themselves by large denomination shares with low deposits, could not pay the calls on their shares. Investors were made bankrupt, companies were deprived of the capital they needed. Banks failed. Merchants and manufacturers retrenched. Workers were laid off. Large-scale economic dislocation was the result.[48] Novelists presented such calamities vividly. Here is Dickens on the disaster following Merdle's collapse:

> The admired piratical ship had blown up, in the midst of a vast fleet of ships of all rates, and boats of all sizes; and on the deep was nothing but ruin: nothing but burning hulls, bursting magazines, great guns self-exploded tearing friends and neighbours to pieces, drowning men clinging to unseaworthy spars and going down every minute, spent swimmers floating dead, and sharks.[49]

Quite legitimately has Barbara Weiss described the Victorian conception of bankruptcy as a 'social apocalypse', whose implications stretched far beyond the personal, to engulf whole communities.[50]

Large-scale investment in joint-stock schemes implied too great a transfer of property at one time, which would destabilise the economy. An anonymous pamphleteer, writing in 1825 about the range of proposed joint-stock schemes, argued that 'the vast transfer of capital required to carry them into simultaneous effect' meant it was difficult to ignore 'the utter absurdity of a great number of them, with a view to the benefit of anybody or anything, except the projectors'.[51] The railway mania intensified these fears. Even if many of the schemes were legitimate, it was impossible that they could all be carried out at once. 'Whence is to come all the money for the construction of

---

47 Anon., *Beware the bubbles*, 1–2.
48 See, for example, Smith, *Bubble of the age*, 6–7.
49 Dickens, *Little Dorrit*, 711. See also C. Lever, *Davenport Dunn; or a man of our day*, London 1859, 683.
50 Weiss, *Hell of the English*, ch. viii.
51 Anon., *The South Sea Bubble, and the numerous fraudulent projects to which it gave rise in 1720, historically detailed as a beacon to the unwary against modern schemes . . . equally visionary and nefarious*, London 1825, 140–1.

the projected railways?' asked *The Times* in 1845. Answering its own question, the newspaper predicted 'an immense and ruinous derangement of existing employment of capital'. The millions sunk in the railways would have to be withdrawn from other branches of industry. 'The tradesman will have to take his capital out of his business; the farmer will have to diminish, or not to renew his stock; the landlord will have to build less, or repair less, or drain less.'[52] The destructive effects of speculation were also conveyed visually. The very real dangers of railway explosions and crashes were evoked in order to suggest the equally dangerous potential of speculation in cartoons such as George Cruikshank's 'The demon of 1845' (*see* plate 3). This cartoon takes us through the three stages of a promotion boom. Initially, shares are at a premium, and the investing public dances joyously around the bubble-blowing railway engine. After the enthusiasm has worn off, shares fall to par; bubble production slows, and uncertainty creeps in, with the engine balanced precariously on its tightrope. Finally, the inevitable crash comes, shares fall to a discount, the limbs of the demon shoot off in all directions, taking several heads with them and crushing many more helpless bodies. The target of the cartoon was not the railway itself, but the excessive speculation surrounding it, fed by false hopes and a desire to get rich quick. Railway engines were employed as a topical and resonant symbol for this malevolent and devastating new social force.

The great Mammon club

Nineteenth-century diatribes against greed and the sordid pursuit of wealth are familiar, but less acknowledged is the frequency with which these attacks referred directly to stock market speculation. Such views were not new, for there was a long tradition of hostility to the trade in stocks and shares, and to the practitioners of this trade in particular. Samuel Johnson had been speaking for many when he defined the 'stockjobber' in his *Dictionary* as 'a low wretch who gets money by buying and selling shares in the funds'.[53] The growing trade in government funds in the second half of the eighteenth century had obliged these 'wretches' to move from the coffee houses where they had traditionally operated and to establish a separate home, the 'Stock Exchange' at the corner of Threadneedle Street and Sweetings Alley. Henceforth, this became the focus of attack for opponents of speculation. Thomas Mortimer, an early investment adviser and author of the best-selling *Everyman his own broker*, which went through fourteen editions between 1761 and 1807, consistently railed against the curse of stock-jobbing which was carried out in '*the sleight-of-hand theatre, the Stock-Exchange*'.[54] In 1802 it

---

[52] *The Times*, 1 July, 14 Oct., 4 Sept. 1845. See also the earl of Dalhousie's speech in the Lords: *Hansard*, 3rd ser. lxxxv. 868 (23 Apr. 1846).
[53] Cited in Kynaston, *World of its own*, 20.
[54] T. Mortimer, *The nefarious practice of stock-jobbing unveiled*, London 1810, 60.

Plate 3. 'The demon of 1845'.
Source: *George Cruikshank's Table-Book* i (May 1845), opposite p. 93.
By permission of the British Library (shelfmark PP5985.ba)

moved to purpose-built accommodation at Capel Court on the corner of Throgmorton and Old Broad Streets. The new building, unlike the old one, excluded the public, which may have fed a suspicion of 'the oblique arts of stock-jobbing'.[55] Certainly, mistrust of the institution did not die away; indeed 'Capel Court' was often invoked as the symbol of the ills of a society corrupted by avarice. Despite the growing *rapprochement* between the aristocracy and the commercial middle classes which was the wellspring of 'gentlemanly capitalism', Tories were to the fore in attacks on the Stock Exchange.[56] In a series of articles in the 1830s, *Fraser's Magazine* set out its views on the institution at some length. It argued that the Stock Exchange 'has been a curse to the empire. It has corrupted her citizens, it has drained her resources, it has blighted her trade, it has destroyed her stability'. The magazine stretched its capacity for metaphor to the limit in order to do justice to the evils of the Stock Exchange. It was a 'temple of vice' where 'vampires of the stock market' sought out prey. It was a 'city hell', 'a modern monument of debasement and crime'.[57] The 'locusts of the Stock Exchange' were blighting English capital.[58] Dealers were guilty of dragging property 'within the vortex of Capel Court'.[59]

But this anger was far more than a 'country' critique levelled by disaffected Tories, for stock market speculation also offended middle-class sensibilities. For George Sala, the Stock Exchange was 'the great Mammon club'.[60] The members of this club were thought of as showy gamblers. David Morier Evans remarked that the 'young bloods' of the city were 'great patrons of the turf. They hunt, and ride, and keep their dogs, and make strict holidays for the "Derby," and the "Ascot Cup," with which no description of business is allowed to interfere'. They also displayed 'great anxiety to be peculiar in their dress, which occasions a rage every now and then among them for strangely-fashioned hats, deep striped shirts, long-waisted coats, and other articles of clothing, which meet the eye, and make a sensation'.[61] One pamphleteer expressed dismay that the Stock Exchange was coming to be seen as 'a necessary and irremediable evil'. It was tolerated only because the full extent of its evils was not public knowledge. The institution was a 'monstrous destroyer of souls and bodies', and its members 'agents of a corruption infinitely worse than ever infested society from any other imaginable source of evil'. Men whose vocation was in Capel Court were 'engaged in a pursuit utterly inconsistent with honour, religion, and morality'.[62] It was the opinion

---

55 Anon., *South Sea Bubble*, 11.
56 Kynaston, *World of its own*, 21.
57 Anon., 'Stock Exchange, no. I', 577–85.
58 Anon., 'The Stock Exchange, no. III', FM v (Mar. 1832), 155–65 at p. 155.
59 Anon., 'The Stock Exchange, no. II', FM iv (Jan. 1832), 714–26 at p. 721.
60 [G. Sala], 'The golden calf', HW x (1854), 437–41 at p. 437.
61 [Evans], *The City*, 190–1.
62 Anon. ['Dot'], *The Stock Exchange and its victims*, London 1851, 4, 6, 14.

of another author that 'millions' of pounds were drawn from the public each year by a 'system of iniquity' in order to fund the extravagant lifestyles of the members of the Stock Exchange, that 'Ungodly Brotherhood of Capel Court'. The main focus of the author's venom was the growth of time bargains, which caused evils worse and demoralisation more extensive than all the 'gambling Hells' could ever produce. Colluding brokers and jobbers meant it was only possible for the public to win on the exchange with inside information. 'The game is safe to those who play with loaded dice.' But the gambling game 'wears the cloak of a commercial speculation', so that 'day by day fresh gamblers rush in'. He wanted to see all who engaged in gambling speculations made liable to a criminal indictment.[63]

The London Stock Exchange was not the single focal point of criticism. Stimulated by the railway booms of the 1830s and 1840s, a growing number of provincial stock exchanges emerged to cater for the growing numbers of investors through the country.[64] These provincial exchanges were believed to demonstrate many of the flaws associated with the London Stock Exchange. Matthew Dobson Lowndes, a solicitor, was far from hostile to joint-stock companies and the traffic in shares, but thought that the 'viciousness of the system' prevailing on the Liverpool Stock Exchange was such that brokers needed to be protected from their principals, principals from their brokers and brokers from each other.[65] Nevertheless, the London Stock Exchange attracted the most attention. For Marx, this was 'where little fishes are gobbled up by the sharks, and sheep by the stock-exchange wolves'.[66] As long as the Stock Exchange existed in its present form, wrote one anonymous critic, 'jobbery, corruption, breach of trust, imposture, fraud, and all immorality, must be its inseparable concomitants'.[67] For Trollope, the problem was the City itself, which he presented as a desolate, godless place:

> Oh, the city, the weary city, where men go daily to look for money, but find none; where every heart is eaten up by an accursed famishing after gold; where dark, gloomy banks come thick on each other, like the black, ugly apertures to the realms below in a mining district, each of them a separate little pit-mouth into hell.[68]

This 'famishing after gold' was widely condemned in Victorian society. Carlyle famously condemned 'Mammonism', that worship of the 'deity' of Mammon, that 'leaving all to "Cash" ', where the 'Hell of England' was 'not making money'.[69] One playwright was moved to exclaim: 'All our morals lie

---

63 Anon., *Exposure of the Stock Exchange and bubble companies*, London 1854, 5–20.
64 J. R. Killick and W. A. Thomas, 'The provincial stock exchanges, 1830–1870', *EcHR* xxiii (1970), 96–111.
65 Lowndes, *Liverpool Stock Exchange*, 4, 8.
66 Marx, *Capital*, iii. 571.
67 Anon., *Stock Exchange and its victims*, 11.
68 Trollope, *The three clerks*, 432.
69 Carlyle, *Past and present*, 202.

in dividends!'[70] The moral decline which speculation induced was vividly described. Once hooked, a speculator was plunged 'into the abyss' and became 'a regular and a desperate gambler'. To pay his debts, 'he will strip his dearest relative or his best friend of his last shilling, under the most false and unjustifiable pretences, inspired by the hope, implanted by the Devil himself, that his future speculations will enable him to pay his creditors'.[71] Cobbett warned his readers that the life of the speculator was 'a life of constant anxiety . . . constant apprehension; general gloom, enlivened, now and then, by a gleam of hope or of success'. Speculation beyond one's means brought nothing but 'ruin, misery, and suicide'.[72] The Cruikshank cartoon 'Mr John Bull in a quandary' (see plate 4) illustrated what remained when the gleam of hope had vanished, leaving only despair and ruin. As the accompanying text commented, thousands of railway speculators in the 1840s had incurred liabilities far beyond their means, and the results were horrifying. Railway calls are depicted as a host of imps, who have invaded John Bull's home, and are swarming all over his person and property. They rip at his clothes and are attempting to tear him apart. They are taking his wallet and watch, raiding his cash box, and making off with his personal effects. Items of his property bear auction tickets; even his home will be sold off to make good his debts. Bull is paralysed with shock at the failure of his investments, and can do nothing to fend off the imps.

Speculation broke up homes and destroyed families. It was this invasion of the domestic sphere that made speculation such a terrifying prospect. In *The ladder of gold*, Bell vividly describes what happened when over-speculation led to panic and crash:

> Wherever you went, you met the same evidences of anxiety – the agitation with which the daily newspaper was looked forward to; the whispering fear with which each new disaster was communicated from partner to partner, from husband to wife, from father to son . . . the solitary watch of women, as they waited, with shattered nerves, for the tidings that might in a single hour hurl down their children from affluence to beggary.[73]

Even before the final crash came, however, home life suffered greatly. In his novel *Railway scrip*, A. MacFarlane was keen to depict the uncertainty which daily plagued the speculator: the fear of sudden ruin was always on his mind: 'Not one moment is full happiness allowed him.' Family life was disrupted and vitiated. If shares were down in the morning lists, 'there was goodbye to domestic peace all the day':

[70] The words are those of Affable Hawk, a swindling company promoter: Lewes, *Game of speculation*, 55.
[71] Anon., *Stock Exchange and its victims*, 8–9.
[72] W. Cobbett, *Advice to young men, and (incidentally) to young women, in the middle and higher ranks of life*, London 1906, 66–7.
[73] Bell, *Ladder of gold*, i. 226–7.

Plate 4. 'Mr John Bull in a quandary, or the anticipated effects of the railway calls'. Source: *George Cruikshank's Table-Book* i (Nov. 1845), opposite p. 237. By permission of the British Library (shelfmark PP5985.ba)

Many a loving wife never saw her spouse in such sorry plight before. He looked as black as if he had been sleeping up the flue all night; his tongue vibrated with all the velocity of lightning; his eyes fairly gleamed and gloamed with fury; his face redden to its deepest crimson hue; and, as for his whole visage, you would as soon meet a hungry bear in a forest, or a tiger in a jungle.[74]

MacFarlane told his readers, 'We lose a heaven of happiness, at many times, by the restless desires we indulge for something looming in the distance.' In his novel, the unworldly teacher Andrew McLeod enjoys a simple yet idyllic life in Woodville Cottage, Craven, with his wife and two children. Like many of his neighbours, he succumbs to railway speculation when three lines are projected through Craven. His early speculations are successful, and he is easily persuaded to invest more heavily. He neglects his family, spending an increasing amount of the summer holidays speculating in Leeds, where he lingers amid 'smoke, dust, and noise, instead of passing his hours in rural enjoyment'.[75] When the bubble bursts, rather than getting out, he uses his wife's money and borrows more to continue dealing, and gives up his job to devote all his time to his commercial affairs. His debts accrue, and his reputation in the local community is tarnished. The servants are laid off; and soon after, the bailiffs take the family's furniture and valuables. A humble teaching post becomes available a few miles away. He takes it to oblige his wife, and resolves to give up speculation, but he soon drifts back into bad habits. His wife dies, and only then does McLeod realise the error of his ways and is cured of his addiction to speculation.[76]

The hell of the home torn apart by failed speculation was a common theme in nineteenth-century fiction. In Thackeray's *The great Hoggarty diamond*, the West Diddlesex Company collapses, and we see in some detail how the speculating head clerk's family suffers for his *naïveté* and greed. The family is broken up, he goes to prison, they lose their house and Mary and her son have to live in cheap lodgings. Their baby son dies, and Mary is forced into service. It is a similar story in *The three clerks*. Alaric Tudor is found guilty of speculating with his trustee's money and is imprisoned. The house and the furniture is sold. His wife, who gives birth to a second child during Alaric's sentence, is aged by the ordeal, and when he is released, the family have to emigrate to Australia in order to start afresh, separating Alaric's wife Gertrude from her loving mother and sisters for ever.

In 'The railway dragon' (*see* plate 5) Cruikshank again provided the visual accompaniment to the text. Here a terrifying demonic railway engine is shown smashing into a comfortable middle-class home at Christmas, knocking the children to the floor and grabbing the family's Christmas

[74] MacFarlane, *Railway scrip*, 42, 48.
[75] Ibid. 6, 35.
[76] A similar picture is presented more briefly in H. Martineau, *Illustrations of political economy. No. XI: For each and for all*, London 1832, 110–11.

Plate 5. 'The railway dragon'.
Source: *George Cruikshank's Table-Book* i (Dec. 1845), opposite p. 261.
By permission of the British Library (shelfmark PP5985.ba)

dinner. The father has been speculating, and now the results of his gambling are brought home to his loved ones, the innocent victims of his improvident behaviour. He holds his head and wails, 'Oh! my beef! and oh! my babbies!!!' But the monster ploughs on remorselessly.[77]

The commercial fungus

Compulsive speculation spoiled the ordinary pleasures of life and tore families apart. The desperate speculator would stop at nothing to feed his habit: all moral considerations, all rational calculation, were suspended. In this way, as G. R. Searle has noted, speculation was closely linked in the popular imagination to disease and mental illness.[78] Contemporaries saw similarities between the periodic peaks of speculative activity and the epidemics of cholera, typhus, typhoid and other diseases which rampaged so destructively through nineteenth-century towns. By associating the urge to gamble in financial markets with this terrible and seemingly insoluble phenomenon, critics of speculation were able to key into a central fear and preoccupation of the age. Contemporaries referred to 'the contagion of Stock Exchange speculation'.[79] The 'Stock Exchange influenza' ravaging the population was a greater threat than the cholera, which only killed the afflicted, while 'the influenza of Capel Court exterminates the victim, beggars his family, taints his connexions, and blights his memory'.[80] The 'wild spirit of speculation . . . like the periodical visits of an epidemic, from time to time, bursts upon the land'.[81] Critics of speculation bemoaned 'this morbid appetite for schemes, this epidemic . . . a chronic rather than an inflammatory complaint'.[82] The railway mania was described as a 'paroxism', a 'contagion' and a 'fever'.[83] The company promoters behind this mania were 'a commercial fungus – a financial mushroom'; they were 'signs of the times – emblems of our era; just like the Cholera'.[84] In Dickens's *Little Dorrit*, the growth of the corrupt financier Merdle's influence is described in a chapter entitled, 'The progress of an epidemic'. Dickens stressed the potency of these epidemics: 'Bred at first, as many physical diseases are, in the wickedness of men, and then disseminated

---

[77] The cartoon also suggests the destruction wrought by railway lines running through people's homes, facilitated by railway companies' powers of eminent domain.

[78] Searle, *Morality and the market*, 85–6.

[79] Anon., *Stock Exchange and its victims*, 4.

[80] Anon., 'The Stock Exchange, no. II', 726.

[81] Anon., *Stock Exchange and its victims*, 10.

[82] Anon., *Remarks on joint stock companies*, 28.

[83] Owen, *Business without Christianity*, 27; D. M. Evans, *The commercial crisis of 1847–1848*, Newton Abbot 1969, 14, 3. Lord Brougham condemned 'the gambling disease and fever of speculation': *Hansard*, 3rd ser. lxxxv. 880 (23 Apr. 1846).

[84] Boucicault, *School for scheming*, 34; Lever, *Davenport Dunn*, 64.

in their ignorance, these epidemics, after a period, get communicated to many sufferers who are neither ignorant nor wicked.'[85]

This language did justice to what contemporaries believed were the cataclysmic effects of speculation. It also emphasised the way in which speculation could rob a man of his self-control, undermining the sense of restraint central to middle-class notions of character.[86] The ultimate manifestation of the shedding of all self-control was the descent into insanity, which was often used as a metaphor for speculation, most obviously with the term 'mania' to describe periods of intense speculation. Joseph Parkes, solicitor and parliamentary agent for many joint-stock companies, and a keen collector of company prospectuses, referred to the enthusiasm for joint-stock companies in 1824–5 as 'the national epidemic . . . at that time the public were mad'.[87] Similarly, for the novelist Henry Cockton, the 'blind recklessness' which fuelled speculation amounted to 'a species of madness'.[88] As railway speculation reached a climax late in 1845, *Punch* increasingly saw the frenzy for shares as a species of collective lunacy. One cartoon showed all the projected railway lines running into an asylum.[89] The following week, the magazine printed the 'Song of the railway maniac', which concluded:

> I am not mad, I am not mad;
>   See where the shares on whirlwinds fly:
> Off! – give me back the wings I had,
>   To mount and catch them in the sky.
> Maniac, I say! – you torture me! –
>   You crush me in that iron grip;
> Madman, away! and leave me free
>   To chase my railway shares and scrip.

There soon followed 'A medical lecture on the railway mania', describing the course of this most serious form of insanity. 'By degrees, reason is prostrated, and the moral feelings are perverted, so that the sufferer becomes deprived of the power of taking care of himself . . . Under these circumstances he writes frantically for Shares in Lines that are, and always will be, imaginary.' The piece continued that early seclusion was the best treatment. 'If allowed to go about at all, his hands should be muffled, to prevent him from writing for Shares; and his mouth gagged, to hinder him from persuading others to commit the same folly.'[90]

These ideas were worked out with more serious intent by Charles Reade in his novel *Hard cash*, originally serialised in *All The Year Round* in 1863.

85 Dickens, *Little Dorrit*, 571–82.
86 N. Rose, *Powers of freedom: reframing political thought*, Cambridge 1999, 105.
87 *Select committee on joint stock companies*, PP 1844, 225.
88 H. Cockton, *George St George Julian, the prince*, London 1841, 97. For similar language see *The Times*, 31 Oct. 1845.
89 *Punch* ix (18 Oct. 1845), 177.
90 Ibid. ix (25 Oct. 1845), 179; (22 Nov. 1845), 228.

Lunacy is a running theme. The banker, Richard Hardie, becomes embroiled in railway speculations during the mania of the 1840s. With a reputation for commercial soundness – he was 'a walking column of cash' – and for moral uprightness, Hardie had condemned the foolish speculations of others as based on the 'Arithmetic of Bedlam', but had been so jealous of their easy profits that he had joined in.[91] His speculations fail, and he is forced to the edge of bankruptcy. He first tries to salvage his situation honestly, in 'a long and steady struggle' of self-denial and thrift. But temptation is too strong to resist: 'now came a change, a bitter revulsion, over this tossed mind: hope and patience failed at last, and his virtue, being a thing of habit and traditions, rather than of the soul, wore out . . . No honest man . . . repented of his vices so sincerely as Richard Hardie loathed his virtue'.[92] He descends into vice, and chooses the path of grotesque swindling to stay afloat, first using money from his children's trust fund to cover his losses, then stealing from his bank's clients, culminating in taking £14,000 deposited with him by his old acquaintance, David Dodd. Dodd, driven mad by this thievery, ends up in a lunatic asylum. When Hardie's son discovers the embezzlement, he threatens to expose his father, who has him committed to a lunatic asylum. Out of these unpromising materials, Reade contrives a happy ending, but not for Hardie. In the final chapter, we see him begging in the streets of London, even though he has amassed a large fortune. He is mad, obsessed with money, and 'writhe[s] under imaginary poverty'. He dies, 'his end being hastened by fear of poverty coming like an armed man'.[93]

Responsibility

Speculation, then, in discouraging honest enterprise and promoting gambling and the base pursuit of wealth, was conceptualised as a dangerous disease of the body and the mind. The free transferability of shares which facilitated this speculation was thought to enable speculators to shirk responsibility for their actions, allowing them to pass their liabilities to others when things went wrong. This transferability therefore became a focus of criticism. Shares were not solely assets, they could also be liabilities. They represented a right to a share of the future profits of a company, but also a responsibility to make good the debts of a company. Thus to transfer shares meant transferring commitments and undertakings, which was both morally and legally dubious. Free transferability undermined the individualistic notions of contract, agency and personal responsibility central in the nineteenth-century mind to the fair conduct of trade. Private property came with responsibilities as well as rights, and that property-owners would fulfil their moral duties was one of

91 C. Reade, *Hard cash: a matter-of-fact romance*, London 1894, 165, 101.
92 Ibid. 102–3.
93 Ibid. 473.

the key justifications of the institution of property. Joint-stock enterprise with transferable shares, on the other hand, was a depersonalised form of business, in which the owners, often only transient owners, of capital had little say in how their capital was used, and could not therefore ensure that it was being deployed in a manner consistent with high moral standards. Free transferability weakened the responsibilities but left intact the right to unrestricted profit. It made it possible for speculative investors to get out of trouble if their investments disappointed. Bribes were commonly given by holders of stock in failing companies to others to take on the shares, in order to shed their responsibility. Joseph Parkes had seen much of this. He told a select committee

> The other day a gentleman, who represented 50 shares in a company, a gentleman of considerable fortune and station, was in great distress fearing proceedings in equity, knowing that the company was involved to the amount of 50,000*l*. or 60,000*l*. beyond the assets, in consequence of the failure of a London bank, and he gave 500*l*. to a party to take the assignment of his shares, and to run the risk of all litigation and liability; and I have assigned shares for gentlemen of considerable pecuniary responsibility to men of straw, in order to avoid the responsibility. It has been a frequent practice of late years, in extricating persons from bubble and ruin companies.

Parkes admitted that such a practice, in relieving parties of their liabilities, was 'to a certain degree, a fraud upon the continuing partners and upon the public'.[94] Nevertheless, many unincorporated companies, in an effort to attract investors, held out the lure of freely transferable shares, assuring the public that by the sale of these securities, the purchaser immediately stood in law in the place of the vendor. It was in order to prevent such practices that the courts endeavoured to enforce high standards of commercial responsibility. They did this by declaring illegal unincorporated companies which boasted of transferable shares.

In *Duvergier* v. *Fellows* in 1828, Chief Justice Best ruled the Patent Distillery Company illegal because it claimed that its shares were transferable. 'There can be no transferable shares', argued Best, 'except the stock of corporations, or of joint-stock companies created by acts of parliament.' Transferability meant that 'the assignee was to be placed in the precise situation that the assignor stood in before the assignment; that the assignee was to have all the rights of the assignor, and to take upon him all his liability'.[95] But this was impossible, for a share was not merely an asset, it could also be a debt, and indefinite and uncertain debts could not be transferred in this way. The assignor would remain fully liable in law for every debt contracted by the company before he ceased to be a member. Vice-Chancellor Shadwell

94 *Select committee on joint stock companies*, PP 1844, 239–40.
95 *Duvergier* v. *Fellows* (1828), 5 Bing. 248, 130 ER 1056, p. 1063.

reached a similar decision nine years later in *Blundell* v. *Winsor*, declaring the Anglo-American Mining Company illegal because it held out to the public the 'false and fraudulent representation that they might continue partners in the undertaking just as long as they pleased, and then get rid of all the liability that they had incurred by transferring their shares to some other person'. The company claimed that shareholders assigning their shares to someone else would cease to have any responsibility, and that the assignee would stand in the shoes of the assignor. For Shadwell it was clear that 'this could not be done'. Anyone who claimed that it could was guilty of promoting a fraudulent scheme, and 'The more such schemes are discouraged by Courts of Justice, the better it will be for Her Majesty's subjects.'[96]

These notions had support outside of the courts. By enforcing contracts made and responsibilities incurred, the state was not interfering in trade, merely reinforcing the natural order. J. R. McCulloch thought that 'In the scheme laid down by Providence for the government of the world, there is no shifting or narrowing of responsibilities, every man being personally answerable to the utmost extent for all his actions.'[97] Likewise, William Hawes, a merchant, argued that the under the 'moral influence' of the law of partnership, the nation's commercial greatness excited 'the envy and admiration of the world'. This law imposed upon every man of business the obligation 'to liquidate to his last farthing, every obligation he has incurred either by his agents, or himself'.[98] Legal authorities tried to warn the public of the consequent dangers of investing in unincorporated companies, pointing out that by the sale of a share in an unincorporated company, the buyer did not stand in the place of the vendor. John George warned that such a transaction 'cannot by law have this effect in perhaps one case in a thousand'. Contracts entered into which had not been completely executed, and debts owed by or to the partnership meant that the vendor was still involved by law in the affairs of the company: 'the vendor in law continues answerable for the performance of the contracts on the part of himself and copartners'.[99]

Stupid money

That such warnings were required indicated a great degree of public ignorance regarding the legal status of unincorporated companies, and the implications for investors in these bodies. This was unfortunate, for the

---

[96] *Blundell* v. *Winsor* (1837), 8 Sim. 601, 59 ER 238, pp. 242–3. Legal authorities in the 1820s and 1830s took free transferability to be evidence of illegality: Gow, *Practical treatise*, 43–4; Collyer, *Practical treatise*, 625.
[97] McCulloch, *Considerations on partnerships*, 10.
[98] W. Hawes, *Observations on unlimited and limited liability; and suggestions for the improvement of the law of partnership*, London 1854, 12.
[99] George, *View of the existing law*, 51.

public were frequently misled, as a glance at the notices on the front page of the *Morning Chronicle* of 7 November 1807 reveals. This was a period of frantic company formation, and to attract interest, promoters were not above making deceptive claims. The Eagle Insurance Company invited applications for its £50 shares thus: 'only 5*l.* per Share payable by instalments is at present required, as 200,000*l.* will thus be raised, it is more than probable no further call will ever be made'. Companies often made this assurance, inviting people to buy more shares than they could really afford, leaving them open to ruin if these calls were ever made. Further down the same page the London Genuine Wine Company claimed that 'The advantages that will accrue from this institution is [sic] obvious; as the subscribers will, *without risk*, be sure to gain at least 20 per cent. on their respective Shares.'[100] Such claims, divorcing the prospect of great gain from the concomitant prospect of great loss, were typical in promotion booms, and had an obvious appeal to passive investors. But they were highly misleading, and their outrageous claims were extensively satirised in newspapers and magazines, which published spoof company notices. *John Bull* carried several of these during the mania of 1825. One such was for the 'Resurrection Metal Company', which, to capitalise on the current high prices of metal caused by railway construction, proposed to raise all the cannon balls fired during the last war from the bottom of the sea.[101] In the hands of *Punch*, these spoofs became an art form:

> A great deal is said of a new company, whose object is to take advantage of a well-known fact in chemistry. It is known that diamonds can be resolved into charcoal, as well as that charcoal can be ultimately reduced to air; and a company is to be founded with the view of simply *reversing the process*. Instead of getting air from diamonds, their object will be to get diamonds from air; and in fact the chief promoters of it have generally drawn from that source the greater part of their capital . . . It is intended to declare a dividend at the earliest possible period, which will be directly the first diamond has been made by the new process.[102]

Such spoofs were of course on one level frivolous froth. But they had a serious aim as well, to highlight that toxic combination of greed and gullibility which was thought to keep the joint-stock system afloat. The ease with which dubious promotions managed to raise capital during boom years seemed to bear out Bagehot's conviction that 'at particular times a great many stupid people have a great deal of stupid money'.[103] Others shared Bagehot's view that the public was only too willing to buy shares first and ask questions later, if at all. George Farren, director of the Economic Life Assur-

---

100 *Morning Chronicle*, 7 Nov. 1807. Emphasis added.
101 *John Bull*, 27 Feb. 1825.
102 *Punch* i (4 Dec. 1841), 245.
103 Cited in D. Newsome, *The Victorian world picture: perceptions and introspections in an age of change*, London 1997, 77.

ance Society, was convinced of the ignorance of many who invested in companies which had obtained acts for suing and being sued. These acts did not incorporate the companies in question; therefore the shareholders who invested in them were still subject to unlimited liability. This fact, Farren argued, was entirely lost on the investors, for 'even the statutes which are of public interest are seldom examined by people in private life'. The result was that ninety-nine out of a hundred investors did not look upon their investments as sources of danger. 'The inconvenience and disquietude, which a man would labour under, if he were aware of such responsibility attaching to him, cannot be adequately described.' Denied a hand in the management of the company, such an investor would be quite unaware that the company was facing litigation and that he faced a heavy liability if the decision went against him:

> Little could he fancy at the moment, that, if satisfaction of the judgment should be delayed, either by the want of funds, or by the contumacy of those who control them, the very bed on which he slept might be seized on for the amount; – nay, that the very knocker at his hall-door might shortly announce the arrival of the holder of a writ of execution, by which his person must be imprisoned if the money should not be paid.[104]

George Henry Lewis agreed, arguing that the 'ignorance' and 'negligence' of speculators left them open to 'serious consequences'.[105] Exacerbating the situation was the fact that among those who invested were some of the most vulnerable sections of society, who were easy game for unscrupulous parties. Joseph Parkes commented of the investors of the boom of 1834–7, 'it was astonishing what a number of ladies and clergymen signed bubble subscription lists'. These were people 'who could not, from their want of knowledge of the world, be on their guard against fraud, or gambling or speculation'.[106]

This level of ignorance regarding the actual workings of the Stock Exchange and the activities of those who manipulated it meant that the public stood in a position of some disadvantage in relation to the informed stockbrokers and promoters who worked on the inside. The contrast between tricksters and tricked is highlighted in *Nicholas Nickleby* by the fortunes of two brothers, Ralph and Nicholas. Nicholas inherits his father's farm and continues in a modest way, unlike his flashier and wealthier brother. He marries, and has two children. When they are nineteen and fourteen, he considers ways of repairing his capital, greatly reduced by the expenses of his children's education.

'Speculate with it,' said Mrs Nickleby.

'Spec – u – late, my dear?' said Mr Nickleby, as though in doubt.

---

[104] G. Farren, *A treatise on life assurance*, London 1823, 33–4.
[105] Lewis, *Liabilities incurred*, 79.
[106] *Select committee on joint stock companies*, PP 1844, 227.

'Why not?' asked Mrs Nickleby.

'Because, my dear, if we *should* lose it,' rejoined Mr Nickleby, who was a slow and time-taking speaker, 'if we *should* lose it, we shall no longer be able to live, my dear.'

'Fiddle,' said Mrs Nickleby.

She reminds him of his brother's success at speculation: 'Think of your brother! Would he be what he is, if he hadn't speculated?' Nicholas is persuaded to speculate; the result is disastrous, and predictable. We do not even learn in what scheme Nicholas chooses to invest, such is the inevitability of his fate. Dickens writes: 'Speculation is a round game; the players see little or nothing of their cards at first starting; gains may be great – and so may losses. The run of luck went against Mr Nickleby. A mania prevailed, a bubble burst, four stock-brokers took villa residences at Florence, four hundred nobodies were ruined, and among them Mr Nickleby.'[107]

The potential for investors to be exploited was immense due to the defining characteristics of the joint-stock economy. Shareholders were passive investors who knew little of those to whom they entrusted their money. The decision to invest was based not on personal knowledge but reputation and rumour. Newspapers, filled with puffs for, and glowing reports of, companies and their promoters were central to the creation of the impression of solidity and respectability. In the novel *Davenport Dunn*, Charles Lever describes how the press gave the eponymous swindler a veneer of legitimacy. A character opens a newspaper and is struck by

> the fact that, turn where she would, the name of Davenport Dunn was ever conspicuous. Sales of property displayed him as the chief creditor or petitioner; charities paraded him as the first among the benevolent; joint stock companies exhibited him as their managing director; mines, and railroads, and telegraph companies, harbour committees, and boards of all kinds, gave him the honours of large type; while in the fashionable intelligence from abroad, his arrivals and departures were duly chronicled.[108]

Similarly, in *Little Dorrit*, the 'evening paper was full of Mr Merdle. His wonderful enterprise, his wonderful wealth, his wonderful Bank, were the fattening food of the evening paper that night'. But despite press coverage, no one quite understood Merdle's business activities: 'nobody knew with the least precision what Mr. Merdle's business was, except that it was to coin money'.[109] Such ignorance does not stop investors entrusting these men with their cash, however.[110]

This was a far cry from the ideal of market relations held by many in the nineteenth century. Influenced by the classical republican concept of active

---

107 Dickens, *Nicholas Nickleby*, 12–13.
108 Lever, *Davenport Dunn*, 42.
109 Dickens, *Little Dorrit*, 558, 394.
110 Lever, *Davenport Dunn*, 10.

citizenship, liberals like John Stuart Mill idealised small societies where tradesmen were personally known to the communities they served. Public opinion acted as an effective check on fraud, for if a trader cheated his customers, he could not hope to continue in business. But in great cities, tradesmen were not regulated by local knowledge. 'Success, in so crowded a field, depends not upon what a person is, but upon what he seems.'[111] Public opinion became an irrational force easily manipulated by advertising: the tradesman could swindle his customers, but new ones would enter his shop every day.[112] For many, joint-stock enterprise was another example of this degeneration, since here rumour and hearsay replaced personal knowledge as the prime influence on market behaviour. Solidity could be implied by the mere suggestion of wealth: 'The Age of Appearance', David Morier Evans called it.[113] Company promoters who knew the importance of show and display would secure investment, because appearances implied wealth, stability and safe investments. On the stage, corrupt financiers were invariably well-dressed. The costume directions for Captain Hawksley in Tom Taylor's 1855 comedy, *Still waters run deep*, suggest the swindler's flashiness and lack of substance: 'fashionable frock coat, fancy tweed trousers, drab vest, fancy cravat'. Later, he is seen in 'fancy morning coat and smoking cap, buff jean trousers, fancy vest and cravat'. His apartments are 'gaily and luxuriously furnished'.[114] In William Bayle Bernard's 1842 play *Locomotion*, a farce on the rush and bustle of the railway age, Floss, a crooked auctioneer, avers that, in a world going too fast to dwell upon truth, appearances were all that mattered: 'in our day, success depends on motion – that now mind as well as matter is going at a gallop, the only [way] to get business, is to seem as if you had it'.[115]

But Dickens gives the best account of the centrality of show to, and the actual hollowness of, joint-stock enterprise in his 1844 novel, *Martin Chuzzlewit*. He describes the offices of the Anglo-Bengalee Disinterested Loan and Life Assurance Company, which could be found in a spacious house, 'resplendent in stucco and plate-glass', located in a new street in the city:

> Within, the offices were newly plastered, newly painted, newly papered, newly countered, newly floor-clothed, newly tabled, newly chaired, newly fitted up in every way, with goods that were substantial and expensive, and designed

---

111 J. S. Mill, 'Civilization', *London and Westminster Review* iii/xxv (Apr. 1836), repr. in his *Essays on politics and society, collected works*, Toronto 1977, xviii. 119–47 at p. 133.

112 For further discussion of Mill's views on this subject see E. F. Biagini, 'Liberalism and direct democracy: John Stuart Mill and the model of ancient Athens', in E. F. Biagini (ed.), *Citizenship and community: Liberals, radicals and collective identities in the British Isles, 1865–1931*, Cambridge 1996, 21–44.

113 D. M. Evans, *Facts, failures and frauds: revelations financial mercantile criminal*, New York 1968, 74.

114 Taylor, *Still waters run deep*, 32.

115 W. B. Bernard, *Locomotion*, London 1842, 3.

(like the company) to last. Business! Look at the green ledgers with red backs, like strong cricket-balls beaten flat; the court-guides, directories, day-books, almanacks, letter-boxes, weighing-machines for letters, rows of fire-buckets for dashing out a conflagration in its first spark, and saving the immense wealth in notes and bonds belonging to the company . . . Solidity! Look at the massive blocks of marble in the chimney-pieces, and the gorgeous parapet on the top of the house! Publicity! Why, Anglo-Bengalee Disinterested Loan and Life Insurance Company, is painted on the very coal-scuttles.

This attention to show and display pays off. Tigg Montague, the company chairman, tells Jonas Chuzzlewit, 'There are printed calculations . . . which will tell you pretty nearly how many people will pass up and down that thoroughfare in the course of a day. I can tell you how many of 'em will come in here, merely because they find this office here; knowing no more about it than they do of the Pyramids. Ha, ha!' He continues, 'I can tell you . . . how many of 'em will buy annuities, effect insurances, bring us their money in a hundred shapes and ways, force it upon us, trust us as if we were the Mint; yet know no more about us than you do of that crossing-sweeper at the corner.'[116]

Speculation and the social order

Some might have suspected that sweeper of having a few shares in the Anglo-Bengalee too, for novelists and other commentators frequently remarked on the all-encompassing nature of investment in shares. Factual accounts of the 'South Sea Bubble' stressed the wide social range of investors: 'the lower class of people fell into luxury and prodigality, as well as their betters . . . Persons of quality of both sexes were deeply engaged'.[117] The railway mania seemed to provide an even more striking example of this social gallimaufry. For Reade, the investors who fuelled this boom were 'a motley crew of peers and printers, vicars and admirals, professors, cooks, costermongers, cotton-spinners, waiters, coachmen, priests, potboys, bankers, braziers, dairy-men, mail-guards, barristers, spinsters, butchers, beggars, duchesses, rag-merchants'.[118] Evans remarked that no one who had ever attended a railway shareholders' meeting, 'can have failed to notice the various grades of society thus brought together, from the haughty and aristocratic millionaire, boasting, perhaps, possession of the larger amount of the stock of the concern, to the petty tradesman, holding his little all in an investment of five shares'.[119]

The spectacle of duchesses and spinsters in the share market was particularly alarming. Women were not expected to engage in business: the law

---

116 Dickens, *Martin Chuzzlewit*, 372–3, 410.
117 Macpherson, *Annals of commerce*, 88–9.
118 Reade, *Hard cash*, 100. Bell provided a similar view: *Ladder of gold*, i. 276–7.
119 [Evans], *The City*, 89.

discriminated against married women, refusing to recognise them as partners. They 'died a kind of civil death' on marriage, and could not 'sign Bills of Exchange, make contracts, sue or be sued, collect debts or stand surety'.[120] Though women often played an active role in the day-to-day business of part-nerships, this was a subservient and dependent role. However, joint-stock companies presented women with an opportunity for independent commer-cial activity, and their seizure of this opportunity was seen as incongruous and faintly inappropriate.[121]

The habit of speculation was thought to reach up to the very top of society. The sight of lords, ladies and clergy attending George Hudson's *soirées* attracted much adverse comment, as in the image 'He gives soirées (who goes)?' (*see* plate 6) from Alfred Crowquill's satirical account of Hudson's rise and fall. The prevalence of the speculating urge in high society was a favourite theme for many. 'Speculation', wrote Dudley Costello in his 1856 novel *The joint-stock banker*, serialised in *Bentley's Miscellany*, 'is no longer confined to the areas of Capel-court and the Stock Exchange, but peeps from between the rose-hued curtains of the countess's boudoir, and sits in council with the country-gentleman as he sips his claret in his ancestral halls.'[122] This theme was dwelled upon so obsessively because it set a bad example to the masses, who learned speculative habits from their superiors. In Lever's novel, Dunn's secretary, Clowes, imitating his master, is engaged in the task of promoting the Lough Corrib Drainage and Fresh Strawberry Company, to provide the poor with strawberries.[123] In Henry Cockton's *George St. George Julian*, Peter, the servant of a group of fraudsters, wants to improve his lowly position, but having imbibed his employers' morality, thinks the only way he can do this is by joint-stock enterprise, and wishes, 'If I could only just get up some company, some new association, or something of that sort'. His mind is teeming with ideas, such as the British and Foreign Association for the Reno-vation of White Kid Gloves, and the Imperial Poyaisian Association for the Total Intoxication of Mosquitoes. He fails to see that honest labour is the only route to self-improvement, until the end of the novel when the hero offers him employment on his estate, at £200 a year.[124]

It was speculation among the lower orders that really preoccupied commentators. What was so disturbing was the belief that in the maelstrom of speculative frenzies, society's hierarchies were dissolved and could be reformed in new, unusual shapes. Speculation by the lower orders was facili-tated by the tiny deposits required on shares. Well-to-do Victorians increas-ingly suspected that their servants and workers were dabbling in shares and

[120] Davidoff and Hall, *Family fortunes*, 200.
[121] See, for example, 'A Doe in the City', *Punch* ix (1 Nov. 1845), 191.
[122] D. Costello, 'The joint-stock banker', *Bentley's Miscellany* xxxix (June 1856), 551–66 at p. 558.
[123] Lever, *Davenport Dunn*, 158.
[124] Cockton, *George St. George Julian*, 106, 76, 104, 269.

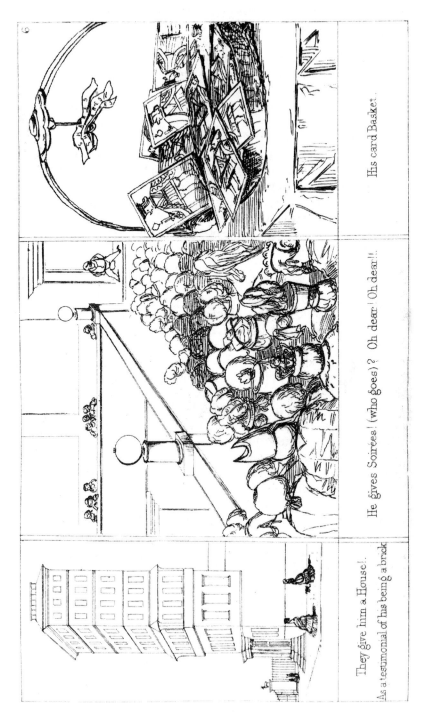

Plate 6. 'He gives soirées! (who goes)? Oh dear! Oh dear!!'.
Source: Alfred Crowquill, *How he reigned and how he mizzled: a railway raillery*, London 1849, 6.
By permission of the British Library (shelfmark Cup.402.d.11)

that the lucky ones might make enormous profits and achieve independence. The amazing turnarounds in fortune that could be occasioned by stock market investment were occasionally employed for comic effect. Thackeray's *Diary of C. Jeames de la Pluche, Esq.* was serialised in *Punch* in 1845–6, and told the story of James Plush, a footman, who speculated in railways and made a fortune.[125] Most of the stories revolved around his absurd pretentions to gentility. *Punch* carried several cartoons on the incongruity of the poor becoming players on the stock market, such as 'Railroad speculators' (*see* plate 7), published at the height of the railway mania.

Despite these lighthearted views of the levelling effects of speculation, Victorians were clearly unsettled by the democratic implications of such investment. Of the railway mania, the Stock Exchange's Edward Callow later recalled, 'a solicitor or two, a civil engineer, a Parliamentary agent, possibly a contractor, a map of England, a pair of compasses, a pencil, and a ruler, were all that were requisite to commence the formation of a railway company'.[126] Such resources were in the reach of many. Lord Overstone wrote to a friend in the early 1860s that 'Joint Stock Banks and Limited Liability Companies – are the order of the day – and the boldest man seems the most likely to be prosperous . . . The world is going up and down stairs, *without laying hold of the banister.*'[127] All social stability was sacrificed in times of speculation: stock-brokers darted around, 'like messengers of doom, with the fate of thousands clutched in scraps of dirty paper in their hands'.[128] People willingly placed their fates in such unworthy hands. The result was, as Hankes, Dunn's partner in joint-stock crime, opines, 'There is no such thing as rich or poor now, for you may be either, or both, within any twenty-four hours.'[129]

Bell's *The ladder of gold* reveals great concern that the joint-stock system allowed unworthy parvenus to rise above their station. Early in the novel, the young Richard Rawlings, beset by poverty and drudgery, comes to realise the power of wealth and resolves to dedicate his life to its pursuit, at all costs: 'It is the ladder by which men ascend to power over their fellow men. Why should not I, too, plant my foot upon it, and climb as well as others?'[130] His climb is rapid, and he becomes a successful railway director. But his ambitions stretch far beyond power and wealth: he wants to become a gentleman, respected in the highest social circles. He later reflects that, courted by 'a venal crowd of great people [who] insisted upon setting me up for worship in their circles . . . I determined to fix myself there, so that they could not shake me off when I

---

125 The first story in the series appeared in *Punch* ix (2 Aug. 1845), 59.

126 Cited in Kynaston, *World of its own*, 153.

127 Lord Overstone to G. W. Norman, 24 Oct. 1863, in D. P. O'Brien (ed.), *The correspondence of Lord Overstone*, Cambridge 1971, iii. 1017. Norman had recently fallen down a staircase as he had not been holding on to the banister.

128 Bell, *Ladder of gold*, i. 276.

129 Lever, *Davenport Dunn*, 324.

130 Bell, *Ladder of gold*, i. 31.

"HOW MANY HUNDRED SHARES HAVE YOU WROTE FOR?"

Plate 7. 'Railroad speculators'.
Source: *Punch* viii (31 May 1845), 244.

had served their turn'. To this end, he secures the marriage of his daughter into the aristocracy. Other fictional speculators attempt similar strategies, such as Melmotte in *The way we live now*, while in Charles Lever's novel, Dunn calculates 'that a recognised station amongst the nobles of the land was the only security against disaster'.[131]

But their grandiose plans always meet with failure: their financial empires collapse, and they are punished by suicide (Melmotte, Merdle), murder (Montague, Dunn), ruin (Brough, Cassilis) or repentance and the adoption of more wholesome values (Hawk, Rawlings).[132] In each instance, it is made clear that corruption leads only to short-term success: the *status quo* is eventually restored. In this way, the alarming democratic implications of joint-stock investment are contained. Affluent readers would be reassured; working-class readers would be dissuaded from emulating the parvenu speculators. Such views were compatible with broader social opinion, which tended to assume that manias would always end with a 'day of reckoning' when the guilty would be punished.[133] Particularly reassuring for the reader was the story which ended with the chastened anti-hero realising the error of his ways and undertaking to choose the path of honest labour. This is the fate of Richard Rawlings. At the conclusion of *The ladder of gold*, he accepts the centrality of family, love and labour, and renounces speculation. He embarks on

> an industrial career, in which everything depended on quiet perseverance, and in which the reputation of having a genius for creating wealth out of bubbles would have damaged rather than served him. He was glad enough to part with that dangerous prestige, and to address himself to small gains, procured by steady and patient efforts.[134]

Vowing that from now on he will 'labour as a man like me ought to labour', the new Rawlings knows his place, declaiming, 'Let no man who rises from obscurity hope to bridge over with gold the gulf that divides him from them. If he be wise, he will keep in his own sphere.'[135] McCulloch might as well have been reviewing the novel when he asserted that mankind should look for their advancement not to speculation, but 'to the blessing of Providence on their industry, perseverance, and economy, and to nothing else'.[136]

But in spite of the reassuring resolutions to these novels, authors, it

---

131 Lever, *Davenport Dunn*, 338.
132 Gabriel Cassilis is a company director and financier in W. Besant and J. Rice, *The golden butterfly*, London n.d, originally published in 1876.
133 *The Times*, 1 July 1845. See Hilton, *Age of atonement*, 131–6, for views on the trade cycle and retribution for speculation.
134 Bell, *Ladder of gold*, iii. 316–17. One wonders whether George Hudson, on whom Rawlings was closely based, ever read the book.
135 Ibid. iii. 305, 303.
136 McCulloch, *Considerations on partnerships*, 26. For identical sentiments see Anon., *South Sea Bubble*, 7.

seemed, were not attempting to induce complacency among their readers. Neil McKendrick is perhaps mistaken when he argues that evil entrepreneurs were employed in nineteenth-century fiction as scapegoats upon whom all the blame for the instability and insecurity of the Victorian economy could be heaped.[137] These businessmen were certainly set up and knocked down with great regularity in the nineteenth-century novel, but the enactment of the ritual was not intended to make for entirely comfortable reading. In *Davenport Dunn*, Lackington and Twining are complacent about men like Dunn: they have wealth, but not 'prestige', and are ultimately of little consequence. They tell each other that such men exert only 'a passing influence on our society', having some influence when rich, but vanishing as soon as they suffer a reversal, leaving 'no trace of their existence behind them. The bubble burst, the surface of the stream remains without a ripple'.[138] But Lever clearly disagrees. He is outspoken as to the moral failings of the public which had paid 'degrading homage' to money. Gold had become 'the standard of all moral excellence . . . From the highest in the Peerage to the poorest peasant, all were involved in the same scheme of ruin'.[139]

The chief target was not the swindler, but the people, wealthy and poor alike, who allowed themselves to be taken in, for in doing so, they revealed the extent of their moral turpitude. In *George St. George Julian*, Bull, the stockbroker, boasts, 'The world scorns poverty, not wealth: nor does it ever scorn those who possess it . . . What is it to the world where the money comes from, or how it was obtained?'[140] Another fictional speculator reasons 'If the sportsman returned from the field laden with game, who would scrutinize the mud on his gaiters?' He is aware 'how deep a man may wallow in the mire, how thoroughly he may besmear himself from head to foot in the blackest, foulest mud, and yet be received an honoured guest by ladies gay and noble lords, if only his bag be sufficiently full'.[141]

This idea recurred in countless novels. When Meredyth Powell Jones, the 'hero' of Dudley Costello's *The joint-stock banker*, stands for election, the 'excitable inhabitants' of the Welsh borough in question 'got furiously drunk, and rolled about the streets in glorification of "The Man of the People;" and if their brains had not been topsy-turvy already they would have stood upon their heads for "The Man of the People," and have crawled on their hands and knees to worship "The Man of the People" '.[142] In *Little Dorrit*, serialised at the same time as Costello's novel, Dickens reached great peaks of indignation, arguing that by elevating Merdle to the position of a God, the public

---

137 McKendrick, 'Literary luddism', p. xxxv.
138 Lever, *Davenport Dunn*, 64.
139 Ibid. 679, 683, 682.
140 Cockton, *George St George Julian*, 131–2.
141 These are the thoughts of Alaric Tudor, the civil servant lured into corrupt speculation by Undy Scott: Trollope, *Three clerks*, 169, 186.
142 D. Costello, 'The joint-stock banker', *Bentley's Miscellany* xxxix (Apr. 1856), 346–65 at p. 350.

had proved its moral bankruptcy: 'All people knew (or thought they knew) that he had made himself immensely rich; and, for that reason alone, prostrated themselves before him, more degradedly and less excusably than the darkest savage creeps out of his hole in the ground to propitiate, in some log or reptile, the Deity of his benighted soul.'[143] Emma Robinson was equally scathing in her 1851 novel *The gold-worshippers*. The aristocracy is pilloried for its devotion to its 'false god', Mr Humson: 'The idol entered, and all the worshippers were instantly – we cannot exactly say prostrate, except in soul.'[144] 'The idol was certainly worthy of his worshippers', comments Robinson, who continues, 'surely the crawling priests and frequenters of the temple were more to be despised and condemned than the object of their adoration!'[145]

Humson was, of course, Hudson, who had, according to Carlyle, revealed the true aspirations and desires of the general public. The electors of Sunderland may have returned him to parliament, but the greater public had 'voted' for him in a more significant way, by purchasing his shares:

> Hudson the railway king, if Popular Election be the rule, seems to me by far the most authentic king extant in this world. Hudson has been 'elected by the people' so as almost none other is or was. Hudson solicited no vote; his votes were silent voluntary ones, not liable to be false: he *did* a thing which men found, in their inarticulate hearts, to be worthy of paying money for; and they paid it. What the desire of every heart was, Hudson had or seemed to have produced: Scrip out of which profit could be made.

And so a subscription was raised for a statue in Hudson's honour. Statues to such men were 'high columns, raised by prurient stupidity and public delusion, to blockheads whose memory does in eternal fact deserve the sinking of a coalshaft'. Carlyle found them as offensive as 'dungheaps laid on the streets'.[146]

Judgements in the aftermath of the railway mania revealed some unlikely bedfellows. The Revd John Cumming judged: 'What a terrible standard is that by which the city estimates man . . . To be a "respectable" man means to be rich.'[147] Herbert Spencer agreed, condemning the 'indiscriminate respect' which was paid to wealth by 'an immoral public opinion', identifying it as the 'chief cause of the dishonesties' perpetrated by businessmen. People were praising the external signs of wealth rather than the qualities which had produced the wealth, and were consequently guilty of 'idolatry which worships the symbol apart from the thing symbolized'.[148] This idolatry was

---

143 Dickens, *Little Dorrit*, 556.
144 Cited in Russell, *Novelist and mammon*, 180.
145 [Robinson], *Gold-worshippers*, 104–5.
146 T. Carlyle, 'Hudson's statue', in his *Latter-day pamphlets*, London 1911, 225, 244.
147 J. Cumming, 'The age we live in', in *Young Men's Christian Association*, 308–36 at p. 332.
148 Spencer, 'Morals of trade', 140–6. Spencer's article was later republished, with his

THE RAILWAY JUGGERNAUT OF 1845.

Plate 8. 'The railway juggernaut of 1845'.
Source: *Punch* ix (26 July 1845), 47.

satirised in *Punch* in 1845 (*see* plate 8) where the railway was depicted as a 'Juggernaut', a crude Hindu idol.

At an annual festival the Juggernaut was wheeled through the town and worshippers are supposed to have thrown themselves under its wheels. In this cartoon, railway investors can be seen bringing tributes of money bags to their idol, the Railway Juggernaut, and falling down in worship before it, and being crushed in the process. Speculators may have been wise after the event, but this was evidence of hypocrisy rather than a sign that the public had learned its lesson. As soon as news of Davenport Dunn's death spreads, for example, though no-one had hitherto dared to question the man's integrity, society is unanimous in condemning him: 'what noble words of reproof fell from Pulpit and Press upon the lust of wealth, the base pursuit of gold!'[149] The story was the same every time: worship, then rejection, but only once the swindler had been exposed and the bubble burst. Dickens thought the chances of the public ever learning its lesson were nil. After Merdle's collapse, he has one character note: 'The next man who has as large a capacity and as genuine a taste for swindling, will succeed as well. Pardon me, but I think you really have no idea how the human bees will swarm to the beating of any old tin kettle; in that fact lies the complete manual of governing them.'[150]

It is possible to detect a pervasive culture of antipathy to speculation in nine-teenth-century Britain. Attitudes inherited from an earlier age were developed and moulded into a coherent set of beliefs which was sufficiently flexible to be adopted by a wide range of classes and groups. These views, combined with the preference for individual over corporate enterprise detailed in chapter 1, were regularly expressed in the courts and in parliament, and determined executive and legislative responses when applications were made by companies for special privileges. Yet they did not remain unchallenged. They found themselves increasingly assaulted by alternative attitudes to joint-stock investment advanced primarily by the promoters of joint-stock companies. The outcome of this challenge is explored in part II of this book.

---

permission, by the Revd Canon Lyttleton in a pamphlet along with a sermon by the latter on the same subject: Spencer, *An autobiography*, 30.

[149] Lever, *Davenport Dunn*, 683.

[150] Dickens, *Little Dorrit*, 738. For a similar expression of pessimism see Thackeray, *Great Hoggarty diamond*, 341–2.

PART II

THE CHANGE IN THE LAW

3

Change Contained, 1800–1840

Suspicion of, and hostility to, joint-stock enterprise and speculation could be detected at many levels of society in nineteenth-century Britain. But alternative views were being propounded. In the first quarter of the century, these arguments twice received a thorough airing during booms of company formation, once during the Napoleonic Wars, and once after. Both periods were characterised by extensive speculation in the shares of unincorporated companies in a wide variety of trades, though the second boom was on a much greater scale. Most of these companies were, in law, simply large partnerships, and in both periods there was extensive debate on the subject of their legal status. As a result of this debate, the law relating to unincorporated companies was revised in 1825, and during a third period of speculation and company formation in the 1830s the law was amended twice more. It will be argued that these changes in the law cannot be seen as landmarks in the evolution of 'modern' company law, or as evidence that those who supported free incorporation and general limited liability were gaining the upper hand. A consideration of the first forty years of the century reveals a great degree of consistency in the legal position of companies, and in both official and popular conceptions of companies and speculation. The repeal of the Bubble Act in 1825 was promoted by the government partly to redistribute the burden of making decisions on incorporation from parliament to the Board of Trade, and partly to dispense with what had come to be seen as an irrelevant relic of the eighteenth century. Though the measure was certainly inspired by a sense of the benefits some of the companies promoted in recent years were bringing to the country, it did not signal a desire to make access to corporate privileges automatic: firms would still have to approach either parliament, or preferably the Board of Trade, for these privileges. The Whig acts of 1834 and 1837 built on the method of reform adopted by the Tory government in 1825, evincing considerable aversion to parliamentary incorporation after the extent of the corruption of private bill committees had been revealed during the boom of 1824–5. These measures sought to extend access to corporate privileges, while retaining the state's control. Proposals to reform the laws regulating companies in a more radical way were therefore thwarted; the main thrust of the law, that incorporation was a privilege to be granted by the state on a case-by-case basis, rather than a right to be enjoyed by all, held throughout these years.

Justifying the joint-stock company

The resumption of war with France in 1803 promoted an increase in economic activity in Britain, one manifestation of which was a boom in joint-stock company formation between 1806 and 1809. There were two key differences between this period and the 'canal mania' of 1791–4, during which forty-two new canals were authorised.[1] First, in the 1806–9 boom, companies were promoted in many sectors of the economy, not just in internal navigation. Second, whereas the canal companies, because of their need for compulsory powers of purchase, had all been incorporated by act of parliament, the bulk of the companies of the latter boom were trading without any legislative sanction. Both factors combined to make this boom deeply contentious. Whereas canal companies were formed to carry out tasks which private individuals or partnerships would have found impossible, now companies were being projected to compete with existing businesses, causing one trader to complain: 'in every article of consumption, in every species of manufacture, in every line of trade, there are now projects of Joint-Stock Companies going on'. This activity was not restricted to the metropolis: 'every county, every town has now its Joint-Stock scheme; every provincial paper is filled with their plans; every county Banking Shop has its prospectus'.[2] In 1807 there was, Thomas Tooke later claimed, 'an almost universal excitement' which led to 'hazardous adventure'.[3] A correspondent of the *Monthly Magazine* produced a list of forty-two companies promoted during the year (*see* table 1). As can be seen, nearly all of them were formed in trades hitherto carried on by individuals. Many greeted the projects with unwavering contempt. One correspondent of the *Morning Chronicle* avowed his 'intention of taking my wine, beer, milk, and coals from the individuals who have hitherto supplied me with those articles quite to my satisfaction'.[4]

But were they illegal? This was the question posed when an anonymous individual began criminal proceedings against the engineer and entrepreneur Ralph Dodd, who had promoted two companies, the London Paper Manufacturing Company and the London Distillery Company. The attorney-general sought an information against Dodd in November 1807. The prospectuses of both companies had promised transferable shares and limitation of liability by deed of trust, thus seemingly contravening the Bubble Act. The act, passed at the height of the speculative mania of 1720, had sought to curb the excesses of company promotion by preventing unincorporated companies from behaving like incorporated ones. It declared that 'the acting or

---

1   C. Cook and J. Stevenson, *British historical facts, 1760–1830*, Hamden 1980, 189.
2   Letter from 'a plain dealer', *Morning Chronicle*, 5 Nov. 1807.
3   T. Tooke and W. Newmarch, *A history of prices and of the state of the circulation from 1792 to 1856*, London 1928, i. 277.
4   Letter from 'an old-fashioned fellow', *Morning Chronicle*, 9 Nov. 1807.

Table 1
Companies formed during 1807

Sector	Number	Sector	Number
Brewing	7	Provisions	4
Insurance	5	Coal	3
Wine	5	Clothing/textiles	3
Banking/finance	5	Copper	2
Distilling	4	Misc.	4

Source: *Monthly Magazine*, cited in Tooke and Newmarch, *A history of prices*, i. 278–80.

presuming to act as a corporate body, the raising, or pretending to raise, transferable stock, the transferring, or pretending to transfer or assign, any share in such stock, without legal authority, either by Act of Parliament, or by any Charter from the Crown' was illegal. This was because companies which did these things tended 'to the common grievance, prejudice, and inconvenience of the subjects in general, or great numbers of them, in their trade, commerce, or other lawful affairs', and were 'nuisances' which had to be suppressed.[5] Soon after the act's passage, however, the mania for companies subsided, and despite the spread of unincorporated business activity in some sectors of the economy in the late eighteenth century, the act had not been invoked since 1723. The rising tide of speculation in the early 1800s, though, brought the events of 1719–20 back into the collective consciousness. Detailed accounts of the mania were published, describing the 'infatuation' and 'delusion' of that period.[6] The spectre of the 'South Sea Bubble' was revived in parliament.[7] The relevant provisions of the Bubble Act were reprinted in daily newspapers, 'as a caution to the public against incurring the serious penalties of that Act'.[8] Company promoters, several of whom had become public figures by dint of the vigour with which they advertised their schemes, were turned into figures of ridicule. They formed the subject of a print, 'The school of projects' (*see* plate 9), published in the *Satirist* in October 1809.

---

[5] The measure also indicated the political influence of the South Sea Company, which lobbied the government to restrict the flow of investment capital into joint-stock schemes, capital which the South Sea Company wanted for itself: Harris, *Industrializing English law*, ch. iii.

[6] Macpherson, *Annals of commerce*, iii. 76–103; Anon., *An account of the South Sea Scheme and a number of other bubbles . . . with a few remarks upon some schemes which are now in agitation*, London 1806. The latter account was extracted from William Maitland's *History of London*, first published in 1739. For an account of how the concept of a 'South Sea Bubble' took hold from the 1770s and influenced nineteenth-century perceptions of speculation see Hoppit, 'Myths of the South Sea Bubble', 163–5.

[7] In a debate on a gas light bill, one MP warned that the project 'might turn out ultimately a second South Sea bubble'. Another likened it to the notorious Ayr Bank, which had failed in the 1770s: *Hansard*, 1st ser. xiv. 860–1 (2 June 1809).

[8] *Morning Chronicle*, 12 Nov. 1807; see also *Morning Post*, 13 Nov. 1807.

Plate 9. 'The school of projects'.
Source: BM 11439, *English cartoons and satirical prints, 1320–1832.*
© The Trustees of the British Museum.

Centre stage is Frederic Winsor, the promoter of London gas and banking projects, standing in front of a broken gas burner from which flames issue, indicating the perils associated with his schemes. He holds a gas-lighter, forked to resemble the devil's tail. On the left are crouched Ralph Dodd and an accomplice. In addition to his paper manufactories and distilleries, Dodd was engaged in promoting schemes for a tunnel from Gravesend to Tilbury, and bridges at Vauxhall and the Strand. These projects are satirised here: Dodd and his friend can be seen carefully constructing a tunnel between the earth and the moon, which are already connected by a bridge. Towards the right of the scene stands George Leybourne, alleged to have a plan for making sheep grow to the size of oxen. Here he is shown feeding a ram with a prospectus for Dodd's Vauxhall Bridge. On the far right of the picture sits William Brown, promoter and manager of the Golden Lane Brewery and the London Bank, smugly overseeing these happenings. Company prospectuses litter his chair and the floor around him. A statue of Hope looks down on him: at best, these promoters are shown to possess a dangerous optimism, at worst, they are depicted as wicked fraudsters.[9]

The victims of these fraudsters are the subject of another print of 1809, 'Joint stock street' (*see* plate 10). Here, rows of gullible speculators gaze upwards at adverts for what are obviously bubble schemes plastered on a wall outside the 'Hospital for Incurables', a reference to the demented investors below. These range from well-dressed ladies and city men, to country types, to an old Jewish man carrying a sack of clothes, stressing the degree to which the enthusiasm for speculation permeated the whole of society. The schemes advertised are either for spurious enterprises – 'a New Company of Mowers of Beards having discover'd a New Machine to Shave 60 men in a minute', 'a New Cabbage and Potatoe Company Warranted Genuine No cooking required' – or for those best conducted by individuals – a milk company, a coffin company, a blacking company and a match and tinder company with a capital of two million divided into shares of five farthings. In case the point was missed, a sign saying 'Bubble Alley' leads off to the right, above an advertisement placed by Peter Puff. Smoke from chimneys fills the air, a metaphor for the ethereal enterprises advertised below.[10] Such cartoons suggest that the revival of the Bubble Act at a time of extravagant promotions struck a chord with at least a section of public opinion.

The world of company promotion was thrown into uncertainty by this revival, and those connected with companies were driven into print to prove the legality and utility of their businesses. Setting the terms of the debate

---

[9] For commentary on the print see George, *Catalogue of political and personal satires*, viii. 881–2. For more on Winsor see T. I. Williams, *A history of the British gas industry*, Oxford 1981, 6–10, and S. Everard, *The history of the Gas Light and Coke Company, 1812–1949*, London 1949, 17–26. For Brown and the Golden Lane Brewery see P. Mathias, *The brewing industry in England, 1700–1830*, Cambridge 1959, 243–51.
[10] George, *Catalogue of political and personal satires*, viii. 883–4.

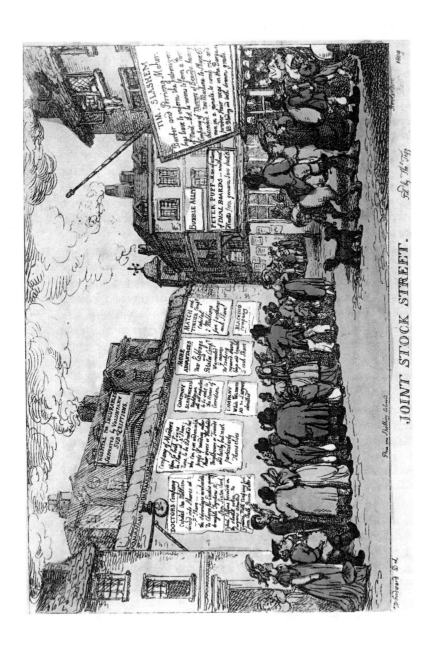

Plate 10. 'Joint stock street'.
Source: BM 11441, *English cartoons and satirical prints, 1320–1832.*
© The Trustees of the British Museum.

which would take place over the next fifty years, they couched their arguments in the language of *laissez-faire* and freedom from judicial and legislative interference. 'Philopatris', a representative of the Golden Lane Brewery, decried the absurdity of the attempts made in the press and elsewhere 'to mislead the Country, to suppose that an Association of Gentlemen for commercial purposes is illegal. Such Associations have existed for centuries past; and are we now, in this age of civil liberty, to be deprived of commercial freedom?'[11] For Henry Day, solicitor to the British Ale Brewery, the case for joint-stock companies was part of the larger argument for free trade and 'against all judicial interference with commercial speculations'. Curiously, given Adam Smith's hostility to extensive joint-stock operations, he invoked Smith in justification of his position.[12]

These writers did not rest their argument on the desirability of freedom from interference alone: they also wanted to show that their companies actively promoted the national interest, and were therefore justified by their public utility. This utility was defined in terms of the extent to which they promoted competition. Challenging accepted opinion, Frederick Eden, author of *The state of the poor*, and chairman of the Globe Insurance Company, in an anonymous pamphlet defending joint-stock enterprise, argued that monopoly was not an essential characteristic of corporate bodies, reasoning that 'the obvious effect of creating non-exclusive companies, in addition to existing traders, is to add to the assortment of dealers which the public possesses, and consequently to increase their chance of benefit from competition'.[13] Having adopted a penname which underlined his patriotism, 'Philopatris' argued that 'public' companies such as the Golden Lane Brewery served the national interest by breaking up existing monopolies established by individuals.[14] Day agreed, arguing that these 'public spirited associations' were 'salutary, reasonable, and necessary coadjutors to the legislature in counteracting fraud, abuse, and extortion'. Companies would help to 'rescue the public from that overgrown Aristocracy of Capitalists, by which it has so long been oppressed'.[15] The proponents of joint-stock schemes in parliament followed suit, challenging the association in the public mind between companies and monopoly. Speaking in support of the proposed Marine Society Fishery Bill in 1803, the independent MPs Sir William Dolben and Sir William Geary reasoned that talk of the society promoting monopoly was misguided, because the public already suffered from 'combinations between

---

11 Anon. ['Philopatris'], *Observations on public institutions, monopolies, joint stock companies, and deeds of trust: shewing the advantages the public derive from competition in trade*, London 1807, 2.

12 H. Day, *A defence of joint stock companies; being an attempt to shew their legality, expediency, and public benefit*, London 1808, 5.

13 [F. Eden], *On the policy and expediency of granting insurance charters*, London 1806, 10.

14 ['Philopatris'], *Observations on public institutions*, 11–12.

15 Day, *Defence of joint stock companies*, 70, 52, 47.

the fishermen, and their agents at Billingsgate'.[16] Seven years later, the promoter of the Marine Insurance Bill argued that the company would not become a monopoly because 'the increased commerce of this country would afford business enough for all'. Furthermore, the bill aimed to repeal the sections of the Bubble Act which gave a monopoly to two companies, the Royal Exchange Assurance and the London Assurance.[17] In this way, company spokesmen attempted to position themselves on the side of the public interest against monopolists and fraudsters and presented their companies as tools to combat these evils by giving consumers greater choice in the marketplace.

Such arguments equipped proponents of companies to contradict claims that all companies which raised a transferable stock without state authority were illegal. They argued that a company's legal status depended not upon whether it had transferable shares, but upon its utility. On their understanding, the Bubble Act only outlawed companies with transferable shares if these companies could be considered nuisances, that is, if they entered trades where there was already sufficient competition. They believed 'that which is of public utility, cannot be a "nuisance", either in common law or in common sense'.[18] In short, utility, rather than transferability of shares, was the test of legality. Companies which promoted competition passed this test. They did not pose a danger to the public: on the contrary, joint-stock funds offered greater security to creditors than what Eden termed the 'personal Responsibility Fund'. This latter fund, though in theory unlimited, was also unknown and uncertain, whereas the joint-stock fund, though sometimes limited, was publicly known and was certain to exist.[19] The emergence of responsible joint-stock schemes was the result of progress, and attachment to individual enterprise should not be allowed to block progress: 'Personal Responsibility, in trade, is well adapted to a state of society in which traffick can be carried on by individuals or partnerships composed of a few individuals. But in the extended operations of mercantile adventure, which are the natural consequence of national improvement, new modes of forming contracts become necessary.'[20] The greater the capital invested in companies the better: 'By enabling individuals to render small capitals productive, these establishments promote the increase of national wealth.'[21] Company spokesmen were unabashed in presenting their interests as identical to the national interest. Such was the amount of property invested in companies that the interests of

16 *Hansard*, 1st ser. i. 1052 (27 Mar. 1803). In 1806 the Globe Insurance Bill was supported in the Commons in the name of promoting competition: ibid. xii. 812 (24 June 1806).
17 W. Manning, ibid. xv. 400 (14 Feb. 1810).
18 ['Philopatris'], *Observations on public institutions*, 26.
19 Eden, *Insurance charters*, 7–9.
20 Ibid. 9.
21 Day, *Defence of joint stock companies*, 72.

companies and of the nation as a whole could not be separated. Litigation threw this property into jeopardy, and therefore threatened the public interest. 'To disturb the repose or prosperity of these valuable Undertakings, would convulse the Nation to its centre, and be fully as alarming as a national bankruptcy.'[22]

In the early years of the nineteenth century, however, the supporters of joint-stock companies adopted cautious positions, arguing not that companies should be permitted in all sectors of the economy, but that they should be allowed to enter trades currently monopolised by a handful of private traders or companies. Advocates of particular companies were anxious to make a distinction between responsible and irresponsible joint-stock activity in order to legitimise their own schemes. 'Philopatris' admitted, 'It is not surprising to me, that good Public Institutions should be calumniated, when there are really so many foolish schemes, which greatly excite the displeasure of the Country.' These 'foolish schemes' included tailoring, coal, wine and milk companies which were all illegal because they were muscling in on trades where sufficient competition already existed.[23] Day followed a very similar line. He thought that 'the present spirit of speculation' had been carried too far, and did not support 'visionary speculations' or companies formed for the purpose of adulteration, price-fixing or monopoly.[24] They did not seek the repeal of the Bubble Act, merely arguing that responsible and useful companies were not prohibited by it. The aim of the act, which was 'a great monument of national morality', was 'to substitute legal commercial speculation founded in judgment, and conducted in industry and honour, for extravagant projects or undertakings, hatched in fraud, nursed in credulity, and terminating in ruin'.[25] The spokesmen of unincorporated companies stressed that they sought no favours from the state, and were confident that they could enjoy the principal benefits of incorporation without obtaining acts of parliament.[26]

But the success or otherwise of such attempts was for the courts to decide. It took several months for the case against Dodd to reach the Court of King's Bench. Day claimed that the delay had left companies 'in a state of anxious suspense'. Uncertainty hung over these companies like 'the sword of Damocles'.[27] But the decision, when reached in May 1808, proved more damaging than the delay. Dodd's defence had employed arguments which had already been rehearsed in print. Transferable shares alone were not sufficient

[22] ['Philopatris'], *Observations on public institutions*, 2.

[23] Ibid. 36–8.

[24] Day, *Defence of joint stock companies*, 4–7.

[25] Idem, *Critical examination of such of the clauses of the act of 6th of George I as relates to unlawful and unwarrantable projects: demonstrating that the present joint stock companies are neither within the letter nor spirit of that act*, London 1808, 6.

[26] ['Philopatris'], *Observations on public institutions*, 14–15; Day, *Defence of joint stock companies*, 31.

[27] Day, *Defence of joint stock companies*, 3, 64.

to make a company illegal: instead it was necessary to look at the aims and conduct of the companies. Each company, the defence claimed, was 'legal in its object and beneficial in its nature'. They only aimed to provide better and cheaper products to the public, in competition with existing traders. Therefore the companies were a public good, and did not come within the letter or the spirit of the law. Chief Justice of King's Bench, Lord Ellenborough, thoroughly rejected these arguments. He ranked the two companies under consideration alongside the 'mischievous projects' currently being promoted. He had no doubt of 'the general tendency of schemes of the nature of the project now before us to occasion prejudice to the public'. These schemes did come under the Bubble Act: they held out 'a false lure' to subscribers that their liability would be limited; they proclaimed 'extravagant hopes of gain' in order to 'allure the greedy'; and persons of modest means were drawn in 'by the facility held out of paying their subscriptions by small instalments'. Furthermore, they both had transferable shares which made it easy for the promoters to evade all financial responsibility for the actions of their companies. Such companies were dangerous to the public, and Ellenborough noted that 'One object of the Legislature was to secure simple individuals against the ruinous consequence of such projects, where great hopes are holden out to the public on false foundations.'[28]

But Ellenborough decided against applying the full rigours of the Bubble Act in this instance. The person who sought an information was not a 'simple individual', but someone who had bought shares in the companies specifically to bring this action. There were other common law actions available to this individual, which he could have pursued before resorting to the act. Most important, however, the long period since the act had last been applied afforded the excuse of ignorance to the defendant and others like him. So Ellenborough declined to pursue the case. But, in adopting this course, he certainly did not want the public to assume that the courts would look favourably on unincorporated companies in the future. He asserted that after this case no one could call the Bubble Act an obsolete law, and concluded by recommending it 'as a matter of prudence to the parties concerned, that they should forbear to carry into execution this mischievous project, or any other speculative project of the like nature, founded on joint stock and transferable shares: and we hope that this intimation will prevent others from engaging in the like mischievous and illegal projects'.[29] Two more cases over the next few months confirmed this ruling, with both the British Ale Brewery and the Philanthropic Annuity Society declared to be illegal.[30]

These three decisions seemed to place companies firmly outside any protection of the law and sent a clear message to company promoters and

[28] *Rex v. Dodd* (1808), 9 East. 517, 103 ER, 670–4.
[29] Ibid.
[30] *Buck v. Buck* (1808), 1 Camp. 548, 170 ER, 1052; *Rex v. Stratton* (1809), 1 Camp. 549, 170 ER, 1053.

investors that the courts would not settle their disputes. In later cases between 1810 and 1812, however, Ellenborough seemed to be travelling in a different direction. In 1810 the Globe Insurance Company, established in 1799, sought to enforce a bond issued in 1803 to secure the faithful services of a clerk. In the spirit of the earlier rulings, the attorney-general argued that despite the fact that the company had secured an act in 1807 allowing it to sue and be sued by its treasurer, the company was not a corporation, but an 'anomalous description of body politic'. The result was that any contract entered into by the members of the company had to be 'governed by the same rules of law as if the individual members had contracted in their own names'. The implication for this particular case was that the defendant was only obliged to abide by the bond so long as the partners to that contract remained constant. As soon as one member changed, the obligation was annulled. But Ellenborough disagreed, arguing that the fact that the contract was made by the trustee of the company and not the partners themselves 'gets rid of all the difficulty'. If the contract had been made by a partnership, the successive partners could not sue upon the contract, 'but a trust may be created for such a body which would extend to those who were successively clothed with the right of the original body'.[31] Ellenborough overruled the attorney-general and found in favour of the company. The decision seemed to offer encouragement to unincorporated companies. Similar decisions were reached in 1811 and 1812, in cases involving the Birmingham Flour and Bread Company and the Greenwich Union Building Society.[32] However, in both cases, Ellenborough drew attention to the restrictions on transfers which were imposed by these companies. The Greenwich Union Building Society was imitating not so much a corporation as a private partnership with its transferable shares, for strict rules were imposed on these transfers: a holder could only transfer his shares on the approval of the purchaser by the society, and by the latter becoming a party to the original articles of the society. Indeed, in a later case, the limits on transferability imposed by these associations were cited as the proof of their legality, in contrast with those companies which allowed unlimited transferability.[33]

Harris, while arguing that the earlier judgements of 1808–9 indicated that the courts were ignoring 'economic developments' and 'the changing reality' of the late eighteenth and early nineteenth centuries, is impressed by the later decisions, regarding them as 'the first signs of retreat' from dogmatic and blinkered attitudes to joint-stock companies, and an indication of 'a more

---

[31] *Metcalf v. Bruin* (1810), 12 East. 400, 104 ER, 156, 159.
[32] *Rex v. Webb* (1811), 14 East. 406; *Pratt v. Hutchinson* (1812), 15 East. 511, 104 ER, 936.
[33] Opinion of J. Bayley, *Josephs v. Pebrer* (1825), 3 B. & C. 639, 107 ER, 872. Bayley pointed in particular to the fact that the object of the Birmingham Flour and Bread Company, to supply its shareholders, the inhabitants of Birmingham, with bread and flour, 'virtually limited the transfer of shares to persons residing in that neighbourhood'.

positive approach to the legality of unincorporated companies'.[34] Perhaps a more convincing interpretation of the slew of cases in these years would be that while the mass of new company promotions was regarded with a sceptical eye, and the unfettered transfer of shares was seen as an unambiguous indicator of illegality, individual companies were able, if they won sufficient political support, secured legitimising acts of parliament, imitated partnerships by imposing strict limits on the transferability of their shares and traded for enough years, to win sufficient respectability and legitimacy to enjoy a degree of protection in the courts.[35]

Elsewhere in the United Kingdom, the story was similar. Some historians have argued that Scottish partnership law was much 'better' than English law in that it was far more accommodating towards the unincorporated company.[36] The development of Scottish partnership law had been influenced more by French and Dutch law than English, with the result that Scottish law came closer to regarding the company as a separate *persona* than English law.[37] But it was not an established principle that companies were able to sue and be sued in the name of the firm. Cases were decided either way in the 1820s and 1830s, creating much uncertainty.[38] That the company's name could indeed be used in lawsuits, along with the names of three individual partners, became the accepted practice only in the 1840s.[39] Assertions that government legislation was irrelevant to Scottish joint-stock activity because of the favourable legal climate in Scotland are belied by applications to the Board of Trade for corporate privileges by several Scottish companies after 1834.[40] And claims made by one Scottish legal authority that in the early nineteenth century investors in Scottish companies enjoyed limited liability, have been shown to be untrue.[41] The differences between

---

34 Harris, *Industrializing English law*, 238–9.

35 The Globe was well-connected politically: no less than thirteen of its directors were at some point also members of parliament: R. G. Thorne, *The House of Commons, 1790–1820*, London 1986, i. 323.

36 Shannon, 'General limited liability', 267 n. 2. R. H. Campbell later took issue with the brevity of Shannon's treatment of the Scottish context, but did not disagree as to the superiority of Scottish law: 'The law and the joint-stock company in Scotland', in P. L. Payne (ed.), *Studies in Scottish business history*, London 1967, 136–51.

37 Campbell, 'The joint-stock company in Scotland', 143; B. Lenman, *An economic history of modern Scotland, 1660–1976*, London 1977, 168.

38 The key cases are covered in D. M. Walker, *A legal history of Scotland*, Edinburgh 1988–2001, vi. 717–18, 722 nn. 147–8.

39 Ibid. 718.

40 R. C. Michie, *Money, mania and markets: investment, company formation and the Stock Exchange in nineteenth-century Scotland*, Edinburgh 1981, 30; Campbell, 'The joint-stock company in Scotland', 139. The Scottish Brewing Company, the Edinburgh Gas Company, the Glasgow Union Banking Company, and the Insurance Company of Scotland were among the Scottish companies that tried (and failed) to secure corporate privileges under the Trading Companies Act of 1834.

41 G. J. Bell made the claim in his *Commentaries on the law of Scotland*, cited in Campbell, 'The joint-stock company in Scotland', 144. McLaren, a later editor of Bell's *Commentaries*,

the two legal systems can therefore be exaggerated; in fact, they were becoming increasingly assimilated after 1707. The Bubble Act was uniformly held to apply in Scotland, and applications by Scottish firms for incorporation were considered by English law officers.[42] It is difficult not to agree with David Walker's judgement that in early nineteenth-century Scotland, 'an unincorporated joint-stock company was still fundamentally a large partnership rather than an entity wholly distinct from its members'.[43]

In Ireland, unlike Scotland and England, limited liability was available on registration, by an act of 1782 passed by Grattan's Parliament, but only to partnerships, and only on several exacting conditions. This act was heavily influenced by the example of the French en commandite partnership where sleeping partners enjoyed limited liability but active partners had unlimited liability, and was adopted explicitly to promote Irish economic development. But many restrictions on access to limited liability were imposed, indicating the awareness of the Irish parliament of the dangers involved in the principle. The act was not to apply to large associations; certainly not to substantial joint-stock companies, for no partnership of over £50,000 could register. The language of the act was vague and could be interpreted as excluding the retail trade, mining, farming and navigation from its benefits, and it explicitly excluded banks. Sleeping partners could not withdraw more than half of their share of the annual profits; the remainder was retained by the firm as a protection for creditors. New partners had to be approved by existing partners. The Lord Chancellor could annul an anonymous partner's limited liability if it was judged that the partner had sought to evade the provisions of the act, or had deceived or defrauded his partners, or creditors of the firm; the partnership could not exist for more than fourteen years.[44] Furthermore the act dwindled into insignificance in the nineteenth century (see table 2).

Thus, the differences in the law between the three different systems were not great: the spate of legal decisions in English courts in 1807–12 was not reflective of backward thinking in England, but was symptomatic of a desire common to all parts of the United Kingdom to limit the scope of joint-stock activity to its proper boundaries.

---

stated in 1870 that Bell's interpretation 'has never been accepted by the profession; and it may be safely be asserted that many hundred thousand pounds have since been paid by the shareholders of joint-stock companies, on the footing of there being no limitation of their responsibility to creditors': cited in Walker, Legal history of Scotland, vi. 715–16; Campbell, 'The joint-stock company in Scotland', 144–8.

[42] Campbell, 'The joint-stock company in Scotland', 137–8.

[43] Walker, Legal history of Scotland, vi. 718. These issues are discussed at greater length in M. Freeman, R. Pearson, and J. Taylor, ' "Different and better?" Scottish joint-stock companies and the law, c. 1720–1845', EHR (2006), forthcoming.

[44] E. A. French, 'The origin of general limited liability in the United Kingdom', Accounting and Business Research xxi (1990), 15–34 at pp. 16–23.

Table 2
Partnerships registered under the Anonymous Partnerships Act, 1782

Period	No. of partnerships formed	Total capital (£)	Average capital subscribed per year (£)	Average capital per partnership (£)
1782–99	109	311,753	17,320	2,860
1800–17	274	1,316,431	73,135	4,804
1818–35	86	356,730	19,818	4,148
1836–53	39	115,051	6,392	2,950
1782–1853	508	2,099,965	29,166	4,134

Source: *Royal Commission on the assimilation of mercantile laws in the UK and amendments in the law of partnership, as regards the question of limited or unlimited responsibility*, PP 1854 xxvii, appendix.

Wild and idle speculation

By the early 1820s the trade depression which had followed the Napoleonic Wars was lifting. War taxes were removed; interest rates were falling. Consols were consequently becoming less attractive and *rentier* investors were willing to consider different outlets for their capital. Loans totalling £17.5 million were arranged for the newly-independent South American states, and accompanying them were schemes to exploit the supposed riches of the continent's mines. At the same time, many domestic ventures were launched. According to Henry English, 624 enterprises were promoted in London in 1824 and 1825, with a nominal capital of over £372 million.[45] Prior to 1825, there were only 156 companies in existence in England, with a nominal capital of £48 million.[46] Development in Scotland and Ireland was also significant in these years. In Edinburgh, in 1825, the securities of more than fifty joint-stock companies were freely traded.[47] In the three years 1823–5 twenty-two limited partnerships were registered in Ireland under the act of 1782, with a capital of £129,555. This was a considerable increase on the previous three-year period, when half this number of partnerships had registered, with a total capital of just £24,945.[48] But it was in England that the

---

[45] These figures excluded those provincial companies, and companies formed in Scotland and Ireland, whose shares were not traded in London: English, *Complete view*.

[46] Ibid. 31.

[47] Michie, *Money, mania and markets*, 45. Several large joint-stock banks were formed in Scotland and Ireland: C. W. Munn, 'The coming of joint-stock banking in Scotland and Ireland, *c.* 1820–1845', in T. M. Devine and D. Dickson (eds), *Ireland and Scotland, 1600–1850: parallels and contrasts in economic and social development*, Edinburgh 1983, 204–18 at pp. 215–16.

[48] *Royal Commission on amendments in the law of partnership*, PP 1854 xxvii.

most dramatic explosion of activity took place. The range of enterprises promoted in London was remarkable (*see* table 3).

Table 3
Companies promoted during 1824–5

Sector	Number of companies	Nominal capital (£)
Investment	28	52,600,000
Canal/rail	54	44,051,000
Mining	74	38,370,000
Insurance	20	35,820,000
Building	26	13,781,000
Gas	29	12,077,000
Trading	11	10,450,000
Steam navigation	67	8,555,500
Provisions	23	8,360,000
Misc.	292	148,108,600
Total	624	372,173,100

Source: English, *Complete view*, 30–1.

But figures of nominal capital are misleading when determining the actual size of the joint-stock economy at this point, for a great many of these schemes existed on paper only. According to English, of the 624, no less than 379 (61 per cent) left no trace of their existence other than their prospectuses or advertisements in the press.[49] Many clearly existed purely to extract subscription money from the public. As a consequence, it should not be surprising that, as in the earlier boom of 1806–9, many of the companies promoted were unincorporated and made no attempt to secure acts or charters. But a significant number did: in March 1824, an early stage in the boom, there were twenty-nine bills for incorporation before the Commons, many more than at previous sessions.[50] This suggests both the uncertain legal climate that continued to prevail after the decisions of 1808–12, and also the difficulties encountered by companies operating under deeds of trust.

The numbers of companies approaching parliament for special privileges worried many, and through the 1824 session voices of opposition to the fashion for company promotion were raised. Some doubted whether the sudden flood of promotions reflected genuine popular enthusiasm for companies. For example, it was revealed that the petition in favour of the Manchester Gas-Light Bill, signed by 700 people, contained 108 duplicates. On further investigation, it transpired that an Irish weaver named Corbett

[49] English, *Complete view*, 26.
[50] *Annual Register* (1824), 2.

had signed 496 of the names.[51] Lord Lauderdale, concerned 'to provide against mischief which was now going on with respect to Joint-Stock Companies', successfully secured changes in the standing orders of the Lords so that company bills could not be read a second time unless three-quarters of the capital had been subscribed.[52] As the session drew to a close, Eldon, who had earlier drawn attention to the evils of speculation in the scrip of a company before it had been incorporated, promised to introduce a bill the following session to compel the register of names of members of companies with the courts, to facilitate both the suing of companies and the recovery of money from all shareholders of companies in such actions, and to negate transfers of liability unless properly registered.[53]

None of this had any significant effect on the glut of promotions. Confidence in the profitability of the schemes being promoted continued to rise through the year and into 1825. Mining shares rose dramatically.[54] But the situation changed in February when, just as in 1807, the question of the legal status of unincorporated companies was raised in dramatic fashion. Immediately after the king's speech on the opening day of the new session, Eldon rose to announce that, as promised, he would move for a bill to check dealing in the shares of companies which had not received the sanction of parliament or the crown.[55] A young Benjamin Disraeli, an energetic, though unsuccessful, speculator in the foreign mines, recorded the impact of Eldon's intervention: 'A great panic took place – everything fell . . . and for some time it was supposed that the whole Commerce with America might be crushed.'[56] A second blow was delivered the next day, when Chief Justice Abbott ruled that the Equitable Loan Bank Company was illegal under the Bubble Act. An earlier trial had ruled against the defendant, who had refused to pay for some shares ordered from the plaintiff, a stockbroker. The defence had unsuccessfully used the argument that the company was illegal and therefore all contracts relating to the purchase of shares were void. But Abbott found in favour of the defendant. The company was acting as a corporate body: it had transferable shares, and it was not acting in the public interest, as it was lending money at the usurious rate of 8 per cent. Abbott used his platform to comment on the broader current of speculation in condemnatory terms:

> we cannot help observing that in other companies and associations the sale and transfer of shares at enormous premiums is carried on to a greater extent than was ever known, except at the period when the statute referred to was

---

51 *Hansard*, n.s. xi. 8–15 (30 Mar. 1824).
52 Ibid. xi. 856 (25 May 1824), 1076–7 (2 June 1824). It should be noted, however, that the impact of this amendment was limited: it was flouted just a week afterwards in the case of an Irish mining bill, despite Lauderdale's protestations: ibid. xi. 1100–2 (9 June 1824).
53 Ibid. xi. 791 (21 May 1824), 1456–7 (18 June 1824).
54 *Annual Register* (1825), 3.
55 *Hansard*, n.s. xii. 31 (3 Feb. 1825).
56 Draft letter, Benjamin Disraeli to Robert Messer [?], Apr. [?] 1825: B. Disraeli, *Letters: 1815–1834*, Toronto 1982, 27.

passed. The necessary effect of such a practice is to introduce gaming and rash speculation to a ruinous extent. In such transactions one cannot gain unless another loses, whereas in fair mercantile transactions each party, in the ordinary course of things, reaps a profit in his turn.[57]

The following month Eldon made a similar ruling, concerning the Real del Monte Mining Company. This case concerned a dispute between a shareholder and the directors: the former was seeking an injunction to prevent the directors from transferring company property to John Taylor, one of their number. Eldon confounded both sides by questioning at the start of the case 'the right of any persons, claiming as proprietors in such a company, to have the aid of a court of justice'. By 'such a company', Eldon meant an unincorporated one, which nevertheless claimed to enjoy all the attributes of a corporation. The Real del Monte's deed of settlement claimed for the company all these attributes: indeed, Eldon commented wryly, 'if the Bank of England, the East India Company, or the South Sea Company, wanted a new charter, they could not do better than copy the deed of regulation of the Real del Monte Company'.[58] The company was clearly acting as a corporate body without the authority of the crown or parliament, and therefore came under the Bubble Act.

Both the Chief Justice and the Lord Chancellor intended their judgements to act as a brake on the wave of company promotions they found so disturbing. But these decisions, combined with the threat of Eldon's bill, had a different effect. Companies applied in ever greater numbers for corporate privileges in order to secure their legality. Parliament was swamped. In the 1825 session 297 petitions were made for bills granting such privileges.[59] Their second response was to rush into print to justify themselves, as they had in 1807–8. Disraeli was occupied through 1825 writing pamphlets urging the companies' case.[60] He produced three works in quick succession, published by John Murray, who had entered into a speculative partnership with Disraeli.[61] In these, Disraeli appealed to principles of commercial freedom, asking, 'ought not the wise legislators of a free and commercial people to encourage and to support undertakings which tend to enrich a considerable body of the

---

[57] *Josephs v. Pebrer*, 3 B. & C. 639 (1825), 107 ER, 872.

[58] *Kinder v. Taylor* (1825), 3 Law Journal Reports, 76, 78.

[59] Hunt, *Business corporation*, 52.

[60] He had been encouraged to do so by his friend J. D. Powles, promoter of several mining companies. The third and final of Disraeli's pamphlets, *The present state of Mexico*, featured only a short introduction by Disraeli: the bulk of the text was written by Lucas Alaman.

[61] Disraeli and Murray were heavily involved in mining speculations. The shares Disraeli purchased were kept in an iron case in Disraeli's room. Profits from them were to be split two-thirds for Murray and one-third for Disraeli: Disraeli to Murray, 1 Apr. 1825, Disraeli, *Letters*, 25–6. For accounts of Disraeli's speculations see J. Ridley, *The young Disraeli*, London 1995, 31–4; R. Blake, *Disraeli*, London 1966, 23–6; and W. F. Monypenny, *The life of Benjamin Disraeli*, London 1929, i. 58–64.

inhabitants of this country?'[62] Similarly, Alexander Mundell, another advocate of joint-stock enterprise, lamented that 'governments do not keep pace with the knowledge and enterprise of the times'.[63] He wanted companies to enjoy complete freedom, arguing that to 'common apprehension it seems difficult to conceive why fifty persons may not associate for any commercial or other purpose as well as five, or five hundred as well as fifty, or five thousand as well as five hundred'.[64] Advocates of the mining schemes developed utility arguments, just as the earlier pamphleteers had done, revolving around the perceived national benefits to be obtained by the expansion of commerce with Latin America. Sir William Rawson, oculist-extraordinary to the Prince Regent and, like Disraeli, a keen speculator, argued that restoring the mining industry of the Americas, as well as proving very profitable to shareholders, would stimulate trade, ensuring a 'mart for our manufactures, which may thus be increased to an almost unlimited extent'.[65] Enlarged trade with the New World would boost the public revenue, and would mean commercial independence from mainland Europe. Britain's enemies would not be able in the future to weaken Britain by combining against her exports, making the nation 'free and independent of Continental politics, Continental dictation, or Continental interference of any kind'. Furthermore, by civilising the new states, Britain would be establishing 'a salutary balance of power, between them and the United States', making British influence paramount in disputes between the two factions, a situation which would also hold in European politics. Britain would become 'the Arbitress of Nations, – holding the Balance of Power in both Hemispheres in her own hands'.[66]

But, just as during the previous boom, the utility argument precluded the blind endorsement of all companies. Proponents of the foreign mines tended to condemn domestic projects, which they thought were unnecessary:

> Joint Stock companies are beneficial, where a larger capital, and more extensive credit are required, than individuals can furnish. They are useful also in opening new channels for commerce of too great magnitude, and where the risk is too much, for individuals to undertake . . . But they are decidedly prejudicial, when directed to objects fairly within the reach of the industry and capital of individuals.[67]

---

62 [Disraeli], *Lawyers and legislators*, 6.

63 A. Mundell, *The influence of interest and prejudice upon proceedings in parliament stated*, London 1825, 1.

64 Ibid. 145. See also idem, *The principles which govern the value of paper currency, with reference to banking establishments*, Edinburgh 1823, 18.

65 Rawson, *Mexican mine associations*, 44. For an account of Rawson's speculations see Charles, Lord Colchester (ed.), *The diary and correspondence of Charles Abbot, Lord Colchester*, London 1861, iii. 443.

66 Rawson, *Mexican mine associations*, 62–3.

67 Ibid. 64–5.

Disraeli was sceptical about all domestic companies, including those projects, like canals and docks, which required large capitals. Companies for 'home improvement' did not make sense as the country was already fully developed: they were 'formed to develope [sic] the resources of one of the smallest, most thickly populated, and most civilized countries in Christendom. The truth is, that in England, there are no new resources to develope [sic]'. They would create an unnatural demand for labour during construction, and when completed, by competing with existing services, would 'injure existing property', eventually ruining both parties.[68] 'Better by far would it be', wrote one Malthusian commentator, 'that we should throw our accumulating riches into the sea, than employ them in creating an unnatural and improvident demand for labour; thus adding a fresh stimulus to a population already too rapidly increasing'.[69]

Supporters of domestic improvements, on the other hand, thought that speculators in foreign schemes were indeed throwing their riches in the sea, condemning the projects as utterly fraudulent and worthless. John Barrow looked favourably on all 'home projects of an innocent character' on the grounds that they provided employment to the poor, even if they ultimately turned out to be unprofitable.[70] Such attitudes were characteristic of Tory thought: back in 1817 Liverpool's government had established the Exchequer Bill Loan Commission which disbursed large sums annually to public works to provide employment for the poor. Canal companies and other labour-intensive infrastructural projects such as bridges, harbours and roads, were major recipients.[71] This preference for domestic schemes continued to colour Tory thought: while it was recorded that the duke of Wellington was unsympathetic to the 'speculating mania' and thought that 'the companies are bubbles invented for stockjobbing purposes', he was 'not averse to those which are formed for improvements in our own Island'.[72] Supporters of domestic companies tried to allay popular fears that these companies would become huge monstrosities forcing private traders out of business by arguing that companies faced intrinsic restrictions on size, with Mundell holding, for instance, that 'The division of profit will always prevent more persons from associating together than will be necessary to raise the capital required'.[73]

Partial though many writers' recommendation of the joint-stock principle was, most insisted that the flaws of some types of joint-stock enterprise must not be used to condemn the whole, and few of them endorsed legislative or judicial action against unsound companies. Rawson admitted that it might be

---

[68] Disraeli, *Lawyers and legislators*, 26–7.

[69] Anon., *Remarks on joint stock companies*, 64–5.

[70] [Barrow], 'Canals and rail-roads', 355–6.

[71] For more on the commission see Taylor, 'Transport, *laissez-faire*, and government policy', 25–37, and M. W. Flinn, 'The Poor Employment Act of 1817', EcHR xiv (1961), 82–92.

[72] F. Bamford and the duke of Wellington (eds), *The journal of Mrs Arbuthnot, 1820–1832*, London 1950, i. 382.

[73] Mundell, *Influence of interest*, 146.

thought desirable to legislate to prevent the establishment of fraudulent companies, but it would be both impracticable and inconsistent for the legislature 'to create new shackles' when it was repealing so many of the long-established restrictions on trade. In any case, the public 'possess so much intelligence and sound sense, that the evil will be sure to cure itself, by the speedy detection of fraud or fallacy'.[74] Disraeli claimed that improvident speculation was the result either of folly or of fraud. Fraud was already covered by the common law ('what law in Christendom traces the ramifications of fraud with keener spirit than the common law of England?'), while 'the folly of man is temporary as it is destructive' and it would be wrong for the government to 'commit the great blunder of despotic states, and *legislate for the individual*'.[75] Whereas justifications of joint-stock enterprise in 1806–8 had been defensive, and had sought to show that particular companies were legal under the Bubble Act, now company propagandists went on the offensive, condemning the act as a restrictive and unfair piece of legislation which ought to be repealed. Disraeli was representative, condemning the statute which had been 'smuggled through the Houses by the promoters and projectors of the South Sea scheme itself . . . a statute which suits rather the meridian of Cairo and Constantinople'.[76]

But to convince the government and the public that joint-stock property deserved the protection of the law, company supporters had to overcome traditional scorn of 'stock-jobbing' and ingrained fears of excessive speculation. They did this by carefully distinguishing between the current schemes and those of 1720. The speculation of 1720 was 'one to which impoverished and ill-governed states must always be liable'. But in 1825 the public possessed 'too much knowledge to become the victims of a South Sea scheme'.[77] Company propagandists stressed the respectability and stability of their associations. Disraeli wrote that the Real del Monte mining company was divided into only 500 shares and had but 120 shareholders, all of whom were original proprietors.[78] John Taylor maintained that the mining companies were respectable concerns which depended upon stable and sustainable investment rather than boom and bust speculation. It was counterproductive for these schemes to attract too much capital, for the number of able managers and experienced workmen was finite. Capital should be limited 'to the amount of which the application can be effectively and judiciously directed . . . I am desirous of seeing the experiment conducted upon that respectable scale which may lead to a worthy and profitable result'. Wild fluc-

---

74 Rawson, *Mexican mine associations*, 67.

75 [B. Disraeli], *An inquiry into the plans, progress, and policy of the American mining companies*, 3rd edn, London 1825, 95–6. This pamphlet was a major success, running into three editions.

76 Idem, *Lawyers and legislators*, 89, 94. See also Rawson, *Mexican mine associations*, 66.

77 Disraeli, *Lawyers and legislators*, 86–7.

78 Ibid. 45.

tuations in share prices were portrayed not as the result of the machinations of self-interested projectors and brokers but of public greed or ignorance. The true value of mining shares was determined by the quality of the mines and the progress made with the mining. The public was guilty of wading in and ignoring these factors, pushing share prices to artificial heights, and when prices inevitably fell to their natural level, the public blamed the companies rather than their own rash behaviour.[79] Disraeli took a different tack, but still exonerated company promoters from wrongdoing, asserting that the share fluctuations which the legislature so deprecated were actually caused by the conflicting signals and opinions emanating from the legislature itself.[80]

Despite their best efforts, however, company propagandists still ran up against traditional suspicion of joint-stock enterprise. The narrative of the 'South Sea Bubble', and its attendant imagery, which had been invoked during the last speculative boom, was again revived. Writers sought to remind the public of the disasters which 'shook the kingdom to its centre' in 1720.[81] Unsuspecting people were advised against risking their property in the 'wild Speculations' which were 'continually arising from the fertile and iniquitous brains of visionary schemers'.[82] Joint-stock activity north of the border was also raising concern, with one Edinburgh citizen viewing many of the new schemes as 'visionary and chimerical . . . the illegitimate offspring of the wanton demon of speculation'.[83] In his *Weekly Register*, William Cobbett regularly denounced 'those mischievous and disgraceful combinations, called Joint Stock Companies'. They encouraged gambling and made honest labour seem unattractive:

> Men, and particularly young men, generally dislike a *slow* operation in getting rich, especially as it must be accompanied with labour, or restraint, or both. How, then, are we to expect them to remain quietly at their trade or profession, when they see, almost every day in the week, a RICARDO leap at once from an orange-basket or pencil-box to a park and mansion and half a million of money, merely by 'watching the turn of the market'?[84]

Individual companies were frequently denounced as bubbles in parliament.[85] Eyebrows were raised at the involvement of society's elite in joint-stock

[79] J. Taylor, *Statements respecting the profits of mining in England considered in relation to the prospects of mining in Mexico: in a letter to Thomas Fowell Buxton, Esq. MP*, London 1825, 51–2, 55–6.

[80] [Disraeli], *Lawyers and legislators*, 33–7, 63, 99.

[81] Anon., *South Sea Bubble*, 3. See also Anon, *A list of joint-stock companies, the proposals for which are now, or have been lately, before the public: from 'The Monthly Repository of Theology and General Literature'*, London 1825, 2.

[82] Anon., *Observations on the establishment of new water works companies*, London 1824, 4.

[83] A. Romney, *Three letters on the speculative schemes of the present times and the projected banks*, cited in Michie, *Money, mania and markets*, 34.

[84] *Cobbett's Weekly Register*, 12 Feb. 1825.

[85] See, for example, *Hansard*, n.s. xi. 99 (2 Apr. 1824); xii. 1049 (16 Mar. 1825).

Plate 11. 'Bubbles for 1825 – or – fortunes made by steam'.
Source: BM 14669, *English cartoons and satirical prints, 1320–1832.*
© The Trustees of the British Museum.

speculations, which many found disturbingly redolent of 1720. *The Times* had been unconcerned in the early days of the speculative boom, when those involved were 'Jew-jobbers and traders', but now feared for 'the moral character of the people of England, when we see our noblemen . . . our country gentlemen . . . and our merchants, which was but another term for integrity and honourable dealing, sharing the general contagion, and even proud of showing their plague-spots, as if they were badges of distinction'.[86] Rawson had argued that the mining companies were 'both patriotic and praiseworthy', but *The Times* was convinced that 'if England becomes a nation of jobbers and speculators, there is an end of all patriotism', because 'our commercial greatness, and our national power' would perish.[87] Lord Colchester, former speaker of the house, managed to resist speculating in what he called 'the monstrous speculations and bubbles'; nevertheless, that many of the middle and upper classes participated could not be doubted.[88] Harriet Arbuthnot, wife of the rising Tory politician Charles, recorded her investments in her journal:

> There is a railway going to be made between Liverpool & Manchester which promises to answer immensely. We have 10 shares in it for which we gave 3£ a piece & which are now worth 58£ each, and they are expected soon to be worth above 100£. I am very fond of these speculations & should *gamble* greatly in them if I could, but Mr. Artbuthnot does not like them & will not allow me to have any of the American ones as their value depends upon political events, & he thinks in his official situation it would be improper.[89]

But backbench MPs saw no conflict of interest. The Conservative weekly *John Bull*, eager to show 'the extraordinary infatuation of gentlemen having brains in their heads', published the names of 129 people who were directors of more than three companies, thirty-one of whom were members of parliament.[90]

These developments were greeted with dismay by many, demonstrated by a series of prints from 1824 and 1825.[91] One such print, 'Bubbles for 1825 – or – fortunes made by steam' (*see* plate 11), published in December 1824, is not a celebration of the economic potential of steam power; rather it is a tribute to the power of hot air. The illustration shows a trio of company promoters on a platform blowing bubbles which represent the wide variety of companies

---

[86] *The Times*, 5 Nov. 1825.
[87] Rawson, *Mexican mine associations*, 66; *The Times*, 5 Nov. 1825.
[88] Lord Colchester to Lord Amherst, 23 June 1826, *Diary and correspondence of Colchester*, iii. 441.
[89] *Journal of Mrs Arbuthnot*, i. 382.
[90] *John Bull*, 6 Feb. 1825.
[91] For further details of prints dealing with specific companies and the promotion mania more generally see George, *Catalogue of political and personal satires*, x, BM 14653, 14666, 14667, 14773, 14814.

Plate 12. 'The bubble burst – or the ghost of an old act of parliament'.
Source: BM 14765, *English cartoons and satirical prints, 1320–1832.*
© The Trustees of the British Museum.

and loans being promoted at this time. There are companies for insurance, gas, bread, steam-washing, pearl-fishing and other objects. Two of the bubbles are cracked and deflating, but this does not dampen the enthusiasm of the investing public, who vie with one another for the attention of the promoters and are desperate to give their money in return for shares in the bubbles being blown. The investors are mostly well-dressed and are handing over large sums, but on the right a fish-wife barges into the frame asking for 'Twenty Shilling worth', indicating the wide reach of the speculative mania. It is clear that the only winners from this situation will be the promoters, who are filling sacks with the public's money. The victims of the scene, the investing public, quite clearly need to be protected from the consequences of their greed and stupidity.[92]

Protection is forthcoming in 'The bubble burst – or the ghost of an old act of parliament' (see plate 12), published in February 1825. Here Chief Justice Abbott is depicted pricking the speculative bubble blown by the public with his judgement of February 1825 against the Equitable Loan Bank.[93] The illustration is interesting for its wealth of anti-speculation imagery. The bubble-blower on the far left stands on a mushroom marked 'Projectors' Schemes', likening these enterprises to a fungus, and suggesting that they are by their nature likely to get out of control. The instability of the bubble, labelled 'Speculation 1825', is underlined by the flames and puffs of smoke issuing from it. The flames carry the names of some of the most dubious of the schemes of the day; clearly, these will prove dangerous to anyone who gets too close to them. Indeed, the despairing speculators who have dabbled in these schemes are depicted outside the Stock Exchange sinking into quick-sand; one holds pistols to his head and wails 'Despair Despair'. Behind them can be seen two boys flying kites, yet another metaphor for speculative activity. In contrast with the chaotic and deranged scene on the left of the picture, Abbott stands solid and calm in wig and gown, dwarfing the specula-tors, and dealing what the illustrator hopes will be the fatal blow to the popular madness with his right hand, while brandishing the Bubble Act with his left. The verse at the foot of the print confirms Abbott as the hero of the piece, guarding the public against the schemes of the promoters, and indeed protecting the public from itself.[94]

Yet while bubbles were roundly condemned, the Bubble Act itself was beginning to lose its supporters, and few saw it as the nation's best defence against fraudulent promotions. The Times, despite opposing 'those transac-tions in the city which are founded in fraud or imbecility', thought the Bubble Act unenforceable. The newspaper held that frauds in company promotion could be adequately prosecuted as misdemeanours under common

---

92 Ibid. 428–9.
93 See pp. 108–9 above.
94 George, Catalogue of political and personal satires, x. 467–8.

law.[95] Eldon came to think so too. In *Kinder v. Taylor*, he stated the opinion that unincorporated companies would be found illegal at common law regardless of the interpretation placed on the act, and he later argued in the Lords that the act was not of great significance, as 'there was hardly any thing in that act which was not punishable by the common law'.[96] He never introduced the bill he had promised at the start of 1825, coming instead to believe that companies could be better regulated through the courts.

Nor did the Bubble Act receive support from the growing number who looked to government to establish a regulatory code to make fraud more difficult. For John George 'some statutory enactments of a regulatory character' needed to be applied to all companies in order to discourage fraudulent enterprise. George set out in some detail such a legal framework: his proposals included punishments for false statements in prospectuses, the drawing up of rules concerning the use of names in company advertisements, obligatory directorial shareholdings and the prohibition of the sale of shares at a premium before the company had commenced its business. He was confident that such a system would contribute greatly towards 'checking delusion, fraud, gambling, and the obtaining of other people's money'.[97] Another anonymous writer set out a plan for the deeds of all partnerships of more than six members to be registered at the Court of Chancery, with the names and shareholdings of all members attached. Transfers of shares would be registered in the same way, and companies would have the power to sue and be sued. Such laws would put a stop to 'disgraceful scene[s] of gambling, delusion, and credulity', and prevent companies 'being made mere engines, in the hands of a few individuals, to enrich themselves at the expense of the community'.[98] Without a legal code circumscribing the powers of directors and protecting the rights of shareholders, it was believed that both the investing public, and anyone who dealt with companies, would always be vulnerable to the acts of fraudsters. One writer claimed that until the property invested in companies obtained sufficient protection, 'the Courts of Directors will be tribunals possessed of unlimited and gigantic powers, and from whose decision there will be no appeal'.[99]

Mere repeal, then, was not enough either for those who wanted laws to curb crooked promoters, or for promoters who wanted laws granting them protection from the rigours of partnership law.[100] The insecurity of joint-stock property was only partly attributable to the Bubble Act and the uncertainty over the legality of unincorporated joint-stock enterprise: it was

95 *The Times*, 4, 5, 8 Feb. 1825.
96 *Hansard*, n.s. xiii. 1350 (24 June 1825).
97 George, *View of the existing law*, 66–72.
98 Anon., *Remarks on joint stock companies*, 92–8, 100.
99 Anon., *Letter to John Taylor*, 4.
100 Some company supporters also saw that measures to protect shareholders would increase the respectability of their companies.

also due to the exposure of these companies in their day-to-day existence to the law of partnership. Much more than repeal would be required to give companies a secure legal status. Prompted by Eldon's threatened bill, Disraeli stated: 'That a bill should be introduced on the subject of Joint Stock Companies there can be no doubt; but it should be one not to regulate their management, but to sanction their existence – to make them amenable to the law, of which, under the present system, they are forced to be independent.'[101] Hudson Gurney, a Whig banker, supported the repeal of the Bubble Act, but held that it was 'impossible that the common law, originating in another state of society, could meet all the exigencies of the present commercial situation of the country'. As a result, he called for 'one general law for the formation and regulation of all joint stock companies'.[102] He supported the continental system of limited liability on registration, stressing the benefits which would ensue to the public from registration: they would be better able to judge the promoters of new speculations, and would therefore be less likely to be defrauded. For Rawson too the interests of promoters and the public were identical:

> the Legislature is called upon, by every consideration, to afford its countenance and support to these Companies, and to place them upon a footing of legal security, which, while it exempts the capitalist from the penal consequences of barbarous and obsolete enactments, and from liabilities beyond the sums he engages to furnish, shall also protect the public against the fraudulent designs of selfish and interested adventurers.[103]

Thus, by 1825, the Bubble Act had run out of supporters: advocates of joint-stock enterprise opposed the act as an obstacle to their activities, while those sceptical of the benefits of company promotion on a large scale no longer saw the act as a guarantee of their interests. This situation explains the sudden repeal of the act in 1825. Peter Moore, an MP involved in several company promotions, introduced a repealing bill in April. The bill claimed that the wave of new companies had been a boon to the public, but that the effect of certain vague clauses in the Bubble Act had been 'to prevent and restrain' many people from investing in these companies 'in case they be subjected to its penalties'. The bill declared that it was therefore 'expedient to repeal such clauses, and to enact other provisions, in lieu thereof'. These 'other provisions' set out rules governing the formation of all companies, to protect shareholders both from the uncertainty of the law in general and from dishonest or fraudulent promoters in particular.[104] The bill passed its first

---

[101] [Disraeli], *Lawyers and legislators*, 95.
[102] *Hansard*, n.s. xii. 1283–4 (29 Mar. 1825).
[103] Rawson, *Mexican mine associations*, 78.
[104] *A bill to alter and amend an act passed in the 6th year of the reign of King George the First . . . for the prevention of frauds in the establishment of joint stock companies*, PP 1825 i. 5, 3, 6–9.

reading but did not receive a second; instead, on 2 June, the attorney-general, John Copley, introduced a government bill of repeal. This passed both houses without opposition, and received the royal assent on 5 July.[105] It looked as if the government had caved in to the pressure placed on it by company supporters.[106] But this was only part of the story. The government measure did indeed repeal the relevant sections of the Bubble Act, but it did not include any of the legal innovations proposed in Moore's Bill. Copley had considered introducing provisions to replace the repealed statute, but 'after having very attentively considered the subject, he had been convinced that to do so would be at once difficult, unwise, and impolitic'.[107] He believed that as no legal enactments regulating joint-stock companies had existed before 1720, no regulatory law was now required. By removing the artificial interference of the statute of 1720, companies would once more be regulated by the common law.

So, while repeal of the Bubble Act is often thought of as the first step on the road to an 'enlightened' company law, the government had not, in fact, done as much to advance the interests of either promoters of, or shareholders in, joint-stock companies, as it seemed. In fact, the measure appealed to the government as much for political as commercial reasons. The origins of the act, passed in the interests of the South Sea Company, and confirming the monopoly of the two chartered marine insurance companies, were distasteful to a Tory government pursuing a policy of retrenchment and attempting to lift itself above sectional interests.[108] The act contained only one innovatory aspect. The government signalled its intention to make some of the privileges of incorporation more easily available in a section tacked onto the end of the act, which permitted the Board of Trade to advise the crown to grant charters of incorporation with unlimited liability. Hitherto, the Board had been reluctant to recommend charters with limited liability for companies which had not already received parliamentary sanction. The act was intended to enable companies to approach the crown direct for privileges, and to increase the chances that such approaches would be successful. This innovation was significant for three reasons. First, it indicated a desire on the part of the government to extend the principle of unlimited, not limited, liability, a point which underlines that attitudes to joint-stock enterprise did

---

105 6 Geo. IV. c. 91.

106 This pressure had been substantial: a committee of all the members of parliament with mining interests had been formed, and sent deputations to ministers urging against a hard line on companies: draft letter, Disraeli to Robert Messer [?], Apr. [?] 1825, Disraeli, *Letters*, 27.

107 *Hansard*, n.s. xiii. 1019 (2 June 1825).

108 For more on these policies see P. Harling, *The waning of 'old corruption': the politics of economical reform in Britain, 1779–1846*, Oxford 1996. See also Harris, *Industrializing English law*, 207–15.

not change dramatically in 1825.[109] Second, it suggested that incorporation by the crown was seen as a less corrupt means of granting privileges than parliament, a theme which will be explored below. Third, it indicated that the government, though appreciating the benefits of allowing some corporate privileges to legitimate concerns, wanted to keep tight control of which enterprises received these favours. The message was clear: exemptions from partnership law would not be granted indiscriminately, but would have to be sought by approaching either parliament, or preferably the crown, and would be decided on a case-by-case basis.

The panic and its aftermath

The boom had already shown signs of slowing in June, before the Bubble Act was repealed. Prices stopped rising, confidence was knocked and with the enormous over-extension of credit came difficulties in paying calls on shares. Country banks, eighty in all, began to close their doors, and the year culminated in a run on the Bank of England. Monthly bankruptcies, which in the summer had averaged sixty-four, rose in November to 142, and in December to 224.[110] In the panic, share prices collapsed, and with them the companies themselves. Of the 624 promotions recorded by Henry English, only 127 were still in existence by 1827, and the shares of most of these were at a large discount (*see* table 4). Only a small portion of the capital had been paid up, and large overhanging liability remained on the shares.

The panic of 1825 led the following year to the legalisation in England (outside London) of joint-stock banks. The perceived flaws of the country banks were contrasted unfavourably with the stability of Scottish joint-stock banks which had weathered the storm far more convincingly. The new banks were given a privileged legal position in comparison to other joint-stock companies, being placed inside a detailed regulatory framework based on registration, upon which they received corporate privileges, excluding limited liability.[111] It was believed that these new banks would rest on a wider, and therefore more secure, stock of money.

While joint-stock enterprise was seen as worthy of encouragement in the field of banking, there was no more general legitimisation of joint-stock enterprise. Indeed, following the collapse of the boom came agitation in parliament both for legislation to prevent further speculative manias, and for an investigation into some of the worst cases of fraud, though these were

---

[109] One legal authority noted that in the act, 'the Legislature appears to have carefully guarded against any alteration in the existing law relative to partnership liability. Indeed, it seems doubtful whether it was not the intention of the Legislature to extend the doctrine in question': Collyer, *Practical treatise*, 653.

[110] *Annual Register* (1825), 333.

[111] Hunt, *Business corporation*, 50.

Table 4
Companies formed during 1824–5 and still existing in 1827

Sector	Number	Nominal capital (£)	Amount paid (£)	Present value (£)	Liable to be called (£)
Insurance	14	£28,120,000	£2,247,000	£1,606,000	£25,873,000
Mining	44	£26,776,000	£5,455,100	£2,927,350	£21,320,900
Gas	20	£9,061,000	£2,162,000	£1,504,625	£6,899,000
Misc.	49	£38,824,600	£5,321,850	£3,265,975	£33,502,750
Total	127	£102,781,600	£15,185,950	£9,303,950	£87,595,650

Source: English, *Complete view*, 30.

successfully resisted by the government.[112] Furthermore, the panic of 1825 left a profound mark on the national psyche. It was to form the raw material for novelists for the next thirty years, even after the railway mania of the 1840s provided them with a more recent example of collective madness. Those who were closely associated with the promotions of 1824–5 suffered damaged reputations. Of the thirty-one MPs who held three or more company directorships, fifteen were either defeated or did not stand in the elections of 1826. Ten of these never made it back into parliament. The boom had not advanced the claims of those who wanted general legislative approval of joint-stock enterprise, and it was clear that the government did not contemplate any revision in the system by which companies which desired exemptions from partnership law had to obtain them from the state.

Committee-room corruption

The 1825 collapse also reaffirmed the link in the public mind between companies and corruption. One key aspect of this corruption stemmed from the relationship between companies and parliament. There was enormous potential for corruption in the procedure by means of which acts of incorporation were sought. Promoters of joint-stock schemes were quite willing to bribe MPs with shares or directorships in order to secure a favourable hearing for their companies. The temptations held out to MPs to become the agents of outside economic interests was huge. Radicals were prominent in highlighting the corruption that existed. In May 1824 Joseph Hume moved a standing order that no Member with an interest in a private bill should be

---

112 *Hansard*, n.s. xiv. 416 (15 Feb. 1826); xvi. 243–84 (5 Dec. 1826). A motion for a select committee to inquire into the 'origin, management, and present state' of the fraudulent companies of 1824–5 was confined on the insistence of government ministers to an inquiry into just one of the companies, the Arigna Iron and Coal Mining Company: *Select committee on the Arigna Mining Company*, PP 1826–27 iii.

permitted to sit on the committee deciding on the bill. He told the House that he 'had been strongly impressed with the impropriety of the existing practice, not merely during the present session, but for many sessions . . . The business in committees above stairs was no longer a question of justice between the parties; it was one merely of canvass and influence'. He stressed that he was not dealing with a few isolated cases, claiming that 'every projector of a new company' found it 'absolutely necessary to have among his subscribers a certain number of members of parliament; without whose aid he could entertain little or no hope of getting his bill passed'.[113] Alexander Robertson agreed, stating that 'it was well known, that in most of the speculations now afloat in the city, some thousand shares were reserved for the use of members of parliament'.[114] Equally, interested opponents of new schemes voted against them without taking into account their merits. Hume thought that the same rule ought to apply to committees as applied to juries, 'namely, that no man should be a judge in his own case'.[115] He managed to secure the appointment of a select committee to consider the question. The committee fought shy of declaring an opinion on the key issue of interested voting, but Hume continued to press for the reform of private bill procedure.[116]

He was far from alone in raising qualms about current practice. A fellow MP objected that 'Persons holding shares to the amount of 50,000*l.*' had voted for the St Catherine's Docks Bill of 1824.[117] One MP disapproved so much of interested voting 'that he had not entered a private committee room for many years', while another 'was resolved never again to enter the door of a private committee room until the business was put on a different footing'.[118] Likewise, Henry Brougham thought that 'the mode of voting on private bills was so scandalous in its nature, that he had made it a rule never to vote upon a private bill'.[119] There were potentially profound conflicts of interest. Henry Bright held that MPs were 'bound to attend to the interests of their constituents in preference to their own; and when a member found that the being a shareholder would prevent his doing his duty, he ought to give up his shares and attend to the interests of his constituents'.[120] Despite these views, Hume's attempts to prevent interested members voting for or against company bills did not win the support of the government. George Canning supported Hume in principle, but argued that his proposals would be too difficult to apply in practice, and concluded that the solution to this delicate

[113] *Hansard*, xi. 910–13 (27 May 1824).
[114] Ibid. xii. 986 (10 Mar. 1825).
[115] Ibid. xi. 913 (27 May 1824).
[116] *Select committee on private business of the House*, PP 1824 vi. 5.
[117] Calvert, *Hansard*, n.s. xii. 612 (22 Feb. 1825). See also the views of Baring, ibid. xii. 638 (23 Feb. 1825).
[118] W. Smith and W. Trant, ibid. xiii. 1013–14 (2 June 1825).
[119] Ibid. xii. 635–6 (23 Feb. 1825).
[120] Ibid. xii. 640.

question 'must be left generally to the honour and the feeling of members'.[121] Peel felt that such a measure would only divert the influences and interests, which were at present openly avowed and unconcealed, 'into secret and hidden channels'.[122]

The end of the promotion boom of 1824–5 relegated the issue to the background, but it was to resurface with the promotion of railways on a grand scale in the mid-1830s. Between 1836 and 1851, thirty-two select committees were appointed to consider matters relating to the private business of parliament, many of which were tasked with solving the issue of interested voting.[123] Parliamentary debates revealed much disquiet at the way in which the legislature dispensed privileges. Daniel Harvey, the Radical MP for Southwark and newspaper proprietor, drew attention to the fact that the committee rooms were being swamped with railway business. These committees were insufficient tribunals and showed 'an excessive indulgence in unwise speculations'. Harvey argued that

> The numbers composing them were too large, the rooms in which they were held too small, the attendance too crowded and confused, and the motives of many Honourable Members too questionable, through private or public prejudice in favour of one line or in opposition to another, to render a Committee of the House of Commons . . . the most correct or impartial tribunal.[124]

The radical Henry Warburton agreed, arguing that 'it had appeared very extraordinary and unaccountable to behold individuals sitting in Committee to consider the propriety of a railroad in which they were themselves Proprietors and Directors'.[125] He was adamant that 'No Member of Parliament concerned in those speculations, or who held shares in them, should sit upon any one of those Committees.'[126]

Individual cases were highlighted and attracted much opprobrium. Sir Samuel Whalley, MP for Marylebone, had voted for a railway of which he was a subscriber, and Lord Granville Somerset successfully moved that his vote be disallowed. The Whig MP and barrister Ralph Bernal called the current situation 'absurd'. He asked whether such a state of affairs would be permitted in any other tribunal. 'In other instances . . . did they permit any men to sit in the double capacity of Judges and Jurors in their own case?'[127] But many similar cases passed by without censure. Indeed, Whalley quite justifiably complained that he was being unfairly singled out, pointing out

---

121 Ibid. xi. 914 (27 May 1824).
122 Ibid. xii. 981 (10 Mar. 1825).
123 O. C. Williams, *The historical development of private bill procedure and standing orders in the House of Commons*, London 1948, i. 58.
124 *Hansard*, 3rd ser. xxxi. 355 (12 Feb. 1836).
125 Ibid. xxxi. 1121 (1 Mar. 1836).
126 Ibid. xxi. 365 (12 Feb. 1836).
127 Ibid. xxxii. 1256 (20 Apr. 1836).

that the evening before his vote, five directors of the Dublin Steam Packet Company had voted on that company's bill, without any complaint being registered.[128]

Whig reforms

It was in this context that the Whig governments of the 1830s approached the question of the laws regulating joint-stock companies. The perceived inevitability of the corruption of parliamentary committees encouraged them to pursue the avenue opened by the Tories in 1825, that of incorporation by the Board of Trade. Such a means of incorporation also had the advantages of making parliament less likely to become bogged down in the discussion of local bills, as had happened in 1825, and of retaining discretion over incorporation to the ministers of the day. Although the Board still nominally included several great major officers of state, such as the Lord Chancellor, the First Lord of the Treasury, the Chancellor of the Exchequer and the Speaker of the House of Commons, in practice the twice-weekly board meetings were usually attended only by the president and vice-president. All correspondence received by the Board, including petitions for incorporation, was read at these meetings and recommendations were made by the members present.[129] For a petition to be successful, then, it was crucial that the president and vice-president were sympathetic to the cause. But this sympathy could not be taken for granted. Indeed, the system established in 1825 did not make for a dramatic extension of the numbers of companies incorporated: in the years between the acts of 1825 and 1834, just thirty applications were received by the Board of Trade for privileges, and only eight of these were granted.[130] In the shorter period 1827–32, twenty-one bills granting corporate privileges were passed by parliament.[131] The chances of securing privileges seemed to be improved by applying to parliament. But Charles Poulett Thomson, president of the Board of Trade, was not keen on this method of dispensing favours, complaining in the Commons of 'private bills being smuggled through the second reading, without the House being generally or at all informed of the contents of such bills'.[132]

Thomson provided the initiative in steps to reform the process by which privileges were conferred in the 1830s. Former Russia merchant, dogmatic follower of Ricardo and a member of the Benthamite circle which included James Mill, Henry Warburton and Joseph Hume, Thomson had been

---

[128] Ibid. xxxiii. 589 (4 May 1836).
[129] L. Brown, *The Board of Trade and the free-trade movement, 1830–42*, Oxford 1958, 20.
[130] Hunt, *Business corporation*, 58.
[131] This does not include utilities and internal transport companies: ibid. 51.
[132] *Hansard*, 3rd ser. xl. 354 (23 Jan. 1838).

vice-president of the Board since 1830.[133] On 6 June 1834, the day after his promotion to the presidency, he ordered that a letter be written to the attorney-general 'respecting the difficulties which have impeded the execution' of the act of 1825 relative to the granting of charters.[134] The letter revealed the president's concerns that individuals of dubious character were establishing and investing in companies. This Thomson attributed to unlimited liability, for to invest in an unlimited company with no say in its management 'would be the highest impeachment of any man's prudence and sober judgement. Companies thus constituted must therefore fall into the hands of necessitous persons who have nothing to lose; or into the hands of improvident and speculative men'. But it was in 'the interest of society at large' that this did not happen. The Board had, in consequence, granted charters limiting the liability of company members to two or three times the subscribed capital, as a halfway house which would both encourage a better class of investor, and protect the public by providing a fund for paying the company's debts. But such security was illusory, Thomson admitted, for when the company was known or even rumoured to be struggling, the richest shareholders with access to the best information would transfer their shares in order to escape liability, thus shrinking the fund to next to nothing. To counter this, it had been suggested that liability should remain after the transfer of shares for a fixed period, perhaps six years. But this posed many questions, such as how to divide liabilities between past and present shareholders, and whether the length of time a share was held affected the liability. Such issues made it difficult to find a rule to determine the claims of creditors against shareholders, and the claims of shareholders against each other. Thomson could not see a way to resolve these difficulties, so he ducked the question, instead proposing a reform which would permit the Board of Trade to grant letters patent conferring solely the right to sue and be sued, without imparting a corporate character to the company thus privileged.[135]

The attorney-general was favourably disposed, and the result was an act the same year 'to enable His Majesty to invest trading and other companies with the powers necessary for the due conduct of their affairs, and for the security of the rights and interests of their creditors'.[136] While continuing to reserve the Board's right to grant charters with limited liability, the five-section act sought to standardise procedure for companies granted the right to sue and be sued. In the interests of circulating information about the companies so privileged, company officers were to submit twice-yearly lists of all company members, including their addresses, to the clerk of the patents. The act also made it clear that judgements against the company officer were to extend to company property and the property of all shareholders, as if they

133 Brown, *Board of Trade*, 17.
134 PRO, BT 5/42, p. 115 (6 June 1834).
135 Letter to attorney-general, BT 3/25, pp. 152–3, 158–9 (7 June 1834).
136 4 & 5 Will. IV. c. 94.

had all been parties to the action. The act did not indicate on what criteria the crown was to grant or refuse privileges. But a Board of Trade minute shortly after it had become law indicates how the Board intended to interpret the legislation. Control over incorporation was not to be diluted to make the grant of corporate powers a formality; rather, these privileges would be carefully guarded:

> My Lords are of opinion, that although the Act . . . undoubtedly confers upon the Crown the power of granting limited privileges to public associations applying for them, and specifically points to that of suing and being sued by their Secretary, as one desirable, not only for the benefit of such associations, but of the public with whom they deal, it is necessary to take care that such powers are not conferred indiscriminately, and that so long at least as the present laws of Partnership remain unchanged, facilities should not be afforded to Joint Stock Partnerships which may interfere with private enterprise carried on under those laws, unless the circumstances and objects of such Joint Stock Companies are of a nature fully to justify such interference, upon the ground of general public advantage.[137]

It is instructive to compare the minute with the opinion of the attorney-general, given back in 1761:

> The Crown has very wisely been always cautious of incorporating traders because such bodies will either grow too great and by overwhelming Individuals become Monopolies or else by failing will involve themselves in the Ruin intendent upon a Corporate Bankruptcy. As Trade seldom requires the Aid of such Combinations but thrives better when left open to the free speculation of private Men, such measures are only the expedient when the Trade is impracticable upon any other basis than a joint Stock.[138]

The persistence of traditional attitudes was further underlined when the Board of Trade minute went on to detail the circumstances where the grant of special privileges would be justified: when the enterprise was too hazardous for two or three large capitalists, when the capital required was too great for individual partnerships, when extended responsibility was required, or when numerous individuals sought to establish literary societies or charitable institutions. By following these rules, the Board was not demonstrating its attachment to an outdated ideology, but was ensuring the application of the principles of political economy to the joint-stock economy. In this period the Board was particularly receptive to these principles. Thomson was a Ricardian; Henry Labouchere, Thomson's vice-president, was a firm free-trader; joint-secretary to the Board was James Deacon Hume, member of the

---

[137] *Copy of the minute of the Lords of the Committee of Privy Council for Trade, dated 4 November 1834, on granting letters patent*, PP 1837 xxxix. 1.
[138] Cited in DuBois, *Business company*, 29.

Political Economy Club and staunch supporter of free trade.[139] The Board's policies cannot, therefore, be written off as backward or reactionary.

The Board rejected the Scottish Porter and Ale Brewery Company's application for privileges in November 1834, and the Board's minute books indicate that ministers subsequently adhered closely to the guidelines set out in 1834.[140] The change of administration in December had no effect on the Board's policy. In January 1835 Alexander Baring and Viscount Lowther, the new team at the Board, rejected the application of the Shropshire Coal Company, as they did not 'think that this undertaking is of sufficient magnitude to require Letters Patent'.[141] The following month they refused the Birmingham District Fire Insurance Company, for its proposed capital of £7,986 was 'so very small'. In March 1837 the Board, again headed by Thomson, agreed to grant letters patent to the Union Plate Glass Company of Manchester: the company's proposed capital of £180,000 was 'larger . . . than individuals would feel inclined to invest'. But the Board was concerned to ensure that the company would not try to enter into competition with private traders, noting 'it is necessary that security should be given for the correctness of the assertion and provision made against the Letters Patent being obtained under this pretext and a competition entered upon with private enterprise which their Lordships are indisposed unnecessarily to encourage'. The Board consequently insisted that as a condition of the grant, at least half of the capital had to be paid up.[142] This figure was uncomfortably high for the company, however, whose representative wrote back asking whether the subscribers would be permitted to pay £24,700 rather than £90,000. The Board did not look favourably upon this suggestion, considering that this 'would be of too low an amount to justify the grant of the Charter since a concern capable of being carried on with this moderate capital ought, in the opinion of this Board, to be left to individual industry'.[143] It should be noted that what was at issue was not a grant of limited liability, but merely letters patent, which would have given the company the right to sue and be sued. The Board's reluctance to permit companies with any form of special privileges to compete with private traders indicates an acute awareness on the part of both Whig and Conservative governments of the potential dangers of exempting too many companies from the rigours of partnership law. This law was viewed as the best means of promoting commercial stability and morality. Thus, while the act did encourage more applications for privileges, these were far from certain to succeed.[144]

---

139 Brown, *Board of Trade*, 24–5.
140 BT 5/42, pp. 260–2 (4 Nov. 1834).
141 Ibid. 316 (20 Jan. 1835), 357 (20 Feb. 1835).
142 BT 5/44, pp. 236–7 (10 Mar. 1837).
143 Ibid. 295–6 (18 Apr. 1837).
144 Between 1834 and 1837 there were 25 applications, an increase on pre-1834 figures, but only 'three or four' were successful: Hunt, *Business corporation*, 58, 60.

But Thomson did not leave the issue here. His letter to the attorney-general had revealed an interest in the principle of limited liability, and as the tide of speculation rose in the mid-1830s, he appointed the barrister Henry Bellenden Ker to inquire into the law of partnership, specifically with reference to limited partnerships. Ker gathered evidence from nineteen bankers, lawyers and merchants. His report indicated that opinion had been divided on the issue of limited liability, with a majority opposed, so Ker left this out of his recommendations. Instead, he focused on the issue of powers of suing and being sued in the name of an officer. The difficulty unincorporated companies experienced in suing and being sued 'often amounts to an absolute denial of justice', claimed Ker. At present, companies had to endure the expense and uncertainty of applying for this privilege from parliament or the crown. The act of 1834 was designed to encourage companies to approach the crown for these powers, but it still conceived of them as a privilege to be granted only when the 'propriety or expediency of the undertaking' could be proven.[145] This was wrong, Ker's report argued, because these powers should be a right. To give large partnerships these powers was the only way to bring them under the jurisdiction of the law, giving protection both to themselves and their creditors. So Ker proposed a system by which the deeds of all partnerships of more than ten–fifteen members had to be registered, within three months of the formation of the concern, with the Enrolment Office of the Court of Chancery. On this being completed, shares could be traded in the concern, and it could sue and be sued in the name of an officer. Ker also proposed that the process of granting charters or letters patent be simplified and standardised.

The government rejected Ker's suggestion that it renounce its discretion over the grant of suing powers, but it agreed to modify existing procedure. Later that year an act was passed repealing the 1834 measure and setting out new procedures for the grant of corporate privileges.[146] The act was much longer than its predecessor, running into thirty-two sections. Companies were required to register more detailed information, including their total capital, the shareholding and liability of each member and details of all share transfers, in order to provide greater security to the public. In return, it was ruled that the grant of letters patent could limit the liability of shareholders, and shareholder liability was to cease not within three years of a transfer as fixed by the previous act, but upon register of the transfer. Here, the government was attempting to balance the rights of shareholders and creditors: the former would be permitted to transfer into and out of companies much more easily, but details of such transfers and other information on companies would have to be registered for the security of creditors.[147]

---

[145] *Report on the law of partnership*, PP 1837, 4, 8.
[146] 1 Vict. c. 73.
[147] But the Board's priority still seemed to be to protect the public rather than extend the scope of joint-stock enterprise: BT 5/44, pp. 439–40 (21 July 1837). Unfortunately, from

Table 5
Companies promoted, 1834–7

Sector	Number of companies	Nominal capital (£)
Railways	88	69,666,000
Banking	20	23,750,000
Insurance	11	7,600,000
Mining	71	7,035,200
Canals	4	3,655,000
Steam Navigation	17	3,533,000
Investment	5	1,730,000
Gas	7	890,000
Conveyance	9	500,000
Cemetery	7	435,000
Newspaper	6	350,000
Misc.	55	16,104,500
Total	300	135,248,700

Source: *Select committee to inquire into the state of the laws respecting joint stock companies*, PP 1844 vii, appendix 4.

The Whigs were criticised for retaining control over incorporation. In the *Westminster Review*, Arthur Symonds argued that the vesting in government of the right of granting and denying charters 'can only be a source of patronage, sought for and obtained by endless begging and intrigue'. He went on to state that 'whatever facilities are now granted by charter or by Act of Parliament ought to be a matter of common right'.[148] Symonds found the grant of privileges by the Board and by parliament equally distasteful, but the powers of the former tended to be more controversial. An anonymous pamphleteer complained that Thomson's policy was a step backwards: parliamentary incorporation was to be preferred because 'in parliament all must be open and straightforward', whereas applications to ministers opened the field to 'back-door influence and private friendship'.[149] Matthew Lowndes, a solicitor, attacked Thomson for his 'prejudice against Joint Stock Companies'. The crown's discretion over incorporation was unfair and corrupt: 'if parties opposed by interest to a Joint Stock Company associated for a particular trade or branch of trade, can win over the president of the Board of Trade to the

July 1839 only unbound rough minutes have been preserved, which are terse and provide little insight into the Board's decision-making process.
148 [A. Symonds], 'Law of partnership', *WR* xx (Jan. 1834), 58–73 at p. 71. For similar views expressed a decade earlier see Mundell, *Influence of interest*, 152.
149 Anon., *Observations on the Trading Companies Bill*, London 1834, 7.

Table 6
The principal joint-stock companies in Scotland in 1837 and 1841

Sector	1837	1841
Banking	13	24
Gas	14	18
Railways	11	17
Fire and life insurance	10	15
Marine insurance	1	10
Misc.	12	27
Total	61	111

Source: John Reid, *Manual of the Scottish stocks and British funds, with a list of the joint-stock companies in Scotland*, Edinburgh 1841, 166–71.

belief that the company is not wanted', then the application was denied and the company had to struggle on unincorporated.[150]

But the government's caution seemed to be justified by events. 1834 saw the beginnings of a boom in speculative activity, led by enthusiasm for railway and banking schemes.[151] Joseph Parkes, a collector of company prospectuses, counted 300 companies promoted in this boom (*see* table 5). In Scotland the boom came later, starting in 1838, but significantly expanded the size of the joint-stock economy. A Scottish stockbroker, John Reid, recorded that fifty new companies were formed in the four years from 1838 to 1841 (see table 6). This survey included only the 'principal' joint-stock companies, therefore excluding those companies of which Reid disapproved, namely those formed to carry out 'the proper objects of private adventure'. But the summary nevertheless indicates the pace of company growth in Scotland in this period.

The fashion for speculation engendered much criticism, however, which closely mirrored the language of 1825. Fears were raised in both houses of parliament about the 'extravagant mania which would doubtless involve and ruin multitudes'. Speculations, many of which 'were undertaken solely for gambling purposes' were being entered into, and they were 'pregnant with national evil'.[152] *The Times* wondered at the 'eager disposition of the public to

---

[150] M. D. Lowndes, *Review of the joint stock bank acts, and of the law as to joint stock companies generally: with the practical suggestions of a solicitor for their amendment*, London 1840, 42. Several pamphlets were published in the 1830s detailing the benefits the growth of joint-stock enterprise would bring. See, for example, Anon., *Remarks on the objections to joint stock banks*, London 1833, and Anon. ['G. H'], *The American mines; shewing their importance, in a national point of view*, London 1834.

[151] Speculation in banks was encouraged by the Bank Charter Act of 1833, which permitted the formation of joint-stock banks in London: 3 & 4 Will. IV. c. 98.

[152] W. Crawford, *Hansard*, 3rd ser. xxxi. 357 (12 Feb. 1836); earl of Winchelsea, xxxvi. 520 (14 Feb. 1837); H. Warburton, xxxvi. 857 (22 Feb. 1837).

embark in Joint-stock Companies, notwithstanding their repeated failures and embarrassments'.[153] Charles Mackay published his *Memoirs of extraordinary popular delusions and the madness of crowds*, which featured a chapter on the 'South Sea Bubble'. Mackay believed that his contemporaries ought to learn lessons from the events of over a century ago: 'The schemes of the year 1836 threatened, at one time, results as disastrous' as those of 1720.[154] In 1837 Thomas Love Peacock published his *Paper money lyrics*, written in 1825–6, and containing ballads satirising the bubbles of those years ('Oh! where are the riches that bubbled like fountains'?), which were, according to the author, 'as applicable now as they were twelve years ago'.[155] Pamphlets were written 'to disabuse the people of this country of the enchantment which of late years has spread its delusive fascination, and produced a kind of moral ophthalmia from one end of the kingdom to the other, in every thing ushered into existence under the paternity of a Joint Stock Company'.[156]

Consequently, there was much popular support for the continuance of the government's discretion over incorporation. The *Circular to Bankers* could in no sense be thought to oppose joint-stock enterprise.[157] But the journal firmly believed that

> The Government should judge and determine whether the objects aimed at by associations be fit and proper to be undertaken by public companies; they should scrupulously discriminate and mark the boundary where trading associations would begin to trench upon, obstruct, and injure individual enterprise, and provide against the waste of capital and labour by granting charters only to eligible and proper applicants.[158]

Some, indeed, thought the board too liberal. The Glasgow Chamber of Commerce wrote to the board complaining of its conferral of exclusive privileges on companies. It stated that the only justification for such privileges was to encourage enterprise when capital was scarce and trade slow, 'but the history of the past year proves but too clearly that this is a period of redundant capital and excessive speculation and that it is much more necessary to apply a drag than to give a stimulus to commercial enterprise'. The Chamber went on to 'express its regret and surprise' at recent attempts 'to revive the exploded system of privileged trading by proposals for establishing Banks,

---

153 *The Times*, 9 Oct. 1840.
154 C. Mackay, *Memoirs of extraordinary popular delusions and the madness of crowds*, Ware 1995, 88.
155 T. L. Peacock, *The works of Thomas Love Peacock*, New York 1967, vii. 123, 99–100.
156 Anon. ['Investigator'], *The Bank of England, and other banks*, London 1840, 3.
157 It bemoaned the loss of the government's 1838 bill on trading companies, which sought to improve the suing powers of company officers, and implement other minor amendments to the 1837 act: *A bill to amend an act for better enabling Her Majesty to confer certain powers and immunities on trading and other companies*, PP 1837–38 vi. *Circular to Bankers*, 17 Aug. 1838.
158 *Circular to Bankers*, 17 Aug. 1838.

Steam Navigation and Manufacturing Companies, with rights and immunities from which the private trader is sought to be excluded'. Such attempts were unfair to those who traded without privileges, would encourage monopoly and would distort the economy.[159]

The courts displayed a similar attitude, and continued to judge unincorporated companies illegal. In a case of 1837 Vice-Chancellor Shadwell decreed that the Anglo-American Gold Mining Company was illegal, 'because it trenches on the prerogative of the King, by attempting to create a body not having the protection of the King's charter, the shares of which might be assigned without any control or restriction whatsoever':

> [It] held out to the public, as an inducement to them to become partners in the working of these imaginary gold mines, a false and fraudulent representation that they might continue partners in the undertaking just as long as they pleased, and then get rid of all the liability that they had incurred by transferring their shares to some other person . . . The undertaking in question appears to have been a wild project, entered into by speculating persons for the purpose of deluding the weak portion of the public of this country, who too often allow themselves to be gulled by any specious scheme that holds out a prospect of gain.

He concluded that 'The more such schemes are discouraged by Courts of Justice, the better it will be for Her Majesty's subjects.'[160] Shadwell's reasoning was consistent with Chief Justice Best's decision nine years earlier, that 'there can be no transferable shares of any stock, except the stock of corporations or of joint-stock companies created by acts of parliament'.[161]

Following in the tradition of F. W. Maitland, some authorities have been bullish about the efficacy of the unincorporated company operating under trust law.[162] Maitland claimed that 'in truth and in deed we made corporations without troubling King or Parliament, though perhaps we said we were doing nothing of the kind'.[163] But the bulk of companies formed in the pre-1844 period were incorporated by the state. Those that were not either operated under a regulatory code established by the state, such as banks, or usually found it convenient to apply for corporate powers from the state, such as insurance companies. Without such privileges, they were regarded in the eyes of the law as partnerships, no matter how many members they had, or how much capital they possessed. Thus the state played a key role in the development of both the incorporated and the unincorporated joint-stock

---

[159] BT 1/330, f. 13, no. 72 (Apr. 1837).

[160] *Blundell v. Winsor* (1837), 8 Sim. 601, pp. 242–3.

[161] *Duvergier v. Fellows* (1828), 5 Bing. 248, 130 ER, 1056.

[162] G. M. Anderson and R. D. Tollison, 'The myth of the corporation as a creation of the state', *International Review of Law and Economics* iii (1983), 107–20.

[163] Cited in Cooke, *Corporation, trust and company*, 86.

economy. This was a role the state took seriously, and grants of corporate privileges were only made if entrepreneurs could convince either parliament or the crown that such grants were in the public interest and would not interfere with individual enterprise.

It is therefore apparent that there had been very little change in popular and official attitudes to joint-stock companies, and speculation in them, by the end of the 1830s. The continuities were obvious. Despite legislation in 1825, 1834 and 1837, companies were in a similar legal position in 1840 as they were in 1800, due largely to the common law interpretation of unincorporated companies, and to the government's desire to maintain its discretion over granting privileges of incorporation. Popular perceptions mirrored the attitudes of the state, and although some voices of opposition to the exercise of the incorporating powers of the Board of Trade were raised, there was widespread suspicion of speculation, and profound fear of the effects of the over-extension of joint-stock enterprise. The numbers of companies, both incorporated and unincorporated, were growing, but these were being contained in what was, broadly speaking, an unchanging legal and conceptual framework. All this was to change after 1840, for reasons to be explored in the next chapter.

4

Reform or Retrogression?
Free Incorporation, 1840–1862

Despite its seeming invulnerability to change, the long-standing consensus on how best to regulate joint-stock enterprise gradually collapsed from the early 1840s, and legislative interventions between 1844 and 1856 created a new legal framework transforming incorporation from a closely-guarded privilege into a freely-available right. The reasons for this break with the past are unclear, though historians have tended to portray the legislation as a result of new, enlightened attitudes to joint-stock enterprise. Legislators, it is argued, had finally come to realise the contributions companies could make to economic growth (and had recognised growth as desirable), while speculation was fast shedding its negative moral connotations. Despite appearances, however, the changes in the law were not proof that traditional fears of the dangers of joint-stock enterprise and speculation had entirely disappeared. Nor were they evidence of a new acceptance of the passive investor who speculated without any sense of responsibility. The legislation in fact concealed a significant degree of continuity in attitudes, for it was designed to bring companies within the law where they would cease to be such a disruptive influence on the economy, and to enable shareholders to perform their regulatory duties more effectively.

The changes culminated in the introduction of limited liability in 1855–6, but this was achieved only in the face of considerable resistance, for the opponents of general limited liability denied that the principle was synonymous with progress, and insisted that calls for its introduction were not consistent with the reforming spirit of the age, but 'a march of retrogression'.[1] Yet the case for unlimited liability was fatally undermined by the fact that the state was the agency by means of which corporate privileges were dispensed and denied. Company law reform became inseparable from political reform since it entailed replacing the state's traditional role with a mechanical, self-regulating system which would exclude government discretion altogether, and establishing a new authority at one remove from central government to oversee the operation of this system, the Joint-Stock Companies Registrar. Consequently, the reform could be portrayed as in harmony with other defining legislation of the post-1832 period, such as the Factory Reform

---

[1] A. Hastie, *Hansard*, 3rd ser. cxxxix. 357 (29 June 1855). All references to *Hansard* in this chapter are to the third series.

Act of 1833 and the reform of the poor law the following year, the currency reforms of 1844 and the removal of indirect taxation accomplished by the budgets of Peel and Gladstone in the 1840s and 1850s. The reform was also facilitated by, and helped to perpetuate, a reconceptualisation of corporate privileges as private rights, and of joint-stock companies as private bodies. With such a realignment, the state's role of delegating corporate powers to selected companies in order to further specific public aims became an unjustifiable 'interference' in private enterprise which had to be removed. In this way, what amounted to a significant reshaping of the commercial laws of the nation could be presented as a free trade reform.

Gladstone's cure-all

Despite the best efforts of the Whigs, by the early 1840s the great majority of joint-stock schemes were still approaching parliament rather than the Board of Trade for privileges. In the five years 1840–4, just nineteen projects applied to the Board for limited liability, and eleven were successful, a success rate of 58 per cent. Parliament had to deal with a far larger volume of applications (see table 7).

Table 7
Selected private bills presented before parliament, 1840–4, and percentage successful

Sector of economy	Bills presented	Acts passed	Percentage successful
Canals/navigations/ferries	35	28	80
Railways	188	137	73
Markets/bridges/cemeteries	49	34	69
Gas/waterworks	63	41	65
'Other' companies	77	49	64
Harbours/piers/docks/fisheries	115	64	56
Total	527	353	67

Source: *Companion to the Almanac; or Year-Book of General Information*, 1841–5.

Although this table includes applications not only for limited liability, but also other corporate privileges, including revisions to existing powers, it nevertheless suggests that company promoters and boards of directors preferred to approach parliament with their requests. Canals and railways were the most successful applicants, partly due to a great degree of consensus by this time on the desirability of incorporating enterprises for inland transport, partly because the large capitals and influential connections of these companies made securing the passage of a bill much easier. 'Other' compa-

nies, made up principally of insurance, iron and coal companies, with a sprin-
kling of manufacturing, colonial and patent schemes of various descriptions,
met with a lower success rate, suggesting that these companies enjoyed less
political backing. Overall, however, it emerges that both parliament and the
Board of Trade were perfectly willing to grant corporate privileges to those
companies which they judged deserving of them. Yet it is clear that applications for privileges were far from a formality, with one in three bills unsuccessful, while applications to the Board of Trade met with a lower success rate
still.

The law regarding joint-stock companies once more became an issue in
1841, when, in the last days of the Whig government, Henry Labouchere, the
president of the Board of Trade, moved for a select committee to inquire into
the subject. However, this renewal of governmental interest was not
prompted by the desire to extend access to privileges; rather, it was a reaction
to a series of insurance frauds which emerged in the late 1830s and early
1840s, highlighting the vulnerability of the money invested in joint-stock
companies. A select committee was formed with a view to identifying
measures 'for the prevention of fraud'; its first task was to gather details of
how the recent frauds had been carried out.[2] The committee was only able to
meet on three occasions in May 1841 before the summer election, however,
and when Peel's Conservative Party was returned, the committee fell into
abeyance. But it was resurrected in May 1843 by William Gladstone, who
had just become president of the Board of Trade.[3] The committee met ten
more times through the summer of 1843, and took evidence from twenty-one
witnesses, who were asked to discuss not only the recent frauds, but also their
suggestions for the improvement of the law regarding joint-stock companies.[4]
Its report laid bare the various 'modes of deception' adopted by companies,
which suggested the danger companies posed to the public as investors in and
customers of these concerns. These included the use of fictitious names; the
use of respectable names without permission; the issue of misleading prospectuses and advertisements; the insertion of puffs and reports of invented meetings in the newspapers; the prevention of shareholders' meetings; the
falsification of share transfer books; the creation of fictitious votes to outvote
the real shareholders; the creation of false accounts to deceive shareholders;
the declaration of dividends out of capital; and the employment of respectable agents to cloak the want of respectability of the company.[5]

The committee concluded that such frauds were facilitated by the unincorporated status of the companies involved. It was simple for fraudsters to set

[2] Ibid. lvii. 842 (2 Apr. 1841).
[3] Ibid. lxix. 806 (23 May 1843).
[4] The witnesses were predominately drawn from the legal profession, with four barristers
and nine solicitors giving evidence, indicating that this was seen primarily as a legal rather
than a commercial reform.
[5] *Select committee on joint stock companies*, PP 1844, p. ix.

up companies, obtain contributions and abscond, as by trading as partner-ships they were beyond the reach of all the controls placed on public compa-nies. There were no registers of shareholders, no rules regarding subscribed capital, no accountability at all. The result was that the property entrusted to these companies by shareholders, customers and creditors, was rendered very insecure. Furthermore, recovery of property from the directors of fraudulent or bankrupt companies in the courts was difficult, for they could exploit the common law illegality of their companies in order to escape punishment: shareholders could not recover from directors if the concerns in question were ruled illegal. But despite this, companies still managed to attract capital. Indeed, the amount of capital invested in companies known on the London market, both incorporated and unincorporated, had grown from around £90 million in 1810 to approximately £210 million by 1843.[6] The security and stability of this capital was becoming wrapped up in the national interest. If it were lost, there would be repercussions through the whole economy. Thus, the idea gained ground that this property needed to be protected. Two cases decided in 1843 by Chief Justice Tindal indicated that this view was winning support in the courts. In both actions the promoters of the companies being prosecuted pleaded the illegality of their schemes as a main plank of their defence. Tindal was unimpressed, holding that 'as the illegality of the company is set up by the very persons who constitute that company, in order to avoid the payment of a demand just in itself, it may be fairly required that the affirmative of the pleas should be established by satisfactory evidence'.[7] Tindal felt that the companies did not succeed in establishing this, for he held that the raising of transferable shares alone did not constitute an offence at common law.[8] A new message was being sent out by the courts, that unin-corporated companies were being brought within the law, and that dishonest promoters who had defrauded investors would be answerable to their victims. The courts did not merely see their role as shielding the public from fraudu-lent or abortive schemes, however; they also began to protect joint-stock property from being exposed to risks of which shareholders were unaware when they had originally invested their money. The Eastern Counties Railway Company wished to establish a steam-packet company to connect to its rail line. The directors proposed to guarantee the profits of the steam-packet company from the capital of the railway company, and, in the event of the failure of the new company, to pay back to its subscribers their invest-ments in full from this capital. The grounds on which Lord Langdale blocked this proposal are revealing: 'Considering the vast property which is now invested in railways, and how easily it is transferable, perhaps one of the best things that could happen to them would be, that the investment should be of

6 Harris, *Industrializing English law*, 223.
7 *Harrison v. Heathorn* (1843), 6 Man. and Gr. 81, 134 ER, 839.
8 Ibid. 840; *Garrard v. Hardey* (1843), 5 Man. and Gr. 471, 134 ER, 652–3.

such a safe nature, that prudent persons might, without improper hazard, invest their monies in it.'[9]

The aims of Gladstone's select committee were in harmony with the trajectory of these legal decisions. As the recent frauds were facilitated by the fact that the companies involved had never had to register themselves, submit returns or fulfil any other requirements, the committee judged it desirable to implement registration and publicity as the best means of combating fraud. Such a procedure already existed with respect to joint-stock banks, obliged under the terms of the act of 1826 to register with the government. This requirement should simply be extended to all joint-stock companies.[10] This would enable the public to obtain full information about a company before deciding whether to invest in or deal with it. Companies were not to be brought within the law because they had achieved respectability, but because they needed to be made respectable. John Duncan, a company solicitor, told the committee that there was 'a strong feeling abroad inimical to joint stock companies, and in many quarters they are treated with unlimited abuse', but argued that it would be 'a fatal error to legislate upon the subject with any design to give way to those inconsiderable prejudices' by increasing state controls over companies, checking investment in them and encouraging companies to operate without the protection of the law. Rather, he supported 'a course of legislation calculated to make every joint stock company respectable, whether successful or not'. This would be the best way to protect the public. Bringing the unincorporated company within the law would 'attract towards it respectable directors and respectable managers, whence will inevitably result respectable transactions'.[11] When this occurred, the public would be safe.

This was a blanket solution: security to the public was to be provided by applying the same rules to all companies, good, bad and fraudulent. This implied that registration would be automatic, ending the state's discretion over incorporation. But there was a difference of opinion among the witnesses on this question. Some, like Edward Bigg, a solicitor and director, were adamant that state discretion should continue:

> I would not allow any society to commence business without having the sanction of some public officer or some public board that the proceedings are *bona fide* in the first instance, that the prospectus is founded on something like reason and good faith . . . and that they should have such a proportion of paid-up capital as to the constituted officer may seem right.[12]

[9] *Colman v. Eastern Counties Railway Company* (1846), 10 Beav. 1, 48 ER, 488.
[10] See, for example, the testimony of Peter Laurie, *Select committee on joint stock companies*, PP 1844, 10 (1841 committee), and Christopher Cuff, ibid. 78 (1843 committee).
[11] Ibid. 162–74 (1843 committee).
[12] Ibid. 96 (1843 committee). The anonymous merchant 'CD' and Joseph Parkes had similar views: ibid. 117, 237 (1843 committee).

Henry Bellenden Ker, author of the 1837 report, agreed with Bigg, believing that 'much evil would be prevented' by insisting that incorporation only be granted by the Board of Trade. This course of action would not inevitably result in hosts of unincorporated companies: 'if the law prohibited joint stock companies unchartered, and consequently made all their contracts and dealings void, I think there would be no danger of any serious evasion of the law'. But he confessed that he was 'aware that this notion is rather out of date, and that another state of law permitting unchartered companies has probably existed too long to admit of such a great change'.[13]

Ker's pessimism was well founded, for the methods by which the state controlled access to corporate privileges were coming under increasing fire. The railways made the corruption of private bill committees an enduringly topical issue. Radicals continued to insist that interested voting in committees lowered the reputation of MPs, and was a corrupt way to dispense privileges. Yet their efforts to overhaul private bill procedure continued to be blocked.[14] As a result, the popular perception of private bill committees as shady affairs endured. This is demonstrated in Anthony Trollope's *The three clerks*, in which interested MPs secure a select committee on the Limehouse Bridge, with the intention of inflating the scheme's share price. The witnesses selected by the proponents of the bridge are all interested in it, and committee members are forced to sit through their self-interested testimonies. To Mr Vigil, one of the committeemen, 'it was all mere nonsense, sheer waste of time. Had he been condemned to sit for eight days in close contiguity to the clappers of a small mill, he would have learnt as much as he did from the witnesses before the committee'. All the committee members had made up their minds on the bridge before proceedings had begun: 'not one of them dreamed of being influenced by anything which had been said before them'.[15] The whole committee was a sham, an absurd ritual. But the other means of dispensing these privileges – application to the Board of Trade – was even more unpopular.[16] Partly, it seems, as a result of this criticism, the Board itself came to dislike carrying out these duties. In a speech of 1844, the sentiments of which would be echoed by subsequent presidents of the Board, Gladstone told the house that the Board's powers of granting and denying charters

> caused him and all connected with him in his office very great anxiety and uneasiness . . . when he was sitting in the Board of Trade with others about him, attending, to the best of his ability, to his duties, there was nothing gave the Board so much uneasiness and annoyance as the exercise of the discretion-

13 Ibid. 185–6 (1843 committee).
14 *Hansard*, xlv. 965–84 (28 Feb. 1839); lix. 679–85 (21 Sept. 1841).
15 Trollope, *Three clerks*, 403, 391–2.
16 See chapter 3 above.

ary powers already vested in them as to the management of commercial matters.[17]

Thus, the growing unpopularity of both means by which the state incorporated joint-stock companies seriously undermined the legitimacy of the state's discretion over incorporation. This was reflected in the committee's attitude to those witnesses who, like Ker, wanted to retain or even increase state discretion over incorporation. Ker was told by Sir William Clay that his 'restrictive policy . . . might perhaps be presumed to be very difficult of adoption in this country after the degree of practical countenance which joint stock companies have received, and the manner in which they have become interwoven with the commercial habits of the people'.[18] The committee looked more favourably on those witnesses who advocated automatic incorporation on registration. Thomas Newman Farquhar, a company solicitor engaged in securing the passage of company bills through parliament, thought it 'monstrous' that companies should have to pay several hundred pounds 'to obtain that which the law ought not to give as a favour, but to impose upon them as a necessity or a duty'. That such views were also held by the committee was made abundantly clear by exchanges such as this:

> Gladstone: You mean to convey to the Committee that in your opinion the advantage is so great to the public of always having some notorious person in whose name they may sue the Company, that although there may be also an incidental disadvantage in giving a sort of *quasi* public sanction to unsubstantial undertakings by the existence of such an officer under Act of Parliament, yet, weighing together the advantage and the disadvantage, you think the advantage greatly preponderates?
> Farquhar: Decidedly.[19]

Predictably, therefore, the committee's report, issued in March 1844, recommended against maintaining the discretion of the state over incorporation, as this method was held to be a flawed means of protecting the public. Neither the legislature nor the executive could guard against companies founded on unsound calculations, for 'any authority appointed to act as censor would be as liable to be deceived as the promoters of the schemes, and it might sometimes sanction bad, and at other times prevent good, schemes'. It was even less likely that they would be able to weed out fraudulent schemes. Instead, the public was to be protected by moving in the opposite direction – by removing state control over incorporation. The committee advocated the construction of a mechanical system of registration which bypassed both parliament and the Board of Trade. This reform was not to eliminate regulation, but to replace state regulation with regulation by public opinion.

[17] *Hansard*, lxxvi. 276 (3 July 1844).
[18] *Select committee on joint stock companies*, PP 1844, 189 (1843 committee).
[19] Ibid. 36, 84 (1841 committee).

Compulsory company registration and publicity would 'baffle every case of fraud' by ensuring the availability of all the information people needed to make informed choices as consumers and investors.[20]

The government introduced a bill based on the conclusions of the committee, which would establish a Joint-Stock Companies Registrar, and which set out a detailed procedure of registration, in all running to 130 clauses.[21] Before any company could advertise itself to the public in any way, it had provisionally to register with the Registrar, setting out the company name, its purpose and the names, occupations and addresses of the promoters. After provisional registration, the company could begin to raise capital, though shares could not be transferred until complete registration had been secured. To accomplish this, companies had to register more detailed information with the Registrar, including details of nominal and subscribed capital, information relating to shareholders and the company's deed of settlement. When a company had completely registered, it had most of the privileges of a corporation. Its responsibilities were not over, however. Companies had to make twice-yearly returns to the Registrar, balance sheets had to be produced at each meeting of shareholders and annual audits were compulsory.[22] Some government opponents feared that the bill would increase the power the Board of Trade possessed over companies. Benjamin Hawes, a radical, thought that 'from beginning to end Joint-Stock Companies were to be placed under the control of the Board of Trade'. John Parker, a Whig, thought that the Bill 'would confer very great patronage on a certain office in Whitehall'.[23] But in fact the Registrar was not to have any power to 'regulate' companies in any meaningful sense. The Bill originally proposed that it should be 'the duty of the registrar to satisfy himself of the legality of any instrument before he affixed the seal of the company to it'. But Gladstone soon removed this clause, telling the House that it was 'a large discretion, and almost amounted to the establishment of a double government of the concern'.[24] The only regulation imposed on companies would be that of public opinion.

The bill passed through its stages easily, remarkably so for such an important piece of legislation. This was because Gladstone had ensured it would appeal to two different constituencies. For those who wanted to improve access to corporate privileges, Gladstone underlined that, under this bill, people would be able for the first time to form companies 'without the fear of interference from any human being whatever'.[25] For those, on the other hand, worried about the lawlessness of joint-stock enterprise, Gladstone

---

[20] Ibid. p. v.
[21] 7 & 8 Vict. c. 110.
[22] See ibid. sections 11, 37, 38.
[23] *Hansard*, lxxvi. 273, 279 (3 July 1844).
[24] Ibid. lxxvi. 101 (28 June 1844).
[25] Ibid. lxxvi. 277 (3 July 1844).

stressed that the aim of the measure was to bring companies within the law, 'to give a statutable position to Joint Stock Companies, subjecting them to general inspection, and providing for their constitution and regulation'.[26] The bill would create a public office 'to which all parties soliciting to take part in Joint Stock Companies might repair, in order to know the real history of these companies'.[27] Indeed, it was the anticipated brake placed on fraud which won the measure most of its plaudits, with the opposition benches hailing it as a 'useful and valuable measure for the protection of the community'.[28] Commentators were optimistic that the measure would limit opportunities for fraud. James Burchell, director of the Mutual Life Assurance Company, thought that the act (the objects of which were 'undeniably excellent'), was 'calculated to enable honest persons safely to enter into engagements with a view to fair profit and benefit either to themselves or families, and to prevent the dishonest from extracting the loose cash from the pockets of their unsuspecting neighbours'.[29] George Henry Lewis, a lawyer, welcomed the act, for hitherto 'The only limits or restrictions placed upon the formation of these companies, were the extent of the will and ingenuity of the projectors; and the mode of operation was equally uncontrolled.'[30] The Times called the measure the 'Anti-Bubble Bill', and thought it was entirely uncontroversial: 'The simple aim and object of the measure, so far as we understand it, is to preclude the growth and to detect the knavery of those fictitious and scheming adventures, which, under the guise and name of trading companies, are continually being devised.'[31]

Gladstone hoped that the act struck the optimum balance between permissiveness and restriction: shares could be transferred, but liability for company debts would continue for three years after transfers.[32] Companies were allowed all the privileges of corporations, but not limited liability, which was still regarded as a privilege too important and too controversial to be made generally available. Accountability would be ensured by obliging companies to allow shareholders to inspect the balance sheets; to register these accounts with the registrar; and to make provision for audit. However, satisfying everyone was more difficult than Gladstone had anticipated, and subsequent events were to convince many that the act had in fact endangered the public.

---

[26] Ibid. lxxv. 475–6 (10 June 1844).

[27] Ibid. lxxvi. 275 (3 July 1844).

[28] J. Brotherton, ibid. 280. See also the similar comments of Conservative MPs James Wortley and Walter James, ibid. 280–1.

[29] J. Burchell, The Joint Stock Companies Registration Act, London 1844, 2.

[30] Lewis, Liabilities incurred, 11.

[31] The Times, 4 July 1844. See also Manchester Guardian, 24 July 1844.

[32] 7 & 8 Vict. c. 110, s. 66.

The Joint-Stock Companies Act in practice

As the Joint-Stock Companies Act was passing through parliament, investment in the leading joint-stock sector of the economy, railways, was beginning to reach unprecedented proportions. The profitability of many of the lines established in the 1830s was noted, and a sequence of good harvests meant that there was a great amount of capital waiting to be invested.[33] The result was a rush on the part both of established companies, and landed and business interests, to promote new lines, culminating in what contemporaries termed a 'mania' for railways in 1845–7. The specialist railway press boomed, while other papers greatly expanded their coverage of railway affairs and share prices. The *Economist* doubled in size in 1845 to accommodate its 'Railway Monitor'; the *Course of the Exchange*, the Stock Exchange stock and share list, recorded 121 different railway securities in February 1845, and 263 in October.[34] The same was true of the provincial press: the *Leeds Intelligencer* had devoted no more than 5 per cent of its column inches to railways in 1836, but by 1845, approximately half of a much enlarged *Intelligencer* was given over to railway business.[35]

The enormous popularity of new schemes created a climate in which overly-hopeful projects could be easily promoted, and, even more harmful, in which fraudsters could set up companies with a view to pocketing subscribers' deposit money and fleeing. As table 8 shows, the newly-established Joint-Stock Companies Registrar was kept busy through late 1845.

Table 8
Companies provisionally registered with Joint-Stock Companies Registrar, 1845

	Jan.	Feb.	Mar.	Apr.	May	June	July	Aug.	Sept.	Oct.	Nov.	Dec.
Registrations	16	31	26	53	92	91	92	176	458	366	87	32

Source: *Report by the Registrar of Joint Stock Companies*, PP 1846 xliii. 3–28.

The majority of these schemes were railway projects. For example, in the week beginning 6 October, when the mania was at its height, 110 schemes were provisionally registered, 92 of which were for the construction of railways.[36] Given such a volume of registrations, it was impossible that all were sound projects. Some were ill-conceived, others were hatched by charlatans cynically cashing in on the massive public appetite for railways. In late

33 Kostal, *English railway capitalism*, 48.
34 *Course of the Exchange*, 7 Feb., 17 Oct. 1845.
35 Killick and Thomas, 'Provincial stock exchanges', 98.
36 *Report by the Registrar of Joint Stock Companies to the Committee of Privy Council for Trade*, PP 1846 xliii, calculated from pp. 22–4.

October, confidence in many railway schemes began to falter. As the extent of the frauds perpetrated became known, doubt turned to panic. Investors rushed to offload their scrip, prices dropped dramatically: the result, in the words of William Aytoun in *Blackwood's*, was 'a grand interment of capital'.[37] The inflation of popular hopes of railway enterprise to such unrealistic proportions through the course of 1845, and the sudden disappointment of these hopes at the end of the year, left a serious mark on perceptions of railway schemes in particular, and joint-stock companies in general, for many years to come, and led to lengthy disputes between directors, shareholders and creditors.[38]

The railway mania provided ammunition for moralists of all descriptions. The Church railed against the lax morals which fuelled the speculation. The Revd John Cumming told his audience at the Young Men's Christian Association that the 'railways came to be all but canonized. A whole generation offered all they had as incense, and rushed as victims to the irresistible mania of railway enterprise'.[39] Several novelists in the late 1840s and 1850s tackled the railway mania, a theme around which they constructed moral tales of warning.[40] One such described the mania as 'one of the most swindling movements that ever disgraced any country or age'.[41] But railways were not the sole targets, for the joint-stock economy was expanding significantly: in the ten years between the passing of the 1844 act and the limited liability debates of 1855, more than 3,500 companies were provisionally registered, and nearly 900 completely registered (*see* table 9).

The profusion of these companies contributed to a perception that commercial standards were being dragged down. One anonymous author claimed that 'in the "haste to be rich," things are done, and done deliberately, of which a delicate conscience would disapprove; that conscience is frequently lulled to sleep by the assertion, "Everybody does so: why should I pretend to be nicer than my neighbours?" '.[42] The problem, as some saw it, was the increasingly common, yet false, belief that religious rules did not regulate commercial behaviour. A. J. Morris condemned the prevailing feeling '*that religion and business are two distinct things; that they belong to different departments, and have different rules and principles*'.[43] For the Revd J. B. Owen, a London minister, a code of loose mercantile morals

---

[37] [W. Aytoun], 'The champions of the rail', *BEM* lxx (Dec. 1851), 739–50 at p. 739.

[38] Kostal, *English railway capitalism*, ch. ii. While the collapse of 1845 did not cripple railway investment, with new promotions emerging in great numbers in 1846–7, share prices did not return to their 1845 levels.

[39] Cumming, 'The age we live in', 331.

[40] For example, Robert Bell's *The ladder of gold*, and Emma Robinson's *The gold-worshippers*.

[41] MacFarlane, *Railway scrip*, 1.

[42] Anon., *Commercial morality; or, thoughts for the times*, London 1856, 3.

[43] A. J. Morris, *Religion and business; or, spiritual life in one of its secular departments*, London 1853, 10. For similar complaints see Bickersteth, 'Introduction', p. vi, and Owen, *Business without Christianity*, 17.

Table 9
Companies provisionally and completely registered, 1845–54

	1845	1846	1847	1848	1849	1850	1851	1852	1853	1854	Total
Provisionally registered	1,520	292	215	123	165	159	211	414	339	239	3,677
Completely registered	57	112	98	63	68	57	63	110	124	132	884

Source: *Reports by the Registrar of Joint-Stock Companies*, PP 1846, 1847, 1847–8, 1849, 1850, 1851, 1852, 1852–3, 1854, 1854–5.

'infects the public and has a tendency to generate crises of epidemic specula-tive mania'.[44]

It began to seem that the best way to remoralise commercial behaviour was to reform the legislative framework within which companies operated. Glad-stone's Joint-Stock Companies Act came under heavy fire. Designed to combat fraud, it had in practice facilitated swindles. The *Railway Record* urged the government to 'act with lasting honour to itself, and with lasting benefit to the community at large', by imposing greater controls on the regis-tration of all joint-stock companies.[45] A series of insurance frauds in the late 1840s and early 1850s led others to similar conclusions. J. Hooper Hartnoll, proprietor and editor of the *Post Magazine*, devoted himself to exposing these frauds. In an attempt to influence government opinion, Hartnoll set out his views on the joint-stock economy in a pamphlet of 1853. Provisional regis-tration gave an unearned gloss of respectability and state sanction to sham enterprises, and lured innocent investors to their ruin. He appealed to the president of the Board of Trade to 'reflect upon the extent of individual suffering that . . . must continue to result, so long as every scheming vagabond who can scrape ten pounds together to take to the Registrar, is permitted to set up an Assurance Company, and announce that it is "Empowered by Act of Parliament" '. The Board of Trade had been rendered a 'convenient . . . vehicle for the operations of some of the greatest villains London can produce'. More stringent measures were needed to filter out dishonest appli-cations for incorporation. Without them, the greater part of the £5m annu-ally paid by the public on policies would continue to pass into the hands of 'dishonest persons' and 'needy adventurers'.[46]

---

44 Owen, *Business without Christianity*, 22. See also the Revd C. Stowell, *The Christian man in the business of life*, London 1856, 22–3.

45 *Railway Record*, 24 July 1852.

46 J. H. Hartnoll, *A letter to the right hon. E. Cardwell, M.P., president of the Board of Trade, on the inoperative character of the Joint Stock Companies Registration Act, as a means of preventing the formation of bubble assurance companies, or of regulating the action of those honourably and legitimately instituted*, 2nd edn, London 1853, 19, 38–9.

The Joint-Stock Companies Registrar, Francis Whitmarsh, was also deeply critical of the working of the 1844 act. At the end of 1849 he signalled to the Board of Trade the need for a thorough amendment of the act, and the following February produced no less than thirty-eight pages of recommended alterations.[47] Inspired by the examples he had witnessed of the deception of the public and the evasion of the law, these were designed predominantly to redress the balance of power between directors on one hand, and their shareholders and the general public on the other, which he believed was currently skewed in favour of the former. Among the most important of his proposals were that the signatures of three promoters be required for a certificate of provisional registration, rather than the one currently required; that certificates of provisional registration be renewable only once rather than indefinitely; that all clauses in the deed of settlement fixing remuneration for promoters must be approved by a general meeting of the company, and that all contracts made previous to, or during, provisional registration, be confirmed at a general meeting after complete registration; that compulsory registration of prospectuses, abolished by an act of 1847, be reintroduced; that one-tenth of the company's capital be paid up and deposited with the company banker before the deed was signed; that penalties be imposed on directors for 'insufficiencies' in the deed of settlement; that the annual returns required from companies be made more detailed, and that penalties be levied for incorrect returns; that returns be made to the Registrar of the minutes of all general meetings; and that companies refusing to make returns be referred to the attorney-general. Whitmarsh also attached a letter from George Taylor, the assistant registrar, proposing to make companies' balance sheets more accurate. From an inspection of the balance sheets registered at the office, argued Taylor, 'it was clear that the existing provisions as to the preparation and audit of accounts had almost entirely failed in effecting the objects for which they were enacted' – to allow shareholders and the public insight into the financial condition of every registered company. Taylor thought that by requiring the registration of balance sheets, the legislature had placed itself 'under a moral obligation to use all reasonable means of securing that the information conveyed by the Balance Sheet shall be accurate and trustworthy'.[48]

Thus it can be seen that the government was coming under pressure from a number of quarters to restrict access to corporate privileges, and to make the terms by which these privileges were granted far more demanding. Seemingly, if there were any legislative innovations in the field of joint-stock enterprise in the 1850s, these would be to tighten up the law in order to protect the public. Yet exactly the reverse occurred, for despite the wide circulation of these arguments, many others held the opposite view that the act, in withholding the privilege of limited liability, did not go far enough.

[47] BT 1/475/3171/220 (17 Nov. 1849); BT 1/477/431/50 (7 Feb. 1850).
[48] BT 1/477/431/50 (1 Feb. 1850).

The course of reform

The initiative was seized by a member of the latter camp, Robert Slaney, a backbench Liberal MP who had chaired committees on education and the health of the working classes. He succeeded in securing the appointment of successive committees on middle- and working-class savings and on partnership law in 1850 and 1851, both of which he chaired.[49] The majority of witnesses were selected for their knowledge either of partnership law in other countries, or of the trading or investing habits of the working or middle classes, and, as intended, they set out the case for amendment of the law in some detail. The current law was an unfair restraint which tied up capital. Reform would allow those with small capitals to engage in commercial activity. It would encourage the formation of useful schemes for local improvements which were currently impractical as they did not promise great returns on capital. To continue to insist on unlimited liability was nonsensical since the repeal of the usury laws.[50] The enthusiasm for limited liability expressed in Slaney's draft reports was, both in 1850 and 1851, toned down by government representatives on the committees. But in 1852 Slaney succeeded in securing the passage of the Industrial and Provident Societies Act, which brought industrial associations of workers under the law of friendly societies, thus exempting them from unlimited liability and allowing them to settle disputes among partners without recourse to Chancery.[51] His ambitions went further, however, for he aimed to extend access to limited liability to all. In February 1852 he and William Ewart called for a commission to consider measures to remove legal obstacles to investment and industry. They met with a favourable response. While the Whig president of the Board of Trade, Henry Labouchere, reiterated his opposition to general limited liability, he told the House that the government was anxious to allow careful consideration of the subject, bearing in mind 'the enormous amount of capital existing in this country, and the great changes which had of late years taken place in the commercial relations of the whole world'.[52] Consequently, Labouchere signalled his intention to establish a Royal Commission on the partnership laws, but before he could do so, Russell's ministry fell. The short-lived Conservative administration which followed, with Joseph Henley at the Board of Trade, seemed disinclined to involve itself in the matter.

[49] *Select committee on investments for the savings of the middle and working classes*, PP 1850; *Select committee on the law of partnership*, PP 1851. For more on Slaney see P. Richards, 'R. A. Slaney, the industrial town, and early Victorian social policy', *Social History* iv (1979), 85–101.

[50] M. Clark, *Select committee on the law of partnership*, PP 1851, 131; E. V. Neale, *Select committee on investments of the middle and working classes*, PP 1850, 21; J. Stewart, ibid. 36; J. Howell, *Select committee on the law of partnership*, PP 1851, 23.

[51] 15 & 16 Vict. c. 31. See Cottrell, *Industrial finance*, 48.

[52] *Hansard*, cxix. 674 (17 Feb. 1852).

The formation of the Aberdeen coalition in December 1852 led to the appointment of the third president of the Board of Trade in less than a year. Edward Cardwell, who had been Financial Secretary to the Treasury in the later stages of Peel's second ministry, and had remained loyal to his leader, proved more determined than his predecessors to clarify the state of the law regarding joint-stock companies. To this end he distributed a memorandum setting out his views to the Cabinet in January 1853.[53] He believed that resolution of the question of limited liability should be a priority, for Labouchere's promise of an inquiry into the law of partnership had a created 'a vague expectation out of doors' that some action was to be taken, and the time was right for the government to make a public declaration of its policy.[54] The great number of applications with which the Board was faced made a decision on limited liability all the more desirable: in the three years 1850–2, the Board received sixty-two applications, one more than it had done for the entire period between 1837 and 1849.[55] Cardwell believed that Henley had been too liberal, granting limited liability to eighteen out of the thirty companies that applied during his brief tenure of office. This policy had encouraged even more applications, but if the Board continued to 'virtually abrogate the law' by granting charters too freely, private enterprise would be discouraged. Cardwell thought 'the extraordinary progress of trade of late years' was evidence that even enterprises requiring heavy investment could be carried on by private partnerships without special privileges. He stressed that he was no enemy of joint-stock enterprise: 'I rejoice in the repeal of the Bubble Act, and in the permission to associate in joint stock.' But he did not see 'why the law should give to such associations a privilege denied to private firms. I think the whole history of joint-stock companies would lead us to an opposite conclusion'. Cardwell's advice was unambiguous: that 'the present law should be steadily maintained both in spirit and in practice'.[56]

Cardwell followed this memorandum with a letter to Lord Aberdeen in February. He continued to urge the government to take a definite line on limited liability, and for the matter to be discussed by the Cabinet, as he thought it 'essential that the Cabinet should be decided in the views which they wish the members of the government to express upon the subject of the Law of Partnership'. Cabinet discussion did not result in the emergence of a clear government line, however, so Aberdeen wrote back to Cardwell with the usual solution in such situations: a Royal Commission.[57] Cardwell

[53] The office of president of the Board of Trade was not of Cabinet rank at the time.
[54] E. Cardwell, 'Limited liability', confidential memorandum, 14 Jan. 1853, Gladstone papers, BL, MS Add. 44570, fos 169–73, p. 1.
[55] Six applications were received in 1850, 15 in 1851 and 41 in 1852. These figures exclude applications for supplemental charters by companies which had already been granted privileges: Returns of all applications to the Board of Trade for grants of charters with limited liability, PP 1854 lxv.
[56] Cardwell, 'Limited liability'.
[57] Lord Aberdeen to E. Cardwell, 19 Feb. 1853, Aberdeen papers, BL, MS Add. 43197, fo. 261.

announced the decision in the Commons two days later.[58] Although Cardwell had wanted ministers to dismiss the issue without resorting to public inquiry, it seems that some campaigners for limited liability were also disappointed with the government's action.[59] Indeed the Royal Commission amounted to little more than a stalling device allowing the government to defer judgement on the question: it was not proof that Aberdeen was bowing to demands for a change in the law. Furthermore, Cardwell used the fact that the law was under consideration as an excuse to all but suspend the grant of charters: out of twenty-seven applications received, he granted limited liability to only three concerns, two of which were associations for building model dwellings.[60] None the less, from 1853, limited liability became a prominent political issue, discussed in newspapers, magazines, quarterlies, pamphlets and even in debating societies. The Political Economy Club in London debated the topic four times between 1853 and 1857.[61] The Union Society of London debated the subject in 1856.[62] Both the Birmingham and the Edgbaston Debating Societies tackled it in the early and mid-1850s.[63]

The evidence accumulated by the commission, which reported in 1854, gave only qualified encouragement to supporters of general limited liability. The commission conducted a thorough survey of commercial opinion, distributing detailed questionnaires to merchants, manufacturers, chambers of commerce, bankers, lawyers, academics and MPs. Opinions from seventy-four individuals and organisations were received from within Britain, giving a reasonable snapshot of opinion in the commercial community.[64] While a majority (forty-three to thirty-one) supported some form of extension of limited liability, opinion was far more evenly split on the question of joint-stock companies (*see* table 10).[65]

The balance of opinion thus was narrowly in favour of retaining some form of state discretion over the grant of limited liability to companies, to be exer-

---

58 *Hansard*, cxxiv. 348–9 (21 Feb. 1853).

59 E. W. Field, *Observations of a solicitor on the right of the public to form limited liability partnerships, and on the theory, practice, and cost of commercial charters*, London 1854, 8.

60 *Returns of applications to the Board of Trade*, PP 1854.

61 Political Economy Club, *Minutes of proceedings, 1899–1920, roll of members, and questions discussed, 1821–1920*, London 1921, 67, 72, 75.

62 Union Society of London, London Guildhall Library, MS 22405.

63 Birmingham Debating Society, Birmingham City Library, MS 607/133; MS 607/3.

64 The method of gathering evidence adopted by the commission meant that the survey was probably reasonably representative of opinion. Seventy-six questionnaires were sent out to particular individuals, but a further sixty were distributed to twenty of the largest chambers of commerce in the UK, for distribution to nominees of the chambers: as a result, by no means all of the responses received by the commission were directly solicited.

65 The figures for opinions on limited liability in general are from R. A. Bryer, 'The Mercantile Laws Commission of 1854 and the political economy of limited liability', *EcHR* l (1997), 37–56. It is harder to provide a definite figure for opinions on limited liability for joint-stock companies in particular, as in a small number of cases the opinions expressed were so vague or brief as to render interpretation difficult. These have been counted as supporters of limited liability for joint-stock companies.

Table 10
Opinions of witnesses before the Royal Commission on the law of partnership on whether limited liability should be extended to joint-stock companies by right

Occupation/residence	Yes	No
Merchants/manufacturers	17	18
Legal profession	9	6
Bankers	3	14
Academics/MPs	7	0
London	18	15
Rest of England	9	11
Scotland	5	10
Ireland	4	2
Total	36	38

Source: *Royal Commission on am the law of partnership*, PP 1854 xxvii.

cised by the Board of Trade, parliament or some other authority.[66] The biggest concentrations of support for a change in the law could be found in the legal profession and among academics and MPs, and, geographically speaking, in London and Ireland. The bare figures conceal the fact that the pro-limited liability stance was far from a monolithic one: those who wanted a change in the law did not all agree on what the new law should look like. Many supported not the unconditional adoption of limited liability, but the much less sweeping form of *en commandite*, popular in France, whereby the liability of non-directing members only was limited. Several qualified their support of limited liability by stipulating that liability should continue for a fixed period after the transfer of shares, that liability should be set at double or treble the value of the shares, or that the past six years' profits should be liable, along with the capital, for the debts of the company.[67]

Therefore, it is not surprising that the commissioners noted in their report that they had been 'much embarrassed by the great contrariety of opinion entertained by those who have favoured them with answers to their questions. Gentlemen of great experience and talent have arrived at conclusions diametrically opposite'. This division was reflected within the body of the commission itself. Five of the eight commissioners put their names to the

[66] For detailed restatements of traditional opposition to general limited liability see the evidence of James Andrew Anderson, James Freshfield, John Kinnear, Lawrence Robertson, James Clark and William Hawes: *Royal Commission on the law of partnership*, PP 1854, 61–3, 67–70, 86–90, 102–5, 105–9, 191–4.

[67] See, for example, the opinions of James Perry, William Thomson and John Brooke, ibid. 67, 76, 159.

report, which recommended against the adoption of general limited liability, but three declined to do so, each of whom registered separate opinions on the question. These three, George Bramwell, Kirkman Daniel Hodgson and James Anderson, all supported limited liability for companies, with Anderson also recommending a system of special loans at rates of interest varying with the profits of the company. But the majority report arrived at the conclusion that the proposed alteration of the law would not 'operate beneficially on the general trading interests of the country'.[68] The commissioners restated the traditional line, that limited liability was only required for large-scale enterprises which could not be funded by private partnerships, and for local improvements which did not attract the capital of wealthy investors. These exceptions should continue to be granted limited liability by a public authority on a case-by-case basis.

The Aberdeen government had passed the question of limited liability on to a commission to avoid having to reach a decision itself. The resulting evidence collected and the opinions expressed by the commissioners hardly pointed to an obvious course of action. In light of the division of opinion, the only valid course seemed to be to do nothing. This is what the government appeared to want to do, but opinion in the Commons meant that this was impossible. All three MPs who had responded to the commission's questionnaire had supported limited liability, and they were representative of their colleagues' views: despite the deep division of opinion in the country, the principle had majority backing in the Commons. Soon after the publication of the commission's report, the backbench Liberal MP Robert Collier moved a resolution in the Commons that the law of partnership was 'unsatisfactory' and should be modified to enable people to contribute capital to businesses without incurring unlimited liability.[69] Collier's resolution received support from most of the subsequent speakers in the debate, Liberals and Conservatives alike. Cardwell tried to stall, conceding that the law as it stood was far from perfect, but opposing making decisions on limited liability before the report could be digested. Two of his colleagues, Sir Alexander Cockburn and Palmerston, the Home Secretary, also attempted to induce Collier to drop his resolution, as they did not want to be bound by an abstract principle. But it was clear that a difference of opinion existed within government, for both Palmerston and particularly Cockburn undermined Cardwell by expressing much sympathy with Collier's aim of making limited liability more available. Collier was happy to follow the government's instructions, the debate already having indicated much support for an extension of limited liability, but the House 'by loud cries . . . expressed its wish that the Motion should not be withdrawn', and it was duly agreed to.[70]

The debate had suggested a government split on the issue, and this was

---

68 Ibid. 5.
69 *Hansard*, cxxxiv. 754 (27 June 1854).
70 Ibid. cxxxiv. 800.

indeed the case. Cardwell's scepticism on limited liability was echoed by fellow Peelites including Gladstone, Chancellor of the Exchequer, and also by Russell, at this time Lord President.[71] In addition to Palmerston and Cockburn, however, limited liability also had the support of Lord Granville and the duke of Argyll.[72] Boyd Hilton has suggested that the crucial event breaking this deadlock and paving the way for limited liability was the fall of Aberdeen's ministry in January 1855 and the formation of a new administration soon purged of Peelites, headed by Palmerston.[73] In fact, shortly before it fell, Aberdeen's administration acceded to the demand for limited liability, announcing in December 1854 that it would introduce a limited liability bill.[74] This was no idle promise, for the following month Cardwell announced his intention to move for leave to bring in a bill to amend the law of partnership on 29 January.[75] Yet this was the day that Abderdeen's government lost a vote of confidence on the Crimean War in the Commons by 305 votes to 148, and the proposed bill was lost in the wreckage of the ministry.[76]

The Palmerston administration, with Edward Bouverie at the Board of Trade, presented two bills in 1855, one proposing to grant joint-stock companies access to limited liability, the other to allow creditors of partnerships to receive interest varying in proportion to the profits of the concern without being classed as partners.[77] While the latter failed, the former passed the Commons easily, and was driven vigorously through the Lords at the tail end of the session. This short measure was essentially an extension of the 1844 Joint-Stock Companies Act, allowing registered companies to acquire limited liability.[78] Like the 1844 act, it applied only to companies of twenty-five members or more, but unlike the 1844 act, it did not apply to companies with shares of less than £10. Banking and insurance companies were also excluded. The requirements imposed by the 1844 act, such as compulsory filing of accounts and returns of shareholders, and annual audits, continued to apply. The following year, when Robert Lowe had succeeded Bouverie at the Board, two further bills were presented. Again, the measure applying to partnerships stalled, but the other passed, which extended access

---

[71] Russell told J. R. McCulloch, 'I am much disposed to agree with you about limited liability': Russell to McCulloch, 5 May 1856, *Overstone correspondence*, ii. 646.

[72] Hilton, *Age of atonement*, 258; G. D. C. Argyll, *The unseen foundations of society: an examination of the fallacies and failures of economic science due to neglected elements*, London 1893, 555–6.

[73] Hilton, *Age of atonement*, 258.

[74] *The Times*'s 'Money Market' column welcomed the news, but complained that many months would pass before such a measure would become law at a time when many applicants for privileges required them immediately: *The Times*, 20 Dec. 1854. For a negative reaction to the announcement see *Law Times*, 23 Dec. 1854.

[75] *Economist*, 27 Jan. 1855.

[76] For details of the vote see O. Anderson, *A liberal state at war: English politics and economics during the Crimean War*, New York 1967, 43.

[77] For the text of this bill, and its successor in 1856 see PP 1854–5 v.; PP 1856 v.

[78] 18 & 19 Vict. c. 133.

to limited liability to companies of seven or more members, and scrapped the £10 share qualification.[79] In addition, the annual audit and the presentation of balance sheets now became voluntary, though Table B of the act set out a detailed list of suggested regulations for managing companies, which companies were free to adopt if they wished.[80]

Social healing

Historians have advanced various explanations for the change in the law in 1855–6. Underlying much of the early, whiggish, historiography was the assumption that the state was merely responding to economic necessity, and the introduction of limited liability was ultimately inevitable.[81] But such views have been undermined by more recent arguments that reform was introduced in advance of economic pressures.[82] The fact that it was not until the final two decades of the century that the banking and manufacturing sectors began to convert to limited liability on a significant scale also lends weight to the argument that economic pressures were not driving reform.[83] The simplistic notion that the legislation was the product of the state's belated realisation that it could no longer hold out against economic realities (or the pressures of history) must be rejected. But there remains the question why general limited liability was instituted when it was, and in the form it was.

Donna Loftus has recently argued that the introduction of general limited liability was as much a social reform as an economic one. Limited liability, by drawing greater numbers into the world of joint-stock capitalism, would be providing possibilities for the education and improvement of groups hitherto innocent of business.[84] Indeed, earlier views that company formation and company investment were both improper, even dangerous, spheres for women and workers to inhabit began to lose their force. Women, with the backing of authorities such as Mill, began to exploit the joint-stock company form to establish their own businesses.[85] Mill also urged the working classes to do the same.[86] While Cobbett, Hodgskin and others had railed against specu-

---

79 19 & 20 Vict. c. 47.

80 These regulation included the presentation of balance sheets and an annual audit.

81 See particularly the views of Hunt and Shannon which are discussed in the introduction above.

82 See, for example, the arguments of Cottrell which are explored in the introduction above.

83 P. L. Payne, 'The emergence of the large-scale company in Great Britain, 1870–1914', EcHR xx (1967), 519–42.

84 D. Loftus, 'Capital and community: limited liability and attempts to democratize the market in mid nineteenth-century England', VS xlv (2002), 93–120.

85 J. Rendall, ' "A moral engine"? Feminism, liberalism and the *English Woman's Journal*', in J. Rendall (ed.), *Equal or different: women's politics, 1800–1914*, Oxford 1987, 118–19.

86 J. S. Mill, *Principles of political economy*, books IV, V, Harmondsworth 1985, 258, 267.

lation, others now saw the joint-stock company as an extension of the collective principle already embedded in working-class life in the form of trade unions, mutual societies and co-operative forms of production and exchange. Chartist leaders in the 1830s and 1840s wrote enthusiastically of the power of the joint-stock company to enfranchise the working classes and change the face of society.[87] Watered-down versions of these arguments also won support in more mainstream circles.[88]

But there is little evidence that their arguments carried much weight with policymakers. It is true that the language used in the Commons and in the press in support of the limited liability bills was in some instances theatrically democratic. Palmerston, not known for his commitment to democracy, portrayed it as a contest 'between the few and the many'.[89] But such rhetoric was little more than a debating tool to isolate and discredit opponents of reform as reactionaries and enemies of the people. Loftus admits that the idea of 'operatives' performing the regulatory functions required of shareholders, such as examining accounts and interrogating directors, was for many Victorians utterly inconceivable.[90] The social dimension of the debates, though prominent in the earlier 1850s, particularly so in the select committees of 1850 and 1851, was beginning to fade by the time of the Royal Commission, and was largely absent in the parliamentary debates of 1855. When Bouverie presented the limited liability bill to the Commons, as one cynical commentator remarked, 'the Honourable Member thr[ew] overboard all the working-class claims'.[91] The failure of the partnership bills of 1855–6, which aimed to help small firms, illuminates the priorities of the legislature better than any number of soundbites.[92] While the 1856 act lowered the number of members required to obtain limited liability from twenty-five to seven, and abandoned the £10 minimum share stipulation, the extent to which the legislation would encourage the formation of working-class enterprises was at best debatable. Although the social context of the limited liability debate helps to explain the popularity of the principle in radical circles, and enabled it to be presented as a measure of social reform, which certainly did not hinder its progress, we have to look elsewhere to understand its adoption by the state in the 1850s.

---

[87] W. Lovett, *Manifesto of the general convention of the industrious classes*, London n.d.; R. Lowery, *Address to the fathers and mothers, sons and daughters, of the working classes, on the system of exclusive dealing, and the formation of joint stock provision companies, shewing how the people may free themselves from oppression*, Newcastle 1839; J. F. Bray, *Labour's wrongs and labour's remedy; or, the age of might and the age of right*, London 1968, 170.

[88] J. Lalor, *Money and morals: a book for the times*, London 1852, 203; *Morning Advertiser*, 3 July 1855; *Lloyd's Weekly Newspaper*, 5 Aug. 1855.

[89] *Hansard*, cxxxix. 1389 (26 July 1855).

[90] Loftus, 'Capital and community', 116.

[91] Anon. ['A Manchester Man'], *The law of partnership: a reply to the speech of the right hon. E. P. Bouverie, MP*, London 1855, 14.

[92] P. W. Ireland, 'The rise of the limited liability company', *International Journal of the Sociology of Law* xii (1984), 239–60 at pp. 241–4.

Growth or stability?

Numerous historians have argued that the reforms of 1855–6 were the fruit of a decisive shift in the state's economic policy priorities. In his aged but still influential thesis, James B. Jefferys claimed that the limited liability legislation marked the 'victory of the investing classes over the industrialists'.[93] A united front of commercial and landed interests, professionals and MPs, frustrated by the lack of profitable investments open to them in the early 1850s, conspired to secure the passage of limited liability to extend outlets for *rentier* capital. Such a reform was possible, David C. Itzkowitz has more recently argued, because of the emergence of new attitudes to joint-stock investment. Encouraging us to view the limited liability legislation in the context of the 'domestication' of speculation which occurred in the first half of the nineteenth century, Itzkowitz writes that 'henceforth, speculation increasingly came to be seen as a reputable activity and speculators as respectable economic actors'.[94]

The framework of the law was therefore restructured in order to encourage what was now seen as a legitimate, and in fact beneficial, form of economic behaviour. Mary Poovey agrees that speculation had become respectable, but holds that this was because the moral concerns which had previously prevented its acceptance were no longer thought to be relevant. The legislation marked the moment when 'the economic domain was relieved of its moral component'. By severing the link between failure and ruin, limited liability signalled that traditional moral considerations were no longer thought to apply to joint-stock investment.[95] Most influentially of all, Boyd Hilton makes the case that the legislation signalled a new prioritising of economic growth by the state. Peelites, traditional and evangelical in their economic outlook, favouring stability over growth and prudence over speculation, stubbornly resisted limited liability, but Palmerston's government, less hidebound by these ideas, did not view speculation as a sin, and thought growth something to be encouraged by government policy. Whereas visions of a static or cyclical economy had hitherto held sway, growth now seemed at once possible and desirable.[96]

Certainly, it could be argued that, by mid-century, Britain was a nation seduced by the expansionist potential of limited liability. The benefits delivered by limited companies were inescapable. The rapid development of the railway network was the most obvious example. In 1837, just 540 miles of track had been laid; by 1851, this had risen to 6,802 miles, more than a

93 Jefferys, 'Trends in business organisation', 53.
94 D. C. Itzkowitz, 'Fair enterprise or extravagant speculation: investment, speculation, and gambling in Victorian England', VS xlv (2002), 121–47 at pp. 122, 144.
95 M. Poovey, *Making a social body: British cultural formation, 1830–1864*, Chicago 1995, 22–3, 155–81.
96 Hilton, *Age of atonement*, 255.

twelve-fold increase. In a period of just five years (1846–50), no less than 4,028 miles of track were laid.[97] In addition, steamship companies began in the 1830s to establish rapid and reliable passenger and goods services with other continents. Telegraph companies were improving internal communications, and 1851 saw the successful laying of the Dover–Calais cable.[98] Advocates of limited liability were not slow to highlight the fact that these highly visible and useful benefits had been delivered by the agency of joint-stock companies operating with limited liability. According to the *Morning Post*, limited liability had 'covered our country with railroads, canals, and great public works' and had 'set on every sea magnificent fleets of steamers'.[99] Robert Collier argued that but for the violation of the law of limited liability, 'we should still have travelled in stage coaches, and voyaged in sailing packets'.[100] Consequently, it was foolish to retain outdated and irrelevant laws which hampered economic development.[101] Arguments that reform was unnecessary because Britain was already sufficiently rich were flawed, since no one could predict the economic benefits which would ensue if all restrictions were removed. After all, 'It is not every Watt that has found a Boulton.'[102] Perpetual growth was to be encouraged.[103]

The Great Exhibition of 1851 provided further impetus to such arguments. While certainly representing an 'assertion of British pride and prosperity', the Exhibition also engendered fears in some circles that Britain was in danger of falling behind her rivals industrially and scientifically.[104] Innovations in company law abroad were extending access to limited liability, and whereas traditionally the freer availability of limited liability elsewhere had been cited as proof that the privilege was an artificial stimulus only required in less developed economies, by the 1850s some were beginning to doubt that Britain could afford to forsake the economic and legal structures enjoyed by her rivals. Mirroring the change in English law in 1844, American states were beginning to replace the special charter system with general incorporation

---

97 P. Mathias, *The first industrial nation*, London 1969, 280.

98 Connections with Ireland and Holland followed in 1853: D. Read, *The power of news: the history of Reuters, 1849–1989*, Oxford 1992, 13.

99 *Morning Post*, 27 July 1855.

100 *Hansard*, cxxxiv. 755 (27 June 1854). See also Bouverie, ibid. cxxxix. 311 (29 June 1855).

101 *Observer*, 12 Aug. 1855; *Morning Post*, 30 June 1855; *Morning Chronicle*, 11 Aug. 1855.

102 J. Howell, *Select committee on the law of partnership*, PP 1851, 25. See also the evidence of R. Fane, ibid. 81.

103 G. Bramwell, *Royal Commission on the law of partnership*, PP 1854, 27. For similar arguments see Anon., 'Partnership with limited liability', 390–1.

104 H. Cunningham, *The challenge of democracy: Britain 1832–1914*, Harlow 2001, 54; J. H. Auerbach, *The Great Exhibition of 1851: a nation on display*, New Haven 1999, 122–6. The Great Exhibition was also significant in another sense: Collier reminded the Commons that if the principle of unlimited liability had been strictly adhered to, 'that greatest work of modern art and science, the Crystal Palace', would not have been possible: *Hansard*, cxxxiv. 755 (27 June 1854).

statutes, including New York between 1847 and 1854, and Massachusetts in 1851. By 1855 most states had adopted such statues. Unlike England, however, these statutes granted access to limited liability.[105] In France, companies were not granted free incorporation until 1867, but from the mid-1820s large numbers of entrepreneurs formed *en commandite* partnerships which did not require state sanction and allowed non-managing partners to enjoy limited liability.[106] In this international context, it began to be suggested that Britain's attachment to unlimited liability could prove lethal: 'such a country as Great Britain cannot stand still, it must either rapidly advance or be overtaken by more energetic nations . . . without a new impetus our manufactures and commerce will henceforth decline'.[107] 'If we would not be left behind in the great race among the nations for wealth and power and commercial prosperity', argued another, 'we must break off those legal fetters which encumber the energies of our people'.[108] Once associated with corruption and degeneracy, it was now argued that the urge to speculate had helped to secure Britain its dominant place among the nations. If this drive were curbed, the nation's greatness would be jeopardised: 'When Englishmen will be satisfied with the tame security of the Three per Cents, their career will have been run. They will have fulfilled the task allotted to them in the great Scheme, and will be required to make way for a stronger race.'[109] Speculation was now portrayed as essential to the economic health of the nation. Unlimited liability, by restricting investment, was obstructive and harmful: 'capital was dammed up';[110] it was 'constantly struggling to break the bonds which beset it'.[111] Limited liability would allow capital to flow freely throughout the economy, enriching the population and creating 'healthful enterprises'.[112] It would encourage a more even and healthy spread of capital across the economy rather than driving it into one sector of the economy, as had happened with the railway mania of the 1840s.[113] The current law had the unfortunate effect of diverting British capital into the pockets of 'insolvent or rival states', which made Britain's competitors 'more

---

105 There were safeguards, however. In New York, for example, the 1848 statute applying to manufacturing corporations provided for double liability until shares were fully paid up. In Massachusetts, companies with capitals of less than $5,000 or more than $200,000 were excluded from the scope of the act: R. E. Seavoy, *The origins of the American business corporation, 1784–1855*, Westport, CT.1982, 1–7, 177–93; E. M. Dodd, *American business corporations until 1860*, Cambridge, MA. 1954, 384–7.

106 Freedeman, *Joint-stock enterprise in France*, and *The triumph of corporate capitalism in France, 1867–1914*, New York 1993.

107 E. Moss, *Remarks on the act of parliament, 18 & 19 Vict. c. 133, for the formation of companies with limited liability*, London 1856, 10.

108 E. Warner, *The impolicy of the partnership law*, London 1854, 54.

109 Anon., 'Partnership with limited liability', 401.

110 *Hansard*, cxix. 683 (17 Feb. 1852).

111 Ewart, ibid. cxix. 684.

112 A. Parsons, *The Limited Liability Act and its legal interpretations*, London 1855, 3.

113 Lord Hobart, *Remarks on the law of partnership liability*, London 1853, 20.

formidable'. As a result, taxes were forced upwards to pay for additional arma-ments.[114] General limited liability would stop the flow of capital abroad by encouraging investors to be patriotic.[115] A change in the law would also encourage Irish economic development, dragging the country out of poverty and preventing mass emigration from her shores.[116]

However, once the over-enthusiastic pronouncements are peeled away, we glimpse a set of attitudes which had altered barely at all, the longevity of which cast much doubt on the idea that visions of growth drove the reform of the 1850s. First, and most important, Victorians still believed the individual to be superior to the company. While reformers advocated the opening up of all trades to limited companies, and thought that businessmen should be permitted to choose how they would organise and raise money, it was still assumed that joint-stock enterprise operating outside its proper sphere could never thrive. In an argument which echoed that of Disraeli over twenty-five years earlier, Robert Fane, a commissioner in bankruptcy and a keen supporter of limited liability, explained to the 1851 select committee that there were natural limits to the application of the joint-stock principle resulting from the inherent superiority of private enterprise. Fane held that a steam-washing company, for example, would never displace washerwomen, 'because it is utterly impossible that a company could wash so cheaply as indi-viduals can'. Such companies were misapplications of capital, but were adequately punished by the failure they would inevitably encounter.[117] Simi-larly, William Thomson, an Edinburgh shipbroker, supported the extension of limited liability, but was 'quite satisfied joint stock companies never will successfully compete with private enterprise and management in any well-known business, and within the range of ordinary capital'.[118] Limited companies would not enjoy the same degree of credit as unlimited firms, a fact which placed a natural limit on their growth, but which did not mean they would not be useful in certain situations.[119]

It might be suspected that these arguments were deployed principally to try to quell concerns often voiced that limited companies would drive private enterprise out of business, but they did in fact reflect the views of many in the 1850s that general limited liability would not herald a new dawn of commerce, but that it was simply a modest adjustment of policy which would have little immediate impact on the economic landscape. After all, under the 'restrictive' system, limited companies had still been allowed to leave their mark, for even the bitterest opponents of making limited liability generally available supported the principle when confined to important public

---

114 Warner, *Impolicy of the partnership law*, 42–3.
115 *Hansard*, cxxxiv. 793 (27 June 1854). See also *Lloyd's Weekly Newspaper*, 1 July 1855.
116 *Hansard*, cxxxiv. 778 (27 June 1854).
117 *Select committee on the law of partnership*, PP 1851, 71.
118 *Royal Commission on the law of partnership*, PP 1854, 76. See also W. D. Fane, ibid. 171.
119 J. Howell, *Select committee on the law of partnership*, PP 1851, 23; W. Cotterill, *Royal Commission on the law of partnership*, PP 1854, 70.

works.[120] This, allied to the natural confines imposed on the limited economy by the superiority of private enterprise, made it difficult to see where the much vaunted economic benefits would come from.[121] The current law, argued the *Economist*, another supporter of company law reform, was not throttling legitimate trade, but merely causing it a degree of inconvenience by forcing businesses to approach parliament or the Board of Trade for limited liability. These powers were already granted to legitimate companies; the new law would merely make access to them cheaper and more straightforward:

> We look for a moment at any kind of directory in which lists of public companies appear, and their number is so great, *embracing all kinds of objects which companies are fit to carry into effect* – banking, insurance, carriage – that the law as it at present exists appears scarcely to be an impediment to their formation. It is said, indeed, that they exist only by setting aside the law, and that to set it aside requires in each case a considerable expense, which is very properly urged as a reason for amending the law; but when it is so easily, and is already so continually set aside, this is a strong reason for concluding that those who expect much benefit from the change will be deceived.[122]

It is unlikely that many believed enterprises such as Shaeffer's Patent Oil Grease Company, the Quartz Reduction Company or the Seamless Leather Company (all established in the first months of the new regime) to be the means by which Britain would maintain her economic superiority over the rival nations snapping at her heels.[123] Even those who wanted to extend access to limited liability believed that the dynamism of the British economy relied upon the individual risk-taking spirit, working within the private partnership system. For this reason Mill was a prominent supporter of the principle of differentiation in debates on income tax reform in the 1850s and 1860s, arguing that investments in joint-stock companies ought to be taxed at a higher rate than profits deriving from active trade. In the latter case, 'the reward of industry and talent forms part of the income', and this element of the income was more precarious, and also terminated with the life of the entrepreneur.[124] By taxing this income at a lower level than share dividends, risk-taking would be encouraged. As Martin Daunton has argued, 'The entire thrust of liberal, free trade, economics was in favour of active participation in small firms and associations, rather than passive investment.'[125] This remained the case in the second half of the nineteenth century.

---

120 Anon., *Law of partnership*, 23.
121 K. D. Hodgson, *Royal Commission on the law of partnership*, PP 1854, 38.
122 *Economist*, 27 Jan. 1855 (emphasis added). See also *Economist*, 1 July 1854. For similar views see *Standard*, 31 July, 11 Aug. 1855; *Manchester Guardian*, 3, 27 July 1855.
123 All three companies had been dissolved by 1864.
124 *Report from the select committee on income and property tax*, PP 1861 vii.
125 Daunton, *Trusting leviathan*, 157.

Indeed, limited liability was as much about stability as growth: its adoption signified not the conversion of the British polity to grandiose expansionist visions, but rather the belief that traditional aims of encouraging sound enterprise and stable growth were best pursued by extending access to limited liability. Limited liability had traditionally been associated with speculation and unsoundness. But after the commercial crisis of 1847, it was becoming increasingly difficult to argue that unlimited companies were any more stable than their limited cousins. Indeed, evidence heard by the 1851 select committee from solicitors engaged in the winding up of unlimited companies suggested that unrestricted liability actually encouraged instability. Many unlimited companies, though patently unsound, had been permitted to trade for long periods because of the reckless credit facilities extended to them by 'large capitalists' and banks.[126] These creditors were willing to lend money so freely because the law of unlimited liability excused them from making careful assessment of the risks involved. They knew that in the event of failure, provided there were some wealthy individuals among the body of shareholders, they could recoup their money by enforcing payment against them.[127] Unlimited liability therefore allowed unstable bubbles to inflate to huge proportions before finally bursting, causing disruption and loss to the public. It followed that 'nothing would drive out panics so much in England as *sociétiés en commandite*'.[128] With a system of limited liability, creditors would have to be much more circumspect with their money, for they could only look to the capital of the company for repayment. Companies would not be starved of capital, because what they lost in credit they would gain in capital. In the words of the deputy governor of the Bank of England, limited liability would substitute 'responsible capital in the place of credit'.[129] Unlimited companies had 'a double capital': the nominal capital, and another 'invisible' capital: the sum wealth of all the investors. It was on the latter, once the first was wasted, 'that borrowers and lenders ran riot together'. Indeed, unlimited companies could 'command almost what funds they pleased', leading to extravagance and mismanagement, and ultimately 'some tremendous crash, with an amount of debt and distress appalling to contemplate'.[130] Limited liability would lead to 'better and more cautious management', as directors could no longer rely upon unlimited credit, but would have to make do with a limited amount of capital.[131] Supplies of capital

---

[126] T. C. Lietch, *Select committee on the law of partnership*, PP 1851, 137; E. W. Field, ibid. 145–6.

[127] Lietch, ibid. 138.

[128] T. Wilson, *Select committee on investments of the middle and working classes*, PP 1850, 38.

[129] T. M. Weguelin, *Royal Commission on the law of partnership*, PP 1854, 124.

[130] *The Times*, 26 Mar. 1859.

[131] *Economist*, 13 Feb. 1858. See also J. M. Ludlow, *Select committee on investments of the middle and working classes*, PP 1850, 7.

would be plentiful, however, as shareholders would be protected from unlimited loss.[132]

Furthermore, these shareholders would be of a superior moral quality to the irresponsible gamblers who invested their money in unlimited companies. Whereas unlimited liability had previously been thought to be the best means of guaranteeing that only those of good character would engage in business, by the 1850s the experience of unlimited companies led growing numbers to argue that unlimited liability attracted only the lowest class of investor who was reckless or stupid enough to risk his or her fortune in a single investment. Henry Morley, writing in *Household Words*, claimed that the law of partnership, with its insistence on unlimited liability, 'perverts wholesome enterprise into a gambler's risk, and controverts numerous undertakings into speculations which would otherwise be fit for prudent men to patronise . . . It filters out sensible people, and lets the reckless pass through'.[133] *Lloyd's Weekly Newspaper* agreed, arguing that the partnership laws were excluding from business 'those who would be glad to risk a certain amount of their wealth, but are prudent enough not to run the possible chance of being completely beggared'.[134] Legislators agreed: for Bouverie, limited liability would ensure that 'men with large means and with the judgment enabling them to know what they were about' bought shares in and managed joint-stock companies, rather than the feckless and brainless.[135] Thus, limited liability was not so much the dividend companies received for having attained to a position of respectability as the reform which would enable them to achieve respectability. It was a response to the belief that the behaviour of those involved with unlimited companies currently fell far short of acceptable standards. As in 1844, the aim was to reform joint-stock constituencies; only the means were new.

The moral character of shareholders mattered because they were still thought to have responsibilities to the companies in which they invested beyond providing capital. This may seem surprising: after all, a chief justification advanced in the 1850s for limited liability was the lack of control shareholders possessed in practice over management.[136] Additionally, that limited

132 H. J. Prescott, *Royal Commission on the law of partnership*, PP 1854, 129. Richard Malins made similar points the following year: *Hansard*, cxxxix. 337–40 (29 June 1855). For Bouverie's opinion, see ibid. 321–2. The widespread currency of these views was confirmed by reactions to the commercial crisis of 1857 in which many unlimited banks collapsed: Dunbar, ibid. cl. 538 (13 May 1858); Headlam, cxlviii. 360–5 (8 Dec. 1857); W. E. Baxter, cxlviii. 1179–80 (11 Feb. 1858).

133 [H. Morley], 'The penny saved; a blue-book catechism', *HW* ii (1850), 81–4 at p. 82.

134 *Lloyd's Weekly Newspaper*, 1 July 1855. See also the views of J. M. Ludlow, *Select committee on investments of the middle and working classes*, PP 1850, 4.

135 *Hansard*, cxxxix. 321 (29 June 1855).

136 See, for example, Ludlow, *Select committee on investments of the middle and working classes*, PP 1850, 6; W. Thomson, *Royal Commission on the law of partnership*, PP 1854, 76; Hobart, *Law of partnership liability*, 8–9.

liability allowed those unable to devote themselves to business, and therefore traditionally restricted to government securities, to 'participate directly in the profits of trade' was viewed as a decisive argument for a change in the law.[137] But attitudes here were contradictory, and the retreat from notions of the responsibilities of shareholders seemingly marked by the limited liability acts was at best only partial, for traditional, evangelical-tinged, attitudes towards speculation, improvidence, debt and failure endured. In practice, contemporaries felt uncomfortable accepting the behaviour by investors the law seemed to encourage. This was at its most apparent in the aftermath of commercial frauds, moments when sympathy for the defrauded shareholder might be expected to be at its peak. While the plight of shareholders often did attract pity, denunciations of their ignorance, greed and inattention to their own interests also proliferated. Thus, following the railway frauds of the 1840s, neglectful shareholders were blamed for allowing their directors to fleece them. By the time the crash came, wrote *The Times*, 'an audit of accounts is demanded loudly enough. But then the day for any audit that would be beneficial to the interests of the shareholders is gone by'. Committees of investigation were appointed, but these were *post-mortems*, not audits.[138] Similarly, after a number of joint-stock failures in 1856, the *Economist* was scathingly critical of investors: 'The public, always unreasoning and generally unreasonable, want the security of Consols without submitting to the low interest – they want the high profits of speculating businesses without incurring the risk attending them, and without taking the labour and trouble of looking after them.'[139] Such views did not suggest a society entirely at ease with passive investment.

Furthermore, the persistence of traditional notions of the duties of shareholders to play an active role in their companies determined the form limited liability took in 1855. The government adopted an undifferentiated mode of limited liability rather than introducing the *en commandite* model popular on the continent, and among supporters of limited liability in Britain, whereby the liability of the sleeping partners was limited, and the liability of the directors was unlimited.[140] Such a system appealed to many as a halfway house between two systems, combining the best of both. Capital would be readily available given the inducement of limited responsibility held out to passive investors, while the potential for lax management or outright fraud would be greatly circumscribed by the unlimited responsibility of directors. Yet the system rested on the assumption that investors would remain passive: interference in management meant that sleeping partners lost their privileged

---

137 *The Times*, 30 June 1864.
138 Ibid. 12 July 1849.
139 *Economist*, 17 Jan. 1857. Such views were to persist beyond the 1850s: see chapter 5 below.
140 The witnesses before the 1850, 1851 and 1854 inquiries who advocated *en commandite* partnerships included John Stuart Mill, Leone Levi and G. R. Porter.

status and became liable to an unlimited extent. The precise lengths to which investors could go in supervising the conduct of directors before they forsook their limited liability were uncertain in French law, and although Michael Lobban argues that by the mid-1840s the French courts were recognising the right of *commanditaires* to perform some supervisory functions in order to check fraud, the assumption of shareholder passivity implicit in the *commandite* system clashed fundamentally with dominant attitudes in Britain as to the responsibilities of shareholders.[141] Mill, for example, though supporting the introduction of *commandite* partnerships, thought the form was unsuitable for large businesses such as railway companies. Unlimited liability for railway directors might encourage more prudent management, 'but the additional security would . . . be too dearly purchased by the renunciation of all power in the shareholders to control the directors or to change them'.[142] This was almost certainly the chief factor blocking the system's introduction in Britain.

The persistence of these ideas influenced the shape limited liability took in other important respects. The withdrawal in 1856 of the 1844 act's imposition of compulsory publication of balance sheets and compulsory audits is sometimes regarded as a backward step, a rash lunge towards extreme permissiveness which was only slowly corrected by subsequent legislation.[143] But it was not so much prompted by an excessive attachment to concepts of *laissez-faire*, as by views on the proper role of shareholders. In 1844 statutory regulations protected shareholders from gross fraud, while unlimited liability ensured that they would continue to possess an active role in the governance of joint-stock companies. In 1856 the situation was reversed: limited liability would protect shareholders from fraud, but the lack of compulsory regulatory provisions meant that shareholders would have to attend company meetings and ensure that basic safeguards such as the publication of accounts and competent audits were carried out. Under both systems shareholders retained an acute interest in keeping directors honest, thus ensuring that, while not possessing all the responsibilities of partners in the traditional sense, neither would they be entirely neglectful of their basic duty to themselves and to the public to regulate the enterprises in which they invested. To have adopted limited liability whilst retaining the statutory safeguards would have been to acknowledge that shareholders' sole responsibility was to collect dividends. In the 1850s this was a step too far.

141 Lobban, 'Corporate identity', 414–15.
142 Mill to Lord Hobart, in F. E. Mineka and D. N. Lindley (eds), *The later letters of J. S. Mill, 1849–73*, Toronto 1972, 107.
143 Cottrell, *Industrial finance*, 54.

Intrigue, jobbing and favouritism

While historians have advanced a number of economic and ideological explanations for what happened in 1855–6, the political dimension has by comparison been neglected. Instead, it has been assumed that the concession of limited liability was a straightforward application of the free trade principle to commercial law.[144] But this is something of a simplification. To begin with, as Jefferys pointed out a long time ago, free traders were in fact deeply split on the issue.[145] Political economic orthodoxy was against limited liability. Mill admitted in a letter to his wife that 'there would but for me have been a great overbalance of political economy authority against it'.[146] The scope for confusion was great. In November 1852 Viscount Goderich, the son of the former Chancellor of the Exchequer, Frederick Robinson, wrote to Henley urging him to be as sparing as possible in his grants of limited liability, condemning the audacity of companies who applied for 'artificial props and favours of Government'.[147] Little more than eighteen months later, Goderich gave the principle of limited liability his unqualified support, explaining that it was 'consistent with the whole course of their recent commercial legislation'.[148] When Prime Minister Palmerston impatiently told the House that limited liability was a simple 'question of free trade against monopoly', his assertion was met with cries of 'No, no!'[149] Both supporters and opponents of reform employed free trade ideology to justify their positions; as Hilton points out, free trade in the context of the limited liability debate meant different things to different people.[150] To argue therefore that the legislation of 1855–6 was a natural concomitant of the conversion of the British polity to free trade is entirely inadequate: the picture was more complex than this.

Opponents of limited liability rejected the measure as an unwarranted interference in trade and denied that unlimited liability was a restrictive policy. McCulloch stated that arguments for unlimited liability had 'as much in common with monopoly as they have with the theory of the tides'.[151] Lord Overstone complained that politicians were endeavouring 'through the most flimsy sophistry' to associate limited liability with free trade, 'matters which

---

[144] See, for example, the interpretation advanced by Saville cited in the introduction above.

[145] Jefferys, 'Trends in business organisation', 20. These splits are explored in J. Taylor, 'The joint stock company in politics', in M. J. Turner (ed.), *Reform and reformers in nineteenth-century Britain*, Sunderland 2004, 99–116.

[146] J. S. Mill to H. Mill, 16 Feb. 1855, in F. E. Mineka (ed.), *The earlier letters of John Stuart Mill: collected works*, Toronto 1963, xiii. 332.

[147] *Petitions, orders in council, memorials and correspondence, with the Board of Trade on the grant of a Royal Charter of Incorporation to the London, Liverpool, and North American Screw Steam-Ship Co.*, PP 1852–3 xcv. 90.

[148] *Hansard*, cxxxiv. 760 (27 June 1854).

[149] Ibid. cxxxix. 1390 (26 July 1855).

[150] Hilton, *Age of atonement*, 260–1.

[151] McCulloch, *Considerations on partnerships*, 27.

have the same relation to each other which Darkness has to light'.[152] To introduce limited liability did not entail repealing restrictive legislation, but imposing new laws regulating commercial activity: as had been demonstrated prior to 1844 the common law was not sufficient. It would be to exempt traders from the natural laws governing market behaviour. But this is what the state was already doing on an extensive scale: between 1844 and 1853 the Board of Trade granted charters to sixty-five enterprises, mostly commercial companies. In the same period, parliament passed 135 private bills conferring limited liability, not including the many more railway acts also granting limited liability passed during these years.[153] The claim that the principle of unlimited liability was founded upon the rule of natural justice, that those who shared in the profits of a business should be fully responsible for its losses, was therefore becoming harder to justify.[154] And as the public became more accustomed to the existence of limited companies, the terms of the debate were beginning to shift. Incorporation was no longer the focus of criticism, but privilege: current policy was creating a host of companies unfairly favoured by the state. As it now seemed inconceivable to deny limited liability to all companies which applied for it, the only other equitable option was to grant it freely. The same shift of opinion was happening in America, where 'proponents of anticharter doctrine became advocates of general incorporation laws for business companies' as the only practical means of undercutting special privilege.[155]

These views gained legitimacy because of the extent to which the existing means of granting privileges had become discredited. Admittedly, the process of parliamentary incorporation had been reformed in 1844 when a system of small, impartial committees for railway bills was adopted. Members were henceforth obliged to sign a declaration of non-interest before being appointed to committees.[156] However, interested voting on other private bills was not scrapped, with the result that this method of securing incorporation continued to be viewed as corrupt.[157] But it was incorporation by the Board of

---

152 Overstone to Granville, 21 Mar. 1856, *Overstone correspondence*, ii. 643.

153 *Returns of applications to the Board of Trade*, PP 1854. Acts passed between 1833 and 1844 authorised the creation of 124 railway companies. During the boom of 1845–7 a further 576 companies were authorised. Thereafter, the number of acts decreased, but remained significant: 120 companies were sanctioned by acts between 1848 and 1850: P. S. Bagwell, *The transport revolution from 1770*, London 1974, 93–4. See also *Return relating to railway bills*, PP 1840 xlv. 2–5; *Return of the number of railway bills brought into parliament in each year since 1839*, PP 1843 xliv. 1–2; and H. G. Lewin, *The railway mania and its aftermath, 1845–1852*, Newton Abbot 1968, 473.

154 See the arguments of Collier and Bouverie: *Hansard*, cxxxiv. 754 (27 June 1854); cxxxix. 324–5 (29 June 1855). See also Anon., 'Partnership with limited liability', 377, and *Morning Advertiser*, 3 July 1855.

155 P. Maier, 'The revolutionary origins of the American corporation', *William and Mary Quarterly*, 3rd ser. i (1993), 51–84 at p. 76.

156 Williams, *Historical development of private bill procedure*, i. 85–6.

157 For opinions on private bill procedure see *Select committee on railway acts enactments*,

Trade that generated the most anger, and those company promoters who found themselves thwarted by the Board were vocal in their condemnations of the system. Robert Lamont, a Liverpool shipowner whose applications for a charter to the Board of Trade had twice been refused, told a special meeting of the Liverpool Chamber of Commerce, that he had 'no hesitation in saying that the board was guided by no principles whatsoever in granting charters'.[158] A colleague of Lamont told the 1854 Royal Commission that he did not support the discretion of government agencies such as the Board of Trade. 'They are constantly influenced by pressure more than justice, and "my lords" often do things for one reason or motive, and invent another afterwards as an excuse (which was not the reason), when they are obliged to give one.' He thought that the 'Board of Trade wants reforming, as well as the law of partnership'.[159] Even opponents of general limited liability doubted that the Board was a competent authority to decide on questions of limited liability: it was a political body not suited to making legal decisions, and should be replaced by a special tribunal composed of legal and mercantile members.[160]

Conveniently, the self-interest of those arguing for general limited liability was subsumed by a far more virtuous call to arms to eliminate 'Old Corruption' from the state. The current system operated as an unjust 'tax' on joint-stock enterprise, which paid twice, in cash and in uncertainty, for corporate privileges. By making access to limited liability automatic, the state would in effect be removing this tax, and divesting itself of (an admittedly small) revenue, in the interests of promoting commercial endeavour. The political climate of the mid-1850s made such critiques even more powerful, for the widely perceived mismanagement of the Crimean War led to profound criticism not just of the Aberdeen Ministry, but of the entire system of government: a 'storm of resentment against aristocratic privilege, bureaucracy and bungling', as Olive Anderson described it.[161] While claims by one overexcited contemporary that the war signalled 'the death-blow of the Aristocracy' were obviously hyperbolic, the movement for administrative reform which it engendered was of huge importance, not least for the popular call for

PP 1846 xiv., p. iii; Anon., 'Partnership with limited liability', 405; and [A. Pulling], 'Private bill legislation', *EdR* cl (Jan. 1855), 151–91. Interested voting was finally abolished in 1855: Williams, *Historical development of private bill procedure*, 88.

[158] D. Glick, 'The movement for partnership law reform, 1830–1907', unpubl. PhD diss. Lancaster 1990, 226.

[159] C. Robertson, *Royal Commission on the law of partnership*, PP 1854, 219. See also the opinions of Jeremiah Burroughs, a London merchant, ibid. 238, and those of John Duncan, *Select committee on the law of partnership*, PP 1851, 151. Company solicitors were also contemptuous of the Board's role: Field, *Observations of a solicitor*, pp. iii, 84.

[160] R. Slater, *Royal Commission on the law of partnership*, PP 1854, 49.

[161] Anderson, *Liberal state at war*, 181.

government to be carried out on sound 'business principles'.[162] The superiority of the private sector over the public in making decisions and allocating resources was widely proclaimed, with John Lewis Ricardo holding that 'There is not a clerk in Manchester or the City of London that would not have known how to supply the Army with what it wanted when he had unlimited capital at his command.'[163] Such views fed into the debate on limited liability, and the traditional governmental role of determining which companies deserved privileges became less popular than ever. The press took up the cause of thwarted businessmen oppressed by government interference: the *Daily News* felt that it was wrong for the grant of corporate privileges to be 'dependent on the caprice of Government officials'.[164] The *Morning Herald* believed that 'the power of opening or closing vast sources of wealth and industry should not be placed in the hands of any department of the Government, to be used at its discretion – to be moved by intrigue, jobbing, or favouritism'.[165]

The press's motives for supporting limited liability were not entirely transparent. Hitherto opposed to making limited liability more available, *The Times* changed its mind in the 1850s. Historians of company law have, however, failed to indicate the reason for this change in policy. Rather than symptomatic of an irresistible tide in favour of reform, the shift in editorial line has much more to do with the addition of Robert Lowe to the paper's leader-writing team in April 1851. In the 1850s he was a prolific contributor, sometimes writing two articles a day, and averaging more than three a week.[166] Joint secretary at the Board of Control in Aberdeen's government, then from August 1855 vice-president of the Board of Trade, he soon gained a reputation for using his position at *The Times* to advance his opinions and his career. Lord John Russell complained to his cabinet colleague Earl Granville that if anyone questioned Lowe's proposals, even in private, he could expect to find himself 'gibbetted in the next day's *Times*'.[167] Between 1854 and 1856 *The Times* published a series of leaders supporting the principle of general limited liability and abusing anyone who opposed Lowe's views.[168] However, the rest of the London dailies, regardless of their politics, were equally sympa-

---

162 The words of James Wilson, editor of the *Economist*, as reported by his daughter; cited in G. R. Searle, *Entrepreneurial politics in mid-Victorian Britain*, Oxford 1993, 90, 92.
163 Ibid.
164 *Daily News*, 10 July 1855.
165 *Morning Herald*, 10 July 1855.
166 A. P. Martin (ed.), *Life and letters of the right honourable Robert Lowe, viscount Sherbrooke*, London 1893, ii. 26; S. Morison (ed.), *The history of* The Times, London 1939, ii. 130–3.
167 Russell to Lord Granville, 7 Dec. 1855, cited in J. Winter, *Robert Lowe*, Toronto 1976, 101.
168 *The Times*, 28 June 1854; 1 June, 27 July, 7, 16 Aug. 1855; 22 Mar., 2 June 1856. The article of 22 March 1856 was particularly critical of Overstone. Overstone wrote to Granville that the article was 'no doubt by Lowe – it is fallacious throughout': Lord Overstone to Lord Granville, 23 Mar. 1856, *Overstone correspondence*, ii. 644.

thetic to limited liability.[169] Nor was support confined to the capital. Key provincial papers such as the *Manchester Guardian* were also behind the bills, and it was even claimed in the Lords that no paper in the country except the *Leeds Mercury* would publish an article against general limited liability.[170]

That leader articles failed to reflect the split in public opinion on the issue of limited liability is perhaps explained in part by the economic stake possessed by the press in any measure which might increase the number of company promotions. During the railway mania of the 1840s, one journalist admitted that advertisements of public companies were wildly lucrative to newspapers, and that 'it would not be unfair to estimate the receipts of the leading daily journals at from 12,000*l.* to 14,000*l.* per week from this source'.[171] *The Times* enjoyed its most profitable year to date in 1845, in part due to its advertising revenue.[172] Owners and editors also had more direct interests in the joint-stock economy. William Delane, the treasurer of *The Times* and father of the editor, was a director of the Direct London and Exeter Line, whose shares were puffed in *The Times*; the *Morning Chronicle* was owned by a railway director; both the proprietor and editor of the *Manchester Guardian* were speculating heavily in railways from 1838.[173] Legislators were also interested in the joint-stock economy as both shareholders and directors, and personal economic motives may have influenced the views of not a few MPs. In 1845 parliamentary returns of all subscribers to the 209 railway projects before parliament that session revealed that at least 104 MPs had subscribed sums ranging from £200 to £165,000, to a total value of £1,317,834.[174] By the end of 1845, 157 had accepted railway directorships.[175] Twenty years later 216 MPs were company directors.[176] As Paul Johnson has noted, 'Parliamentarians quite literally "bought in" to the methods and morals of the stock exchange.'[177] Corporate values were also being absorbed

---

[169] For Liberal opinion see *Morning Advertiser*, 28 June 1855; *Daily News*, 10 July 1855; *Morning Chronicle*, 27 July 1855; *Lloyd's Weekly Newspaper*, 5 Aug. 1855; and *Observer*, 12 Aug. 1855. For Conservative opinion see *Morning Herald*, 10 July 1855, and *Morning Post*, 27 July 1855.

[170] Lord Stanley of Alderley, *Hansard*, cxxxix. 1896 (7 Aug. 1855).

[171] [Evans], *The City*, 200.

[172] *The history of* The Times, ii. 12.

[173] Ibid. ii. 14–17; D. Ayerst, *Guardian: biography of a newspaper*, London 1971, 78.

[174] Calculated from *Alphabetical list of the names, descriptions and places of abode of all persons subscribing to the amount of £2,000 and upwards to any railway subscription contract deposited in the private bill office during the present session of parliament*, PP 1845 xl, and *Alphabetical list of the names, descriptions and places of abode of all persons subscribing for any sum less than £2,000 to any railway subscription contract deposited in the private bill office during the present session of parliament*, PP 1845 xl. The total of 104 is almost certainly an underestimate: only definite identifications have been included.

[175] [Evans], *Commercial crisis*, 19–20.

[176] P. Johnson, 'Civilizing mammon: laws, morals, and the City in nineteenth-century England', in P. Burke, B. Harrison and P. Slack (eds), *Civil histories*, Oxford 2000, 301–19 at p. 318.

[177] Ibid.

by the civil service: by 1852 a total of 121 permanent public officers sat on company boards, including four at the colonial office, eleven at the Inland Revenue and Customs, eight at the post office and no less than thirty-four holders of Scottish offices.[178] The same thing was happening on the level of local government, if Francis Whitmarsh was to be believed. In 1850 he told the Board of Trade that the only attempt made thus far to recover a penalty under the Joint-Stock Companies Act had been 'defeated by the magistrates, who themselves threw every difficulty in the way, and it might be expected in other cases, as there are few magistrates who are not in some way connected with the Direction of a public company'.[179] Landed and town elites were drawn en masse into the world of share ownership and company direction by the spread of the railways in the 1830s and 1840s. According to R. W. Kostal, hundreds of English gentlemen 'prostituted' their names to railway schemes with abandon: some accepted directorships to more than thirty companies.[180]

In spite of the influence of the joint-stock interest, however, the concession of limited liability in 1855 was by no means inevitable. Indeed, opponents of the principle exasperatedly drew attention to the absence of commercial demand for reform. Lord Monteagle, a Whig, asked, 'What petitions had been presented to their Lordships' House in favour of this Bill? He knew of none; nor did he know of any great commercial authority which had recommended the measure now under consideration.'[181] Edmund Potter wondered at the general meeting of the Manchester Chamber of Commerce in February 1856 why the government had passed the Limited Liability Bill 'when there had been no solicitation from the country'.[182] Lord Overstone denied that newspapers reflected a ground swell of support for limited liability, commenting privately, 'It is perfectly easy for two or three writers, having connection with the Press, to get up a very fallacious appearance of public opinion.'[183] Even some supporters of limited liability admitted that 'a majority of the commercial community of the country were opposed' to the principle.[184] The chief source of support for reform, argued Hawes, a London merchant who favoured unlimited liability, was ignorant and greedy lawyers. The lawyer was the archetypal 'idle capitalist', who wanted to realise the same profit from his capital, without commercial knowledge, and free of risk,

---

178 *Statement of names of permanent public officers who hold employment out of their office, as directors of life assurance, railway, banking or commercial companies in 1852*, PP 1854 xxxix. 1–5.

179 BT 1/477/431/50, p. 12 (7 Feb. 1850).

180 Kostal, *English railway capitalism*, 57. For more on landed involvement in railways see G. Channon, 'Railways and English landed society', in his *Railways in Britain and the United States, 1830–1940*, Aldershot 2001, 194–216.

181 *Hansard*, cxxxix. 2042 (9 Aug. 1855).

182 Cited in Glick, 'Partnership law reform', 258.

183 Overstone to Granville, 23 Mar. 1856, *Overstone correspondence*, ii. 644.

184 T. Horsfall, *Hansard*, cxxxix. 355 (29 June 1855).

as the man of business.[185] Potter agreed, arguing that 'the whole thing was in the hands of lawyers and certain capitalists in London'.[186] The government could have resisted these pressures, but ultimately it did not want to, partly because limited liability now seemed like a means of stabilising the joint-stock economy, partly because the state's role of deciding on applications for limited liability had become an embarrassment.

It would be a mistake to overlook this latter factor, for in the early 1850s the Board's role was falling under the microscope as never before. In December 1852, when Henley was still at the Board, William Brown, a Liverpool shipowner, moved in the Commons for the publication of all correspondence relating to the London, Liverpool and North American Screw Steamship Company's application to the Board of Trade for a charter of incorporation the previous October.[187] Brown opposed the application on the grounds that all steamship companies should operate on the level playing field of unlimited liability, but Henley successfully resisted his motion. The following February Cardwell rejected the company's application, as the announcement of the Royal Commission had given him the excuse to suspend the grant of charters while the law was being considered, but pressure on the government to make public the correspondence relating to the application continued, and on 27 May it was resolved in the Commons that this correspondence be laid before the House, which was done in June, and the material was printed in July.[188] Nearly one hundred pages long, the return set out in detail the process of petition and counter-petition which inevitably accompanied every such application: letters from Samuel Cunard (head of a rival firm) opposing the company's application featured particularly prominently in the correspondence, and Cardwell's decision could be presented as the result of lobbying from such interested parties. The Board's policy was condemned in *The Times* as arbitrary and unjust, and it is unsurprising that, just as in 1844, the Board expressed unease about its role.[189] Cardwell, despite opposing automatic registration, referred in parliament to 'the invidious power vested in him' of granting charters.[190] Even before the controversy of the summer of 1853, he had revealingly confessed to his colleagues, 'I heartily wish that the law was self-acting, and that the power of interposition did not belong to the Board of Trade.'[191]

---

185 Hawes, *Observations on unlimited and limited liability*, 30.
186 Glick, 'Partnership law reform', 258. Elsewhere, he argued that the press and parliament were the main movers behind the legislation: Potter, *Practical opinions*, preface, pp. 3–4.
187 *Hansard*, cxxiii. 1071–87 (7 Dec. 1852).
188 Ibid. cxxxiv. 772 (27 June 1854); *Journals of the House of Commons*, cviii, 27 May 1853, 520; 10 June 1853, 568; 8 July 1853, 663; *Correspondence with Board of Trade*, PP 1852–3.
189 'Money-Market and City Intelligence' column, *The Times*, 4, 5 Aug. 1853.
190 *Hansard*, cxxxiv. 772 (27 June 1854).
191 Cardwell, 'Limited liability', 9.

So when businessmen interested in extending access to limited liability placed pressure on ministers to rethink their policy in 1854, they received a favourable reception. In December *The Times* reported that 'fresh remonstrances' had been made to the Board by those seeking limited liability, an effort described elsewhere as 'well-organized agitation by some capitalists and speculators, who have been unable to obtain charters from the Board of Trade'.[192] The lobbying was successful, and Aberdeen's ministry announced its intention, which it was not permitted to fulfil, to implement a measure of general limited liability. When Palmerston succeeded Aberdeen, it was no surprise to see the new government introduce, and secure the passage of, a limited liability bill. The bill passed the Commons comfortably by 121 votes to 40, but arrived in the Lords nine days after the deadline imposed by the standing orders. Yet the government forced the measure through in two key divisions, 38:14 and 28:11, which caused much ill feeling in the upper house.[193] John Bright claimed that limited liability was driven through parliament merely because 'the Government was very anxious to say at the end of the Session that something had been done besides voting money for the war'.[194] But more than a way of winning some cheap popularity with the press, it was a means of divesting the government of a role which had troubled it for many years, an opportunity which, in 1855, it seized with some eagerness. Bouverie enthusiastically announced that the market rather than the state would henceforth regulate the corporate economy: 'The true test as to whether these undertakings were of public advantage was their success or non-success.'[195] If they fulfilled a public need, they would thrive, if they did not serve the public, they would fail. The state could thus withdraw from the picture altogether, having no other role than to set up a mechanism automatically granting limited liability, then leave well alone. Thus could the measure be presented as the natural 'corollary to freedom of trade and freedom of navigation'.[196]

But this change in policy did not apply across the whole joint-stock economy: companies which required powers of compulsory purchase or other special powers over property – most obviously railways, but also many gas and water companies – were obliged to continue to apply to parliament for their acts of incorporation. These acts could include a range of regulatory provisions, from publicity of accounts to limitations on prices and profits, designed

---

192 *The Times*, 20 Dec. 1854; George Sweet, *The Limited Liability Act, 1855*, London 1855, p. v.
193 See, for example, the comments of Lord Lyttelton and Earl Grey, *Hansard*, cxxxix. 1901, 1903 (7 Aug. 1855).
194 Cited in A. Redford, *Manchester merchants and foreign trade, 1794–1858*, Manchester 1934, 215.
195 Bouverie, *Hansard*, cxxxix. 325 (29 June 1855).
196 Collier, ibid. cxxxix. 329.

to protect the public, and to a lesser extent shareholders. From the 1840s regulatory provisions were standardised in consolidation acts applying to all statutory incorporations. The 1845 Railway Clauses Consolidation Act specified that all railway companies had to convey annual accounts to the overseers of the poor and the clerks of the peace of the parishes and counties through which the railway ran.[197] Similarly, the 1847 consolidating acts which applied to gas and water companies insisted that all companies provide annual accounts to the clerk of the peace of the county occupied by the works.[198] Companies in these sectors, with their monopolistic powers, had never wholly managed to shed their 'public' image. In other sectors, such as banking and insurance, governments found it more difficult to justify regulation, while in the rest of the joint-stock economy, it did not attempt it at all. The government's willingness to abandon its role outside of these sectors added weight to the gradual reconceptualisation of the joint-stock company as a private rather than a public entity. What were once viewed as public bodies which owed their existence to the state and which possessed responsibilities to the public, were now 'privatised'; limited liability was now conceived as a natural right hitherto unfairly denied companies by an interfering state. This conceptual shift subsequently made it easier for companies to undermine the legitimacy of proposals for government intervention in their affairs, as these could be stigmatised as an interference in the private sector. While this 'privatisation' of the company was facilitated by a sense of the economic benefits limited liability might bring, it was driven by the failure of will of governments in the 1850s, in the face of agitation from company promoters and their allies in the press and parliament, to exercise their customary discretionary powers.

The restructuring of company law between 1844 and 1856 was not carried out primarily in the name of economic growth, but of stability. While some commentators did see this legislation as a means of encouraging growth, many others doubted that it would lead to a significant increase in the number of joint-stock companies. And even with the extension of limited liability to the banking and insurance sectors by acts of 1858 and 1862, the immediate impact of the change in the law was not dramatic.[199] The numbers of company registrations did increase, but not to an extent which would imply that legitimate trade had been stifled by unlimited liability. Between 1848 and 1854 a total of 1,435 companies (excluding railway schemes) provi-

---

[197] 8 Vict. c. 20, s. 107.
[198] 10 Vict. c. 15, s. 38; 10 Vict. c. 17, s. 83. For a thorough discussion of the regulations imposed on joint-stock companies in the nineteenth century see Parker, 'Regulating British corporate financial reporting'.
[199] 21 & 22 Vict. c. 91; 25 & 26 Vict. c. 89.

sionally registered with unlimited liability under the act of 1844 in England and Ireland.[200] Between 1856 and 1862 a total of 2,500 English and Irish companies registered with limited liability (excluding a further 228 existing companies which re-registered under the new act).[201] Many of these were ephemeral or highly speculative concerns promoted in order to cash in on dubious patents or fads: Shannon's survey of the first 5,000 companies established under the act of 1856 revealed that 36 per cent failed within five years of promotion, rising to 54 per cent after ten years.[202] The mainstream business culture of Britain still favoured unlimited liability, and this fact continued to shape the joint-stock economy far more meaningfully than the legislation of 1855–6. While the joint-stock economy did spread into new areas after 1856, most notably into manufacturing, 'traditional' areas of joint-stock enterprise continued to account for many of the new promotions. In England and Ireland 49 per cent of the companies formed between 1856 and 1865 were in what could be described as 'traditional' joint-stock sectors: gas, water, shipping, banking, insurance, public halls, mining and miscellaneous communications, including foreign railways.[203] Continuity was even stronger in Scotland. While the same period saw the formation of a number of manufacturing companies (19.5 per cent of the total), nearly two-thirds (65 per cent) of the 220 companies established were in gas, water, banking, insurance, shipping, mining and public halls.[204]

Furthermore, even after 1856 those concerns which did adopt limited liability found themselves imitating private partnerships in some respects in order to achieve respectability and a reputation for financial solidity. Share denominations in many companies, especially financial institutions, remained high, as it was still widely believed that the only way to attract the right sort of investor was to divide capital into a small number of large shares; low denomination shares drew less responsible shareholders. But the capital on these shares was not usually fully paid up, for companies found that in order to attract loan capital they had to retain a large uncalled margin on their shares, to act as a reserve fund for the security of creditors. Thus shareholders would face a large residual liability on their shares, which in some cases meant unlimited liability in practice. Parliament could not legislate traditional practices away in 1855–6.[205]

But the early 1860s saw an unprecedented boom in company formations, encouraging widespread speculation in shares. When this boom collapsed in

200 Calculated from annual returns, 1849–55. Domestic railway companies had to provisionally register under the 1844 act, but not the 1856 act.
201 Shannon, 'First five thousand', 421.
202 Ibid. 418.
203 Calculated from ibid. 422.
204 Calculated from P. L. Payne, *The early Scottish limited companies, 1856–1895: an historical and analytical survey*, Edinburgh 1980, 54 and appendix table 2.
205 Cottrell, *Industrial finance*, ch. iv.

1866, the laws erected between 1844 and 1856 were placed under intense scrutiny. To many it looked as if the lax legal framework had exacerbated the crisis by facilitating unsound promotions, and one solution seemed to be to restrict access to corporate privileges once more. Would limited liability survive this test?

Limited Liability on Trial:
The Commercial Crisis of 1866

On Saturday 5 May 1866 theatregoers at the Prince of Wales, Tottenham, enjoyed the first performance of *A hundred thousand pounds*, a comedy by Henry James Byron. The principal theme of the play was the illusory nature of wealth: at several points in the play, money which is assumed to exist suddenly vanishes, creating all manner of chaos. In act one, Pennythorne, a livery stable-keeper, is told that he has inherited the eponymous hundred thousand pounds. He makes ambitious plans for the money, but his joy is interrupted when it is revealed that there has been a case of mistaken identity: it is actually Gerald Goodwin, a poor man of good family, who has inherited the money from an estranged uncle in India. Goodwin falls in with Major Blackshaw, a company promoter, who encourages him to set up in fine style on the strength of his imminent fortune. Goodwin runs up extensive bills with tailors and wine merchants, but his uncle returns from India to refute the rumours of his death: he was merely ill with jungle fever. Goodwin's presumed wealth therefore evaporates before his creditors' eyes, and he is faced with massive debts. Alice Barlow, the woman Goodwin loved, but cruelly threw over when he came into his 'inheritance', and who has been left money by her father, forgives his behaviour and offers to pay his debts. But her uncle Joe, who had control of her money in trust, reveals to her that he has lost it, along with his own savings, in Blackshaw's British-Australasian Joint-Stock Discount and General Loan Company, which has just gone bust. Pennythorne does not know this, and, having also lost all of his money in the company, develops an interest in marrying Alice, as the solution to his financial troubles. Joe, ignorant of Pennythorne's losses, and believing his wealth will solve his financial problems, is on the verge of forcing Alice to accept her suitor's advances, when the truth of each man's finances is revealed to the other. Pennythorne, reduced from eligible bachelor to bankrupt, is arrested and taken away, and the play ends with Goodwin's uncle initiating a reconciliation with Goodwin, who sees the error of his earlier profligacy. Alice takes her former lover back, and extols the virtues of modest living: 'Gerald, we shall be happy if we are not too rich. We have seen what money does, so let us be contented with a little.'[1]

Many in the audience may have had cause to reflect on the theme of

[1] H. J. Byron, *A hundred thousand pounds*, London 1866, 47.

vanished wealth the following Thursday, when Overend, Gurney and Co., the country's leading discount company, 'familiar as a household word throughout the kingdom', suspended payments, provoking the next day a panic 'which broke like a thunderclap over the City'.[2] Formerly a partnership, the business had been converted to a limited company in 1865, but its heavy liabilities had been deliberately concealed from the investing public by the company's new directors. Confidence in all financial institutions evaporated: 'The doors of the most respectable Banking-Houses were besieged . . . The excitement on all sides was such as has not been witnessed since the great crisis of 1825.'[3] Lloyd's Weekly Newspaper went further: 'Thursday was, beyond all comparison, the most painful and difficult day ever experienced by the commercial and financial community.'[4] Walter Bagehot, writing in the Economist, doubted 'if there ever was a collapse of credit more diffused and more complete'.[5] At midday on Friday the panic was at its height. 'Lombard Street was actually blocked up by the crowds of respectable persons who thronged the doors of the banks and other establishments.'[6] The Bank Charter Act was suspended. Several banks failed, and many new promotions followed them. Within three months, more than 200 joint-stock companies had collapsed.[7]

As a result of the crisis, the workings of the corporate economy were subjected to intense public scrutiny. A select committee was formed to investigate the Companies Acts, and the law was amended, but the principles of company law as established between 1844 and 1862 were not diluted; indeed in some respects the act of 1867 went further than its predecessors. Hunt rightly argues that this was a crucial moment in the history of company law, but does so for the wrong reason. He presents the reaction to 1866 as the final step on the road to enlightenment by the British: 'After more than a century of struggle against deeply rooted prejudice and widespread misconception, and having weathered the storm of the sixties, freedom of incorporation was a definitively accomplished fact.'[8] This interpretation disguises the fact that while the basis of company law received backing in parliament and in sections of the press, there was far from universal support among the wider population. Public suspicion of joint-stock enterprise was heightened by the events of 1866, and this mistrust was far from fully dissipated in the aftermath of the crisis. But the regime established between 1844 and 1862 was able to resist change thanks to the persistence of the traditional belief that shareholders had a responsibility to look after their own investments. This convic-

---

[2] Lloyd's Weekly Newspaper, 13 May 1866; R. H. Patterson, 'The panic in the City', BEM c (July 1866), 78–93 at p. 79.
[3] The Times, 12 May 1866.
[4] Lloyd's Weekly Newspaper, 13 May 1866.
[5] Economist, 12 May 1866, repr. in Works of Walter Bagehot, ix. 86.
[6] Patterson, 'Panic', 83.
[7] Hunt, Business corporation, 154.
[8] Ibid. 157.

tion had shaped the form limited liability originally took in 1855–6, and its influence was just as strong in 1866. While shareholders were the principal victims of fraudulent companies, they were also thought to be the only effective regulators of company behaviour; consequently, the only legitimate response to the crisis was to encourage them to carry out their regulatory duties. State-imposed safeguards would merely make shareholders less vigilant, and were therefore worse than useless.

The panic and the reaction

1863 marked the start of a boom in joint-stock company promotion. In 1862, 500 limited companies were registered in Britain. Registrations for the next three years were 746, 967 and 992 respectively.[9] A total of 876 companies formed between 1863 and 1866 offered shares to the public, including 283 manufacturing and trading companies, 147 mining companies, eighty-two hotel companies, fifty-eight banks and fifty financial companies.[10] The instability that these limited companies were introducing into commerce was noted. *The Times* realised the opportunities the joint-stock company form gave to fraudsters to cheat the public:

> nowhere are there such astounding illusions as in this city of colossal realities. There are some men engaged in producing the most substantial results, and others by their side blowing the most empty and fragile of bubbles. On your right hand is the most sturdy honesty and plain-dealing, on your left the most gigantic and unscrupulous swindle. There are men there who, if sold up to-morrow, would be worth millions, and others, to all external appearance the same, whose value is hundreds of thousands less than nothing.[11]

The new phenomenon of finance companies was a particular cause for concern.[12] Limited liability had been intended to make it more difficult for companies to obtain loans, but this had not happened, due in part to the emergence of limited companies happy to lend to other limited companies in return for high rates of interest. The profits to be made in financing attracted more companies, whose shareholders saw the chance of an easy 15 or 20 per cent. Competition between these finance companies did not drive down the high rates of interest charged; instead, it drove down the quality of securities accepted by the companies in return for loans. The capital of these companies was therefore tied up in investments which might not prove profitable for many years, if at all. They were unable to raise money on the strength of

9 Shannon, 'First five thousand', 421.
10 Hunt, *Business corporation*, 150.
11 *The Times*, 16 Dec. 1865.
12 *The Times* (2 Feb. 1866) commented: 'to "finance" is a new verb with which our language has been enriched within the last four years'.

their securities in an emergency, because they were bad. Furthermore, calls were difficult to make because of the speculative nature of the market: shareholders held more shares than they could afford, so if calls were made, there was a rush to offload the shares, and the share price plummeted. Thus these finance companies were highly vulnerable in a crisis.[13] They began to hit difficulties in late 1865 and early 1866. Shares in the Joint-Stock Discount Company, floated in February 1863, were at 50 per cent discount in February 1866, after repeated calls.[14] The following month the company collapsed. In April an accountant's report revealed that a large portion of the paid-up capital of the Financial Corporation was lost, and that a far larger sum than the paid-up capital was tied up in inconvertible securities.[15] These and similar cases depressed the market to the extent that shares in ostensibly flourishing finance companies could not be sold, due to a universal fear of calls.[16] By May suspicion was endemic. 'The great moral to be drawn from the present Financial Panic is that money is really not worth 30 per cent', stated The Times.[17]

Even before the fall of Overend Gurney, Russell's government proved itself responsive to the needs of the joint-stock economy by preparing a bill to permit companies to divide their capital into shares of a smaller amount than that stipulated by their constitutions, provided this was not below £10.[18] Promoted by Thomas Milner Gibson, president of the Board of Trade, the bill was designed to try to revive the market for company shares, which was in a state of crisis due to the overhanging liability on the shares of so many companies. Ordered on 3 May, it received its first reading on 7 May, and had passed all its stages in the Commons by 24 May, a fortnight after Overend Gurney's demise, without any debate. The bill met with opposition in the Lords, however. Lord Redesdale, the Conservative chairman of committees, thought the bill would allow companies to 'get rid of a liability to which they were now subject'. Other lords expressed a more fundamental dissatisfaction with limited liability, tracing current difficulties back to the measures of 1855–6. Earl Grey, a Liberal, told the house that it had to take care to frame the law so as 'not to give improper encouragement to a spirit of gambling. The effect of recent legislation had been most mischievous in stimulating such a spirit already too prevalent'. Lord Overstone was even more forceful, calling the shares of the companies in difficulties 'little else but gambling symbols used not for the purpose of promoting industry, but to facilitate practices which had about as much relation to honest industry as the exchange of cards over a gaming table'. He had obtained a return indicating that by May

---

13 Patterson, 'Panic', 82.
14 *The Times*, 2 Feb. 1866.
15 Ibid. 30 Apr. 1866.
16 Ibid. 7 May 1866.
17 Ibid. 10 May 1866.
18 A bill to amend the *Companies Act of 1862*, PP 1866 ii.

PUNCH, OR THE LONDON CHARIVARI.—June 9, 1866.

HOW TO TREAT THE "BEARS;"

Or, Speculating for a Fall,—and Getting it.

Plate 13. 'How to treat the "bears"'.
Source: *Punch*, 1 (9 June 1866), 243.

1864 there was a total of 42 million shares in existence, and that between January 1863 and May 1864 alone, 13.35 million new shares were created. Many more had been created after this date. 'Was it wise', asked Overstone, 'to pass an Act for splitting up and thus causing an extensive multiplication of these shares?' Redesdale, Overstone and Grey were able to muster sufficient support to defeat the bill, 17:14.[19]

The Lords' opinions seemed to have tapped into a vein of popular feeling. The visual and print culture of the 1860s provides plenty of evidence suggesting that the joint-stock economy was just as controversial as it had ever been. The rigid connection between speculation and gambling may have been slowly loosening, but continuities of representation were strong.[20] In the aftermath of the crisis, the 'bears' who were thought to have in part caused the panic by driving down the shares of the finance companies were singled out for particular censure. A *Punch* cartoon of June 1866, 'How to treat the "bears" ' (*see* plate 13), shows Mr Punch drenching a bear in 'Retribution' and 'Contempt', as the bulls of the Stock Exchange, for once not the target, look on approvingly. *Punch* wanted to know 'who conspired Against the Banks, to sink the Shares', and wanted to turn the tables on 'that vile gang'.[21] The members of this gang were no better than criminals: 'For some time past crime has become scholarly and soft, working more safely and successfully with a pen and a smile than with pistol and mask. House-breaking is as old as hunger; Bank-breaking displays all the grace and energy of youth.' The characters involved in City crime were no different to society's more familiar villains: 'JACK SHEPPARD defying recognition with spray whiskers and diamond studs, blocks the entrance to Capel Court, and SYKES, his black eye painted out, lounges along Lombard Street, attended by a Bear instead of a Bull-dog.' A Stock Exchange committee was established to look into the events of 1866, but *Punch* thought that the bank-breaker was 'as much entitled as a burglar to be tried by his peers'. The committee was sure to prove inadequate to drive out the bears, who had 'protectors whose names deserve to be posted elsewhere than on the Stock Exchange'.[22] One of *Punch's* rivals, the recently-established Conservative magazine *Tomahawk* saw one of its roles as helping to curb the excesses of the Stock Exchange: in its first anniversary edition it carried a cartoon, 'The Modern Hercules', which set out the labours facing the new journal. Alongside such tasks as 'Overcoming the monster democracy', and 'Taming the wild boar of South

[19] *Hansard*, 3rd ser. clxxxiii. 2028–34 (7 June 1866). All subsequent references to *Hansard* in this chapter are to the third series.
[20] In an example of changing attitudes, one fictional stock market operator's profession was described thus: 'He was a speculator – a gamester if you will – in his business, but no gambler': C. Clarke, 'How the balance came out: a tale of the Stock Exchange', *TB* xix (1866), 120–37 at p. 125.
[21] *Punch* l (16 June 1866), 255.
[22] Ibid. (23 June 1866), 267–8. See also li (29 Aug. 1866), 261.

Kensington' was 'Tying the stag of Capel Court'.[23] Similar views could also be expressed in more elevated quarters: R. H. Patterson, the Scottish journalist and financial expert, writing in *Blackwood's*, condemned 'the shameful and wicked conspiracy of speculators, who of late have been fattening on the spoils of the community'.[24]

While stockbrokers were often singled out for particular abuse, they were only a small element of a much broader and deeply unflattering critique of the joint-stock economy. The *Weekly Dispatch* remarked that 'Joint-Stock Companies are most justly out of favour. Jobbery and incompetence in the directions are the rule rather than the exception.'[25] Malcolm Meason commented:

> Go where you will, in business parts, or meet who you like of business men, it is – and has been for the last three years – the same story and the same lament. Dishonesty, untruth, and what may, in plain English, be termed mercantile swindling within the limits of the law, exist on all sides and on every quarter.[26]

The illness was not restricted to the joint-stock economy; rather, financial swindling was symptomatic of a more general malaise. For an essayist in the *Fortnightly Review*, 'such audacious, all-pervading roguery, from the highest regions of finance to the smallest detail of petty shopkeeping, has not been known before'.[27] But limited companies bore the brunt of hostile commentary; they had never had a poorer public image. *Judy* carried this barbed comment:

> A Suggestion.
> From the public's experience of the Court of Bankruptcy for the last twelve months, it is suggested that in future limited liability companies be designated as *Unlimited Lie-Ability Companies*.[28]

After the shocks of the 1840s, railway shares had been gaining a reputation for solidity, but this was undermined by the crisis, which exposed the limitations of the contracting system of railway construction which had become popular in the 1860s.[29] The best-known contractor, at least after May 1866, was Liberal MP Sir Samuel Morton Peto.[30] Peto was responsible for financing

23 *Tomahawk* ii (2 May 1868), 177–9.
24 Patterson, 'Panic', 93.
25 *Weekly Dispatch*, 11 Aug. 1867.
26 [M. L. Meason], 'Finance, frauds, and failures', *TB* xvii (1866), 381–95 at p. 393.
27 F. P. Cobbe, 'What is progress, and are we progressing?', *Fortnightly Review* vii (1867), 357–70 at p. 361.
28 *Judy* ii (30 Oct. 1867), 3.
29 The instability of this system is explored in [T. Hennell], 'Railway finance', *QR* cxxii (Apr. 1867), 489–506. See also P. L. Cottrell, 'Railway finance and the crisis of 1866: contractors' bills of exchange and the finance companies', *Journal of Transport History* n.s. iii (1975), 20–40.
30 For more on Peto see P. L. Cottrell, 'Sir Samuel Morton Peto', in D. J. Jeremy (ed.),

the metropolitan extensions of the London, Chatham and Dover Railway, which resulted in a massive over-issue of debentures.[31] His contracting business, which had been in financial difficulties since the late 1850s, collapsed the same day as Overend Gurney, with whom Peto had extensive dealings, and the London, Chatham and Dover was declared bankrupt soon after. Peto became a popular symbol of the decadence of the joint-stock system, in the same way that George Hudson had twenty years earlier. *Fun* depicted him as a clown who had outwitted the railway's shareholders and stolen their money.[32] A story of his life was drawn for *Punch's* 1867 Almanack, charting his progress from 'idle apprentice' to millionaire, in contrast to the life of the industrious apprentice, who invests his life's savings in Peto's railway and loses everything. 'Women and children, with here and there a country parson, fancy that everything connected with rails must be perfectly straightforward', wrote *Punch*. But 'Rails, I have lately discovered, are carried out in very crooked ways, and those who lay down the sleepers are themselves remarkable for being very wide awake.'[33]

As in the past, speculation was thought to be sapping the nation's vitality. The *News of the World* bemoaned the widespread 'abandonment of legitimate enterprise in favour of mere speculation, which no more increases the resources of the country than do the operations of the members of Tattersall's'.[34] *Judy* presented speculation as one of the ills, alongside trade unionism and faction, which were weakening the nation and leaving it vulnerable to foreign rivals. In the cartoon, 'John Bull's dream' (*see* plate 14), Bull is asleep, with impish figures representing the aforementioned evils crouched on his chest. One is sitting on a stack of volumes marked 'Limited Liability Company', and two are brandishing share certificates. Other figures are hiding around and underneath the bed, while Bull, oblivious to the peril he is in, continues to sleep. The accompanying verse rams home the message that the country was in dire threat from these problems. Bull falls asleep with comforting visions floating through his mind, of 'Old England flourishing in wealth and industry', but soon he is troubled by 'Un-English, lying, treacherous' voices:

> Trades Unionism, Faction, Speculation's open theft
> Drained the nation of its heart's blood – no strength was in it left;
> And as it still grew weaker throughout its breadth and length,
> Each Foreign Rival from our loss drew health, and life, and strength.[35]

Dictionary of business biography: a biographical dictionary of business leaders active in Britain in the period, 1860–1980, London 1984–6, iv. 644–53.

[31] In *Punch* the company became the London, Cheatem and Clover: *Punch* li (27 Oct. 1866), 175.

[32] *Fun* n.s. iv (3 Nov. 1866), 81.

[33] *Punch* li (8 Dec. 1866), 237.

[34] *News of the World*, 13 May 1866.

[35] *Judy* i (11 Sept. 1867), 255.

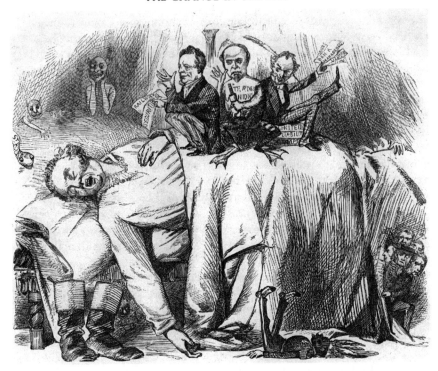

Plate 14. 'John Bull's dream'. Source: *Judy* i (11 Sept. 1867), 258.

The low standards of commercial morality Britain was displaying to the world was damaging the nation's reputation. *Punch* mourned: 'the soil'd name of England, that once stood so high . . . has so fallen, through gold's abject lust, That they who would seek it must look in the dust'.[36] In the 1869 comedy, *New men and old acres*, by Tom Taylor and Augustus William Dubourg, the honest Liverpool merchant Sam Brown reiterates his belief that fortunes should be made not by speculation but 'by fair dealing and hard work. If the world went on my tack, thousands of families wouldn't be ruined to enrich a few score of successful speculators, and British enterprise would not stand in the pillory as it does now, with "Lie" branded on its forehead!'[37] According to Dickens, a new morality had sprung up, based on shares:

> As is well known to the wise in their generation, traffic in Shares is the one thing to have to do with in this world. Have no antecedents, no established character, no cultivation, no ideas, no manners; have Shares. Have Shares enough to be on Boards of Direction in capital letters, oscillate on mysterious business between London and Paris, and be great. Where does he come from?

36 *Punch* lvi (6 Feb. 1869), 48.
37 T. Taylor and A. W. Dubourg, *New men and old acres*, in M. R. Booth (ed.), *English plays of the nineteenth century*, Oxford 1969–76, iii. 313.

Shares. Where is he going to? Shares. What are his tastes? Shares. Has he any principles? Shares. What squeezes him into Parliament? Shares. Perhaps he never of himself achieved success in anything, never originated anything, never produced anything! Sufficient answer to all; Shares. O mighty Shares![38]

For many, one of the chief sources of information about the joint-stock economy would have been the slew of short stories detailing the sordid underbelly of company promotion which appeared in the burgeoning middle-brow press of the 1860s. While such stories had appeared before then in magazines such as Dickens's *Household Words* and even *Blackwood's*, these became much more commonplace in the 1860s, featuring in journals such as *Temple Bar*, *Saint Pauls Magazine* and *All the Year Round*. They were comple-mented by the works of David Morier Evans, which provided inside stories of actual cases of fraud and other sharp practice.[39] As Poovey comments, these writings performed a variety of functions, including to moralise corporate behaviour and to normalise the workings of financial institutions.[40] Yet they also helped to entrench a traditional set of attitudes about what the joint-stock system represented. In few of these stories do we see much in the way of straightforward business dealings: the City is a place men go in order to be fleeced. For the authors, this did not involve presenting an exaggerated or distorted view of the joint-stock economy; the legitimacy of these stories derived from their professed verisimilitude. In one, after describing a particu-larly scandalous piece of financing by the bank at the heart of the story, the author notes, 'This story may be deemed imaginary, but, with alterations of names and circumstances, it is strictly true.'[41]

The stories usually give an inside view of bubble companies, written from the point of view of promoters, directors or secretaries. Sometimes the narra-tors are schemers, out to fleece the public, sometimes they are respectable innocents, induced to invest in companies and sit on their boards while knowing nothing whatsoever about business.[42] In all of them, the sense of the joint-stock system conveyed was one of instability and unsoundness. Specu-lation was something to be avoided, as it led to nothing but mental anxiety and, ultimately, catastrophic loss. In 'Twenty per Cent', an Indian Civil Servant retires to Britain and through judicious speculation, turns his savings of £20,000 and annual pension of £1,000 into £100 a year, and ends his days

---

[38] C. Dickens, *Our mutual friend*, New York 1978, 117–18.

[39] D. M. Evans, *Speculative notes and notes on speculation ideal and real*, New York 1969, and *Facts, failures and frauds*.

[40] M. Poovey, 'Writing about finance in Victorian England: disclosure and secrecy in the culture of investment', *VS* xlv (2002), 17–41 at p. 25.

[41] [M. L. Meason], 'Twenty per cent: a banking tale of the present time', *TB* xvii (July 1866), 473–92 at p. 488.

[42] For examples of the former see idem, 'The Bank of Patagonia (Ltd)', *AYR* xiii (1865), 485–90, and Anon., 'John Skeeme, the promoter', *AYR* xviii (1867), 342–6, 376–81. For the latter see [Meason], 'Twenty per cent'.

living 'in a fourth–rate French country town'.[43] In another, a man with an inheritance yielding £1,200 a year ends up in the Bankruptcy Court, doubting his estate will pay seven shillings in the pound.[44] While the increased dissemination of these stories betrays growing awareness of, and interest in, the joint-stock speculation in the 1860s, their cumulative effect was to reinforce traditional connections between joint-stock speculation and gambling. None of these works were intended to spread the speculating habit. A review of Evans's *Notes* recommended the book as it allowed 'all uniniti-ated people . . . to look beyond the veil, whilst a high-priest of finance himself expounds to us the mysteries of the temple'. But this would not encourage speculation, quite the reverse: a perusal of it 'will clear your vision by giving you a practical insight into the wear and tear, the troubles, anxieties, cares, and disappointments inseparable from all dabbling in the money-market'.[45]

Elsewhere, readers would not struggle to find other warnings to stay away from the 'whirling vortex of money-getting pursuits' and the 'hum and chink of Stock Exchange'.[46] Commentators urged disengagement from the joint-stock economy. The Conservative weekly *Judy* carried 'The railway shareholder's dirge', which ends with a chastened investor learning a valuable lesson: never to trust directors again.

> I no more will prove confiding,
> All their snares I'll flee;
> And by Three per Cents abiding
> Satisfied I'll be.[47]

Punch echoed these sentiments:

> Happy the man who lives content
> On money safe at three per cent.![48]

Punch refused to accept that joint-stock fraud was any less despicable than the penny-pinching ruses resorted to by shopkeepers, and in 'Rogues in busi-ness', a cartoon of 1866 (*see* plate 15), sought to equate the two types of crime. Here, both the director who presents cooked accounts and the tradesman who uses false weights and measures are standing on the same pillory. With each, the crime is the deliberate deception of the public for financial gain, and with each, the punishment should be public scorn. Signif-icantly, it is the director whom Mr Punch confronts: the guilty shopkeeper lurks at the edge of the cartoon, looking suitably shamefaced. The director on the other hand takes centre stage and, in contrast to his fellow rogue, looks

---

43 [Meason], 'Twenty per cent', 492.
44 [Anon.], 'The Stock Exchange', *Saint Pauls Magazine* vi (1870), 605–18 at p. 613.
45 [Anon.], 'City intelligence', *TB* xi (1864), 491–500 at p. 500.
46 [Anon.], 'The poverty of wealth', *TB* vi (1862), 12–25 at pp. 12–13.
47 *Judy* i (7 Aug. 1867), 185.
48 *Punch* l (23 June 1866), 260.

ROGUES IN BUSINESS.

" PILLORY, A SCAFFOLD FOR PERSONS TO STAND ON, TO RENDER THEM PUBLICLY INFAMOUS,
THAT ALL MIGHT AVOID AND REFUSE TO HAVE ANY DEALINGS WITH THEM."   [*See Dictionaries.*

Plate 15. 'Rogues in business'.
Source: *Punch* li (24 Nov. 1866), 213.

on impassively, his face betraying not a trace of contrition. The implication was that society already condemned cheating tradesmen, but that, hitherto, company directors had enjoyed immunity from such censure due to their elevated social position. The satirical press did its best to redress the balance: the level of venom directed against company directors in these years was unprecedented. A long poem 'The Perfect Cure', written by 'a sufferer' and published in *Fun*, listed the grievances the public had with companies. The refrain, 'hang a Director', summed up the frustration felt by beleaguered victims of corporate bad behaviour:

> We've reached a nice crisis in Commerce and Trade –
> How long will it take us to get its effect o'er?
> And the sole satisfaction for all, I'm afraid,
> Is to hang a Director – yes, hang a Director! . . .
>
> We have pinched, in the hope of insuring our lives,
> But the Company proves to a careful inspector
> So rotten, 'tis useless to tell us it thrives –
> So let's hang a Director – yes, hang a Director!
>
> Directors – aye, guinea-pigs, all of the lot –
> Let's make of the tribe, mob, conspiracy, sect, or
> Whatever you call 'em examples: why not?
> Let us hang a Director – yes, hang a Director![49]

The Select committee on the limited liability acts

Yet parliament was not in a hanging mood. Certainly, a select committee to investigate the limited liability laws was appointed, and this has been regarded elsewhere as particularly significant since the crises of 1847 and 1857 had precipitated inquiries into *currency* law.[50] Yet it would be a mistake to read too much into this, as it would have been difficult to find anyone in the Commons willing to speak against the principle of limited liability: Bagehot's claim that the House of Commons was 'almost hostile' to limited liability is impossible to substantiate. Edward Watkin, a Liberal MP and chairman of the Manchester, Sheffield and Lincolnshire and South Eastern Railways, had moved towards the end of the 1866 session for the appointment of a Royal Commission to investigate the causes of the panic, and to consider the currency laws. His attempt failed, though Sir Stafford Northcote, the Conservative successor to Gibson at the Board of Trade, promised that the government would look carefully into the matter.[51] The government remained inactive, so Watkin renewed his efforts the following session,

49 *Fun* n.s. x (13 Nov. 1869), 103.
50 Hunt, *Business corporation*, 154; Cottrell, *Industrial finance*, 57.
51 *Hansard*, clxxxiv. 1706–61 (31 July 1866).

moving in March 1867 for a select committee on the operation of the Limited Liability Acts. In 1866 his proposal had been unpopular, but this time he won support for an investigation. He stressed that joint-stock companies were now a hugely important feature of the economy: there were 2,200 companies with, he estimated, a nominal capital of around £1 billion. But he painted a gloomy picture of the state of the corporate economy. Currently 266 companies were in liquidation, 'and the shares of the rest of the limited companies were, for the most part, either at a discount, or their operations were so circumscribed as to show that they were almost in a state of collapse'. Considering the position of so many joint-stock companies, this was a suitable time for the House to 'carefully review a law containing so much that was novel and experimental'.[52]

The Liberal MP Walter Morrison, who seconded Watkin's motion, agreed, arguing that this was an important subject for the House to consider. 'The ruin which last year brought down so many families to the ground, had affected classes which before had never been known to be much connected with joint-stock enterprises; and, in fact, all classes were involved in it – farmers, tradesmen, domestic servants, peers, and peasants.' He thought that 'no time should be lost in improving the law before the transactions in connection with it became so large that it would be almost beyond the power of Parliament to deal with it'. David Salomons, another Liberal MP who also supported the motion, argued that an investigation was necessary because 'Very great discredit had fallen upon the commercial character of this country in consequence of the ruin into which many of those companies had sunk.'[53]

Watkin put forward several ideas to tackle the problems generated by the existing legislation. One of the principal evils was irresponsible directors. As the law stood, 'any seven persons' might take a share of a farthing each, present a memorandum of association to the Registrar of Joint-Stock Companies, and thus form a corporate body which there was no power to dissolve. He wanted the law to fix minimum share denominations, and a minimum number of shares to be held by every person signing the memorandum, to ensure that those behind a company had a substantial interest in the concern. Furthermore, he wanted to see the French system of *en commandite* implemented: 'It was notorious that a great number of concerns, which had been rotten from the first, were floated in the market entirely on false representations. Such things could not happen if the directors and promoters of these companies were under unlimited instead of limited liability.' Salomons did not support the introduction of *en commandite* partnerships, but only because he believed they would give total control of the capital of a company to one or two *gérants*. He did support measures to ensure companies were 'conducted by capital and not by credit'. This was not what was currently happening. Businesses only called up a small amount of capital, relying for the rest on

---

52 Ibid. clxxxv. 1372–4 (5 Mar. 1867).
53 Ibid. clxxxv. 1380–3.

bills of exchange and other credit accommodation, not what had been anticipated by the legislation of 1855–6. The law thus encouraged 'rash and
immoral speculators' to set up companies with small paid-up capitals, 'and
the only wonder was, that more calamities had not taken place'.[54]

Watkin also proposed that companies be empowered to reduce the capital
of their businesses, and to reduce the denomination of shares. The law as it
stood locked up capital and generated uncertainty, for prudent shareholders
had to keep money in reserve to cover any calls that might be made in the
future. He pointed to 'the enormous amount of money which was kept in
people's pockets and tills, because of the overhanging weight of uncalled
capital'. He also drew attention to the excessive amount of litigation
involved in winding up companies. He proposed that a uniform procedure for
winding up be established. Four different courts were currently involved in
winding up companies, and 'Some liquidators thought it their duty to get as
much as possible for the creditors, while others believed that it was to the
interest of the shareholders they ought to look.' In Watkin's view, liquidators
were a parasitic interest group whose behaviour urgently needed to be
reformed: 'As long as the liquidators had so many guineas a day, it was probable they would continue to find matters constantly arising which required
great deliberation and grave consideration.'[55]

What is perhaps most remarkable about Watkin's speech was not his criticism of limited liability, but the moderate tone in which his arguments were
made, and the limited scope of his proposed reforms. 'He was far from wishing
to be understood as expressing a general condemnation of that principle',
which he believed to be 'essentially sound'. He was confident that the problems with the limited liability system could be easily eradicated, believing
that 'the area of irregularity was very small, and that the evil approached with
boldness might with ease be removed'.[56] Indeed, the last thing Watkin
wanted to do was to restrict access to limited liability, for he himself had
exploited the permissive legal framework, having been prominently involved
in the promotion of two very short-lived enterprises: the East of England
Screw Coasting Company (1857), and the Humberside Iron and Ship-
building Company (1864).[57] His Liberal colleagues couched their comments
in similar terms, with Salomons, for example, wanting to see the defects of
the law remedied 'without interfering with the principle of limited liability'.
Morrison emphasised that 'he firmly believed in the principle of limited
liability, and that it had nothing to fear from investigation'.[58]

Nor was hostility to limited liability to be found on the Conservative

54 Ibid. clxxxv. 1377–83.
55 Ibid. clxxxv. 1379.
56 Ibid. clxxxv. 1376–9.
57 D. Hodgkins, *The second railway king: the life and times of Sir Edward Watkin, 1819–1901*,
Cardiff 2002, 129, 279–81.
58 *Hansard*, clxxxv. 1384, 1382 (5 Mar. 1867).

benches. The government made it clear that it would not countenance any reform which challenged the foundations of the legal regime established in the 1850s. Northcote only decided not to oppose the committee when he learned that it was not Watkin's intention to challenge the principles of the Limited Liability Acts, but that he was restricting himself to 'points of detail'. He was 'anxious to have it understood distinctly that in assenting to inquiry we do not intend to impugn in any way the principle of limited liability'. Northcote defended Palmerston's acts wholeheartedly, arguing that much of the recent crisis had been 'perhaps hastily and without sufficient consideration, attributed to the operation of the limited liability laws. I think that these laws have been made to bear a greater amount of the burden than is really due to them'. Northcote hoped that the committee would be able to help 'distinguish between that which is good and sound in the principle on which they rest, and those things which are only incidental accessories to the working of the principle, but which have perhaps conduced to results we all deplore'. He therefore did not support a radical restructuring of the law, instead advocating measures to make it easier for companies to reduce their capital, and an inquiry into the method of liquidation.[59]

A committee was appointed on 8 March, and met through March, April and May. Watkin had the chair and, as P. L. Cottrell has noted, the committee contained a large 'City' faction.[60] In particular, the committee was dominated by the Liberal triumvirate of William Forster, George Goschen and Robert Lowe, the architect of the act of 1856. The committee heard the testimonies of seventeen witnesses, a cross-section of city lawyers, financiers, company directors, merchants, bankers and civil servants. Nearly all the witnesses supported the principle of general limited liability, which was far from surprising, as most of them had stakes to a greater or lesser degree in the continuance of the system established in 1855–6. Yet these witnesses did suggest a variety of sometimes quite radical solutions to the ills of joint-stock enterprise as revealed by the crisis of the preceding year, including strengthening the powers of the Registrar, curbing the powers of directors and increasing shareholders' access to information. But such suggestions were met with no favour by Forster, Goschen and Lowe, who did their best to discredit all remedies which involved the replacement of individual responsibility by greater state controls. The committee's priorities were not to restrict the actions, or increase the liabilities, of directors, nor to strengthen the regulatory powers of the state. The evidence was heard at a time when depression, prompted by the events of May 1866, continued to hang over trade. The number of company promotions had fallen off dramatically after May 1866.[61] Committee members displayed less interest in combating over-speculation and fraud, and more in measures which would provide a stimulus to trade.

[59] Ibid. clxxxv. 1384–5.
[60] Cottrell, *Industrial finance*, 61.
[61] C. Cook and B. Keith, *British historical facts, 1830–1900*, London 1975, 252.

The committee therefore looked most favourably on those proposals which seemed to offer a means of eliminating the fear and lack of trust which hindered economic recovery. The nostrum which proved most popular was the one that had been suggested the previous year: that of allowing companies to reduce the denomination of their shares. To this was added the further proposal of allowing companies to reduce their total capital. It was believed that these measures would restore confidence in the joint-stock economy by making investment in it safer. The 1866 crisis had revealed that, despite the acts of 1855–6, shareholders could still find themselves facing *de facto* unlimited liability. A large nominal capital was the norm for companies formed prior to 1866, a symbol of wealth which would attract business, but companies found they did not need all of this capital, and the uncalled margin made shares unattractive to investors in the post-1866 climate. The financier and banker William Newmarch outlined the typical situation: 'A company which really required only 1,000,000*l.*, formed itself, with a great flourish of trumpets, two years ago, with a capital of 2,000,000*l.*, and now it finds its shares entirely unsaleable in the market.'[62] William Drake, a company solicitor, told the committee that 'very many hundreds of people have parted with their shares at a ruinous sacrifice rather than face that liability'.[63] The financial agent David Chadwick agreed: 'People will not, after the late crisis, invest their money in the purchase of shares, even in sound trading companies, having so large a margin of capital unpaid.'[64] Echoing Watkin in 1866, Newmarch argued that overhanging liability meant that large amounts of capital were kept in 'suspended animation', as money had to be set aside by shareholders in case of calls.[65] Chadwick made the same point that the prospect of calls kept capital in suspense, telling the committee that 'within the circle of our own acquaintances and our clients, which extends all over the country, many millions of money are held in reserve on that account'.[66]

Hitherto, hostility to low share denominations and fully paid up shares was based on fears that they would lead to an inferior class of shareholders, and provided insufficient safeguards to creditors. Both of these objections were challenged by the events of 1866.[67] This was essentially a rerun of the limited liability debates of the 1850s, when unlimited liability had been rejected

---

[62] *Select committee on the limited liability acts*, PP 1867 x. 64.

[63] Ibid. 40.

[64] Ibid. 54.

[65] Ibid. 33.

[66] Ibid. 55. These public testimonies re-enacted the private pressure the same men had already placed on the government for reform. Chadwick had been involved in a deputation to Northcote in November 1866 which presented the president of the Board of Trade with an outline bill to enable capital reduction; Newmarch and Drake were members of a deputation which approached the Board of Trade in March 1867, while the committee was sitting.

[67] For an overview of the change in attitudes see J. B. Jefferys, 'The denomination and character of shares, 1855–85', *EcHR* xvi (1946), 45–55.

because it no longer seemed to conduce to responsible shareholders; the same objection was now levelled against high denomination shares, for they made for a 'less stable, and less reliable' constituency.[68] They were 'purchased by more speculative and, generally speaking, less responsible parties, thus lessening the security of the creditor'.[69] When asked whether low denomination shares would lead to more ignorant shareholders, Thomas Webster, a lawyer, replied, 'I think not, I think the great flats are the rich men.'[70] It was now thought that a larger number of small shareholders would provide greater security for creditors. Newmarch argued that 'the smaller the shares be made the larger becomes the basis of the company. The creditor has much better security with 10 men holding 100*l.* each than with one man holding 1,000*l*'.[71] The uncalled portion of the share had traditionally been viewed as security for creditors, as it provided a reservoir of capital on which creditors could draw. But the actual benefits of this had come to be questioned. Drake argued that

> Practically, no advantage or security is gained from the uncalled capital upon shares of large nominal amount, say 50*l*. or 100*l*. In the great majority of cases additional security would be given to creditors, if a company so constituted were to divide its shares into smaller denominations, for by so doing it would, by making its shares more readily saleable, increase the number of its members, whilst the individual responsibility of each member would be decreased, and the ability of the whole body of members to meet calls, in case of a winding-up, would be unquestionably greater.[72]

Again echoing the debates of the 1850s, William Henderson, a city accountant, argued that a large nominal capital gave companies credit they did not deserve, and made people more likely to deal with them 'under the impression that the large amount of uncalled capital forms a valuable security' which was revealed as illusory when the company was wound up.[73] In short, instability derived not from limited liability, but from the fact that liability was not sufficiently limited. The committee's report therefore recommended that companies be allowed to reduce their capital, or the amount of their shares, or both, with the permission of company creditors, on notifying the Registrar and advertising the fact.[74]

The committee's other proposals indicated that the main concern was to

---

[68] Watkin, *Select committee on the limited liability acts*, PP 1867, 40.
[69] Drake, ibid.
[70] Ibid. 50.
[71] Ibid. 34.
[72] Ibid. 39.
[73] Ibid. 59.
[74] This is further than the Liberal government had been prepared to go in 1866. Milner Gibson's bill would have allowed companies to subdivide their shares, but not reduce their capital, for he did not see how creditors of 'reduced' companies could be given adequate security: *Hansard*, clxxxiv. 500 (18 June 1866).

restore the vitality of the joint-stock economy after the blow it had received the previous year, not to tackle the wider issues raised by this blow. Newmarch recommended steps to make shares fully transferable. He pointed out that when there was no money left to call on the share, the character of its holder was no longer a matter of concern to a company's creditors: 'the moment a share is paid up to the full amount, it ceases to be a matter of any consequence to the public whether it is held by Jones, Smith, or Robinson, or anybody else'. This meant that there was no reason why companies should not be able to issue certificates to bearer when the money was paid up, a step which would greatly aid the transferability of shares. 'It would certainly add very much to the eligibility of shares in Limited Liability Companies, as a security upon which to raise money', Newmarch argued, 'if certificates of those shares could be made transferable to bearer. They would then be an available security in a very ready form, and would have a great many advantages which do not attach to property which can only be transferred by a personal transfer.'[75] Goschen and Newmarch were in agreement that 'the present regulations for the transfer of shares impede very much the business between foreign countries and ourselves in shares which are issued in London'.[76] The rationale for the residual liability of shareholders after transfer of shares – to protect creditors – was perceived by some witnesses as no longer valid, as this liability offered no real protection. Drake believed that 'no mode has yet been found out by which a shareholder who has been off the register can be made a contributory'.[77] Edmund Church, a chief clerk in the Rolls' Court, thought that it was impossible for creditors to reach previous shareholders in the courts, stating, 'no call has ever been, so far as I know, made upon the past shareholders'.[78] Therefore there was no reason to prevent the fully free transfer of shares with no residual liability.

The committee took up these suggestions which formed part of the report. The committee also responded to the comments of several witnesses on the problem of 'wreckers': people who bought shares in a company purely to present a petition to wind it up, with a view to being paid off by the company directors. The mere presentation of such a petition could damage a company's reputation.[79] The committee recommended that winding-up petitions should have to be signed by one or more of the original shareholders, or by a shareholder of more than six months. The committee also recommended that companies be able to have some shares paid up in full, and others not fully paid up. The committee wanted to see the law amended to help companies out of the slump, and was patently not interested in curbing the powers of company boards. Just two recommendations were offered as a sop to those

---

75 *Select committee on the limited liability acts*, PP 1867, 34.
76 Ibid. 37.
77 Ibid. 43.
78 Ibid. 101.
79 Ibid. 45, 68.

who wanted greater controls on directors: that all companies be obliged to hold a general meeting of shareholders within four months of registration; and that en commandite companies be permitted, but not made compulsory. Directors were not to be forced to be more responsible, or to bear greater liability for their acts than passive investors in their companies. Other ideas aired by witnesses, such as preventing companies from dealing in their own shares, thus making rigging the market more difficult, standardising company constitutions to give less of a free hand to promoters to grant themselves exceptional powers, and forbidding the release of a prospectus until the memorandum and articles of association were registered, were not taken up.[80]

The significance of what was included in, and what was excluded from, the committee's report did not escape Walter Bagehot, writing in the *Economist*:

> The committee of the Commons on the law of limited liability, under great difficulties, did its work exceedingly well. The doctrine of limited liability was extremely unpopular; it had just been grossly abused; it had just palpably and plainly intensified a panic . . . The country was discouraged and suspicious . . . But the committee declined, even by a hair's breadth, to interfere or impair the principle. Many most plausible proposals were pressed upon them, but they said, 'Let people make what contracts they like; if they choose to take shares in bad companies, let them take such shares; if others choose to trust such companies, let them trust them.'

Bagehot realised that the joint-stock system had done more than weather the challenge posed to it by the events of 1866; it had emerged stronger and more entrenched than ever. The committee 'was asked to confine limited liability; it has extended and completed it'. The resulting legislation would remedy 'the evils caused by partial freedom by the wise concession of complete freedom'.[81] The Conservative government framed a bill closely based on the committee's report. As with the 1866 bill, the only opposition was met in the Lords. Lord Redesdale complained that the measure threatened the interests of creditors, and 'appeared to him to be framed in order to enable companies to do anything'.[82] But this time he was unable to block the bill, for the government was determined that it should pass.[83] The continuities with government legislation since the 1830s were obvious, as was demonstrated by a speech by the Conservative earl of Harrowby summing up the rationale behind the measure. He urged

---

[80] E. Curzon, T. Webster and G. Browne, ibid. 7, 48, 70, respectively.

[81] W. Bagehot, 'The new Joint Stock Companies Act', repr. in *Works of Walter Bagehot*, ix. 406, 410.

[82] *Hansard*, clxxxix. 1545 (15 Aug. 1867).

[83] The duke of Richmond, having replaced Northcote at the Board of Trade, told the Lords that 'the measure altogether was one which greatly interested the banking and commercial world, and which they were very desirous should pass in the course of the present Session': ibid.

the very great importance of giving something like stability to joint-stock companies. Great discredit had been thrown on these undertakings, and public confidence in them had been shaken by the disparity which had been found to exist between real and nominal capital; and it was highly desirable, if possible, by removing that disparity, to give solidity to property of this nature.[84]

A particular view of the joint-stock economy shaped the way in which the select committee was conducted, and the form the subsequent bill took. While out-of-doors there was, to say the least, considerable scepticism about the benefits of free access to limited liability, parliament did not share these doubts. Radical reform was at no stage contemplated, for the priorities of both the Liberal and the Conservative parties were to stabilise, restore confidence in, and support, joint-stock enterprise, rather than reform it in any significant way. Politicians had seen nothing in the events of 1866 to shake their adherence to the logic which had impelled them to institute general limited liability in 1855–6. The faults in the system were due to the misguided preference of the business community for large denomination shares with significant unpaid margins. Such shares appealed to speculative rather than solid shareholders, leading to the boom and bust of the mid-1860s, and subsequently preventing economic recovery. The result was the continued existence of a form of unlimited liability, which legislators aimed to discourage. They were equally concerned not to be pressured into resuming any kind of discretionary power over the grant of limited liability, which they had been so eager to shed in the 1850s. But despite the seeming chasm between parliamentary and public opinion, the policy of minimum interference was legitimised by the conviction, held both in and out of parliament, that ignorant and greedy shareholders were the authors of their own misfortunes. Despite popular disenchantment with the joint-stock system, reforms which would permit shareholders to be even more negligent of their own interests were easily discredited.

Criticisms of passive investment

The Victorian state's dogged perseverance with a 'deregulated' system of company law has often mystified historians who lament the abandonment of Gladstone's wise provision for compulsory audits and publication of balance sheets, and point to the superior regulatory systems prevalent on the continent which reduced the scope for fraud.[85] But such systems lessened the need for shareholders and creditors to supervise their own affairs and were therefore incompatible with dominant attitudes to ideal commercial behaviour. It was this, rather than a commitment to abstract notions of *laissez-faire*, that

84 Ibid. 1546; 30 & 31 Vict. c. 131.
85 Cottrell, *Industrial finance*, 54–6. See also Hunt, *Business corporation*, 138–9.

determined the state's limited response to 1866.[86] Thus although several witnesses before the 1867 select committee proposed substantial amendments to strengthen the regulatory powers of the Joint-Stock Companies Registrar and curb the powers and increase the liabilities of directors, these were all unpopular with the dominant faction on the committee.

Witnesses expressed less enthusiasm for extending shareholders' access to company information, largely on the grounds that they did not make use of the information they already had. Edward Curzon, the Registrar, perhaps trying to justify one of the functions of his office, claimed that members of the public could be found at the Registry searching through company records 'all day long . . . for some information or other'.[87] But he was in a minority, for several other witnesses denied that investors were so careful. Drake had 'seen shareholders flock in by hundreds and sign a deed, when they have never even looked at it'.[88] Webster said that 'people come in and sign Articles of Association like sheep, without ever reading them'.[89] Chadwick concurred, estimating that 'not one per cent. of the persons who come into limited liability companies read first the Articles of Association'.[90] But witnesses reached different conclusions as to the implications of this behaviour. Newmarch stated that 'If a person is foolish enough to take shares in a concern about which he knows nothing, and about the directors of which he knows nothing, he must take the consequences.'[91] But others thought differently: though accepting that shareholders were largely ignorant, they refused to condemn them on this score, and thought that they needed protection by the law. The barrister and director George Browne admitted that substantial and experienced capitalists needed no protection, but remarked that the purpose of making limited liability legislation general was to draw in the capital of small capitalists, 'who are not so capable of taking care of themselves, and certainly not so capable of understanding long legal documents'.[92] Lord Romilly, the Liberal Master of the Rolls, received many letters from people injured by joint-stock companies, and while he attributed their plight to 'folly', he thought it 'the duty of the Government and of legislation . . . to protect people who are ignorant and foolish'.[93]

---

[86] George Robb attributes the state's inadequate response to fraud to 'the tenets of *laissez-faire*': *White-collar crime in modern England: financial fraud and business morality, 1845–1929*, Cambridge 1992, 189. Stewart Jones and Max Aiken go further still, attempting to explain the development of company law in the nineteenth century with reference to A. V. Dicey's theories of *laissez-faire* and collectivism: 'British companies legislation and social and political evolution during the nineteenth century', *British Accounting Review* xxvii (1995), 61–82.

[87] *Select committee on the limited liability acts*, PP 1867, 14.

[88] Ibid. 45.

[89] Ibid. 49.

[90] Ibid. 57.

[91] Ibid. 68.

[92] Ibid. 71.

[93] Ibid. 90.

To this end, the financier and insurer Swinton Boult wanted to make incorporation dependent on a preliminary inquiry into the feasibility of the scheme proposed. The certificate of registration misled investors into thinking that the company so registered carried with it the approval of the state, so he argued that only legitimate enterprises should be permitted to register.

> My impression is, that a great many objects for which companies are formed now, are not at all fit objects for companies to undertake, and would not be undertaken with a *bona fide* intention, and that those are the very companies which lead unsuspecting people, and people of small means, and ignorant people, into trouble, and that so long as the law exists in its present state, some means should be found to give those people a protection which they are utterly unable to find for themselves.[94]

But the committee was not interested in introducing such safeguards. Proposals to strengthen the role of the Joint-Stock Companies Registrar, making the office more than a 'mere clerkship' by giving him the power to check companies' articles of association for serious defects and to veto such articles, met with hostile questioning.[95] If implemented, such power would be a step towards the reintroduction of the element of state discretion in the grant of corporate privileges, which might eventually end automatic incorporation, a prospect which was anathema to Lowe, who took great pride in his part in the legislative achievement of 1856.[96] Chadwick's proposals along these lines were seized upon by Lowe, who asked

> Would it not be liable to this objection, that people would put trust in the Registrar more than they should do, and throw all the blame upon him when they found they were mistaken? . . . Is it not the best to do all we can to inculcate in people that they had better trust to themselves than to others in these matters?[97]

George Browne wanted to see greatly increased powers for the Registrar, but Lowe told him that such steps would 'put to sleep all private vigilance'.[98] Curzon did not think it proper for the Registrar to inquire into the 'status' of those signing the memorandum of association, nor did he think that the articles of association should be examined and approved by the Registrar before they took effect, as was the case with benefit societies. But he did think it desirable for the Registrar to compare the memorandum with the prospectus to check for inconsistencies before granting a certificate of registration. Any

---

94 Ibid. 106.
95 Ibid. 25.
96 Winter, *Robert Lowe*, 100.
97 *Select committee on the limited liability acts*, PP 1867, 57.
98 Ibid. 80.

discrepancies would be sufficient reason for the Registrar to refuse the application. This proposal was seized on by Goschen, who asked, 'Would you hold that, if something slipped your attention, the public might afterwards bring a complaint against the Registration Office for having been misled by its having received the certificate?'[99]

Similarly, proposals to restrict the freedom of action of directors or to extend their liability, were received with scorn. Identifying the unsafe levels of debt run up by many companies as an important cause of the recent crisis, the lawyer Charles Wordsworth proposed that companies' borrowing powers be limited. Lowe was sceptical: 'If the Government attempts to limit that which it really cannot limit, does it not deceive people into supposing that it will be limited?'[100] As a further protection to creditors and shareholders, Wordsworth proposed that companies should be obliged to have at least 20 per cent of shares paid up. Forster objected, asking, 'do you not imagine that there would be a danger that the creditors would feel themselves acquitted from the necessity of themselves examining into the position of the people to whom they lend their money, in consequence of the law interfering to protect them?'[101] Wordsworth wanted to make directors and managers more responsible for their actions: 'they have in the management of these concerns an opportunity of plunging the shareholders into great confusion and great expense . . . and the directors themselves do not suffer in any greater proportion than the other members of the company'.[102] But Goschen thought Wordsworth's suggestion that directors be made personally liable for acting *ultra vires* was impracticable and would lead to endless disputes in Equity between shareholders and directors. The MP asked Wordsworth, 'cannot you conceive that there are gradations of operations which would make it impossible to say where one object began and where another left off?'[103] Several other witnesses echoed Wordsworth's sentiments. Webster thought that company managers should be liable to an unlimited extent.[104] Church thought that promoters should be compelled to subscribe for, and pay a deposit on, a substantial number of shares, to ensure that those behind a company were men of some substance, and to bring the interests of directors and shareholders closer together.[105] Romilly thought that all managers of joint-stock companies should be made more responsible, with double or treble liability rather than the same liability as their shareholders. But all of these proposals were opposed by the dominant voices on the committee. Forster, for example, told Romilly that his proposals were 'an interference

99   Ibid. 12.
100 Ibid. 26.
101 Ibid. 28.
102 Ibid. 31.
103 Ibid. 28.
104 Ibid. 49.
105 Ibid. 97.

with the freedom of trade', and accused him of wanting to 'interfere with the liberty and freedom of men of business making arrangements with one another'.[106] Lowe joined in, asking Romilly, 'Do you not think that, in devising these protections for foolish people, you are making fetters for wise ones?'[107]

The committee's unequivocal rejection of these reforms was accepted because their assumptions as to the effects of such reforms on the behaviour of shareholders resonated with a dominant strand of opinion in Victorian society. If 'foolish people' were exploited, this was ultimately their own fault. In the wake of Overend Gurney's fall, *The Times* asked,

> who are really at the bottom of this huge mischief? The true authors are they who are bringing down their own houses over their heads – the public themselves. Such is the universal rivalry, and such the habit of expenditure all about us, that people will not be contented with the tedious three per cent . . . their souls crave for the more solid and savoury profits of the trader. But to trade is to lose caste, and, for the means of living, to lose life itself. So the universal wish is, with a little cleverness and a happy audacity, to reap the rich harvest of trade without undergoing the primeval sweat of the brow.

In 1866 they had proved, once again, to be an 'ignorant multitude . . . wilfully blind' to the realities of their investments.[108]

Needless to say, Overend Gurney shareholders had a somewhat different view. They thought that their very inactivity proved their innocence. The articles of association of the new company specified that no general meeting was to be held for nine and a half months, and the company failed before this time was up:

> During the entire period of business, we never, as a body, did anything or said anything. We never received a dividend, whether out of profits or out of capital; we never had an opportunity of voting for, or against, any measure whatever, good, bad, or indifferent; we never elected a director, competent or incompetent, honest or dishonest, wise or unwise.[109]

They were misled by the company prospectus, and subsequently had no opportunity to realise their mistake until it was too late.[110] But their case, and the cases of others like them, could be undermined by exploring their motives for investing in joint-stock companies. In the short stories which

---

106 Ibid. 91.
107 Ibid. 94.
108 *The Times*, 14 May 1866.
109 Anon. ['1915'], *Overend, Gurney, and Co., or the saddle on the right horse*, London 1866, 3.
110 Some commentators denied that there had been concealment: Anon. ['A Barrister'], *Overend, Gurney, and Co., (Limited): a plain statement of the case*, London 1867, 4, 10.

proliferated in *All the Year Round* and other magazines, the decision to speculate usually stemmed from two basic motives: an unwarranted dissatisfaction
with one's financial lot, and the conviction, based upon the false belief that
everyone else was speculating, that the stock market presented a route to easy
wealth. Neither motive was in the least praiseworthy; neither earned the
victims any sympathy when they were ruined. Because of the overwhelming
need to 'keep up an appearance', Mr X, the hero/victim of 'The Stock
Exchange', spends more than he can afford on expensive servants, carriages,
luxurious dinners and an Eton education for his sons. Eventually, he is forced
to reveal to his wife the extent of his difficulties, hoping she will consent to a
retrenchment. But, just as Mrs Nickleby bullied her husband onto the stock
market thirty-two years ago, so Mrs X tells her spouse that he can make as
much money as he likes simply 'by going into the City'.[111] Foolishly, he
listens to her, and loses everything. In another tale, an officer returns from
India to Britain with a £2,000 a-year income. Despite his affluence, he
decides to supplement his income by becoming a director: 'Like the famous
Colonel Newcome, I believed myself to be a thorough man of business – by
intuition, as it were – and that I had only to "go to the City" every day, sit at a
board, and adopt the jargon of mercantile men, in order to make money.'[112]
His company fails, and he ends up fleeing to France for two or three years
until the scandal blows over.

These stories conveyed the idea that money-hungry shareholders were as
much to blame as directors for the unsoundness of the companies of the
mid-1860s. If directors declared a small dividend, 'the wrath of the shareholders' fell upon them, with the result that cautious measures were usually overruled at board meetings 'purely from fear of what the shareholders would say
if a large dividend was not forthcoming at the end of the half year'. Thus
companies were 'led into' dubious transactions which led to ruin.[113] So
demanding were shareholders that 'when they no longer see the scheme in
which they have taken shares, quoted at a premium – a premium which their
own common sense should tell them must be more or less, a sham – they at
once rush to sell their shares, and thus themselves depreciate their own property'.[114]

Shareholders tried to win public sympathy by drawing attention to the
widows, orphans and spinsters who filled the columns of shareholder registers: these were the chief victims of company failures.[115] Indeed, blameless
shareholder victims began to feature in visual representations of the
joint-stock economy, such as 'Gone to pieces' (*see* plate 16), published in

---

[111] [Anon.], 'The Stock Exchange', 614.
[112] [M. L. Meason], 'Insurance and assurance', AYR xiii (1865), 437–42 at p. 438.
[113] Idem, 'Twenty per cent', 480–1.
[114] Idem, 'Promoters of companies', AYR xi (1864), 110–15 at p. 115.
[115] Anon. ['1915'], *Overend, Gurney, and Co*, 4.

GONE TO PIECES!

Plate 16. 'Gone to pieces'.
Source: *Will-o'-the-Wisp* i (6 Feb. 1869), 253–4.
By permission of the British Library (shelfmark PP5272.c)

1869.[116] Here, limited liability, an unstable craft, has foundered on the rock of panic, and its passengers are washed up, dead, clutching their worthless shares. Yet the accompanying text tempered the tone of sympathy conveyed by the illustration, with the journal aiming to warn 'silly people caught by promises of large percentages from rushing blindly into speculations of which they know nothing'.[117] Distinctions were beginning to be drawn between speculative shareholders who deserved little pity and steady shareholders who looked upon their shares as permanent investments and whose losses were to be regretted. Yet compassion for the latter was curtailed by a conviction that they 'have no more right to speculate than a child has to play with razors'.[118] In any case, as with previous crises, it was the greedy speculator who was taken as representative of the average shareholder. A *Fun* cartoon, 'The road to ruin' (*see* plate 17), published while the Joint-Stock Companies Bill was progressing through the Commons, shows the train of speculation being driven into the ether by Peto. This is more than a criticism of railway schemes. The public in the second carriage of the train are reaching up to catch the bubbles being blown by directors, which include banks, as well as mining, finance and hotel companies. We can see money invested with a bank director falling straight into a bag being held by his colleague, while banknotes flutter in the wind. The bubble imagery employed here displays a remarkable similarity to that of the cartoons of forty years previously on the schemes of 1824–5, indicating the continued purchase of traditional critiques of the joint-stock economy on the Victorian mind.[119]

Shareholders combined naked greed with extreme credulousness. They looked to dividends, but did not make any greater effort to judge the soundness of their investments: provided dividends were high, they probed no further. As a result, shareholders became the milch cows of promoters, solicitors and accountants: 'if shareholders were wise enough to trust their own money to their own management, where would then these professions be?'.[120] Criticisms of 'too-confiding' and 'careless' investors in unsound companies were common.[121] *Punch* thought the 'flats' who fell victim to fraud 'know nothing about business, and any day will walk into a bubble broker's parlour – like the fly into the spider's – if they fancy there is anything which they may gain by going there'.[122]

---

[116] The Albert Assurance Company scandal of 1869 produced cartoons sympathetic to the plight of shareholders and policy holders: *Judy* v (8 Sept. 1869), 195; *Fun* n.s. x (11 Sept. 1869), 7.

[117] *Will-o'-the-Wisp* i (6 Feb. 1869), 252.

[118] [M. L. Meason], 'How the bank was wound up', AYR xiii (1865), 276–82 at p. 278.

[119] For the earlier cartoons see chapter 3 above.

[120] [Meason], 'Bank of Patagonia', 490.

[121] H. Fawcett, 'To what extent is England prosperous?', *Fortnightly Review* xv (1871), 40–52 at p. 45; *Lloyd's Weekly Newspaper*, 30 June 1867.

[122] *Punch* liii (16 Nov. 1867), 204.

THE ROAD TO RUIN.

Plate 17. 'The road to ruin'.
Source: *Fun* n.s. v (6 July 1867), 178–9.

This kind of speculation was driven by a simple greed for gain, and thus its victims could only meet with limited sympathy. Shortly after a Lords decision had confirmed that the Overend Gurney shareholders could not evade their liability by claiming that they were misled by the company's directors, *Tomahawk* published an allegory warning against speculation.[123] Various characters are described making their way to the Temple of Wealth. Work is one path leading there, but this is a difficult route. There is another 'that led straight to the Temple of Wealth smooth as calm water, but as treacherous as the sea, and eternal night dwelt along this highway. I knew that this road was called "Speculation," and was one mass of pitfalls'. We read of one man's attempt along this passage. He makes good progress, but he sees a mass of jewels and gold, and pauses to pick it up. The accompanying illustration 'A sermon for the city!' (*see* plate 18), shows what happens. He steps on a rock marked 'limited liability', and falls 'headlong into the abyss – among flames and utter ruin! . . . he went on falling and falling through the most dreadful horrors until he reached his grave! And when he reached his grave – still he fell!'[124]

Significantly, this cartoon was closely based on an earlier work by George Cruikshank preaching the evils of crime, 'the demon tempter', which lured men to madness and ruin.[125] *Tomahawk* was likening speculation in limited companies to other forms of crime, which could admit only of a personal solution: the temptation would always be present, and it was up to the individual to resist. In such a diagnosis, legislative reforms had little role to play. Similar conclusions had also been drawn after the crisis of 1857: the 'hasting to become rich, which despises industry and scorns application' was the root of the problem, and could not be cured by legislative enactments. 'The evil lies in our moral nature; so does the remedy.'[126] Behaviour needed to be reformed rather than the law, and contemporaries hoped that economic crises would bring about this reform. While it was less usual to see crashes as 'sublime example[s] of special providence' as was common when evangelicalism was at its height, commentators tended to look to the beneficial effects they would bring.[127] On 13 May 1866, when the shock of 'Black Friday' was still fresh, the *News of the World* was convinced that the main effect would be 'to purify the atmosphere of City life, and make us breathe more freely for years to come'.[128] Meason thought the crash merely the first stage of a process which would culminate in 'a whirlwind in the mercantile atmosphere' which would 'purify the air' and lead to sounder business practices.[129] On a practical level,

---

123 For comment on the Lords' decision see *The Times*, 16 Aug. 1867.
124 *Tomahawk* i (31 Aug. 1867), 180–3.
125 'The folly of crime', *George Cruikshank's Table-Book* i (Mar. 1845), facing p. 45.
126 W. R. Callender, *The commercial crisis of 1857: its causes and results*, London 1858, 36.
127 Hilton, *Age of atonement*, 131.
128 *News of the World*, 13 May 1866, 4.
129 [Meason], 'Finance, frauds, and failures', 394.

A   SERMON   FOR   THE   CITY !

Plate 18. 'A sermon for the City!'.
Source: *Tomahawk* i (31 Aug. 1867), 181.

this process of purification entailed shareholders mending their ways and realising the folly of blind greed. *Fraser's Magazine* hoped that after 1866 investors would not support any limited company in which there were large amounts unpaid on shares, in which the articles of association were not distributed with the prospectus or in which the status and remuneration of the promoters was not made clear. It was also up to shareholders to insist that a company's published accounts contained sufficient information for them to judge of its wellbeing. Legislative interference would compromise the principle of 'the supreme control of shareholders over their own affairs'.[130]

A moral case against speculation, combined with a belief in shareholder responsibility, also provided the rationale behind what has been regarded as the marked reluctance of mid and late Victorian society to expose fraudulent directors to the rigours of criminal law.[131] The Royal British Bank fraud of 1856 had prompted the Fraudulent Trustees Act, designed to clarify the law of liability for fraud, and to facilitate prosecutions.[132] The act set out behaviour by directors and managers now deemed illegal, such as taking the money of the company for their own use, falsifying the company's books or circulating accounts which they knew to be false. However, while the maximum penalty fixed was three years penal servitude, the terms of the act made it clear that defendants could only be found guilty if intent to defraud could be proven, which rendered it far less efficient as a regulatory tool against commercial malfeasance than some had hoped.[133] Nevertheless, in 1869 pressure was mounting on Gladstone's government to finance the prosecution of the Overend Gurney directors, as Palmerston's government had done in the case of the Royal British Bank. But the home secretary, H. A. Bruce, told the Commons that he viewed the British Bank case 'not so much as a precedent to be followed as an example to be avoided'.[134] The prosecution had cost the state £20,000, and many did not see why taxpayers should subsidise 'vindictive prosecution[s]' urged by disappointed speculators.[135] The prime minister was eloquent on the subject, claiming that if the state were to step in to seek redress on the shareholders' behalf, there would be terrible effects

> on the future prudence and self-restraint of a generation too greedy of money and too ready to adopt one of the most doubtful means of making money – that of placing their investments in concerns of which they know nothing at

---

[130] Anon., 'The financial pressure and ten per cent', FM lxxiv (1866), 229–42 at pp. 232–4.

[131] Johnson 'Civilizing mammon'.

[132] 20 & 21 Vict. c. 54.

[133] The terms of the act were repeated practically unchanged in the Larceny Act of 1861: 24 & 25 Vict. c. 96.

[134] *Hansard*, cxcvii. 822 (30 June 1869).

[135] Richard Fothergill, ibid. cxcvii. 977 (1 July 1869).

all, with the view of making large and easy gains, of reaping the fruits of industry without its toil.[136]

The structure of the law was determined not by a belief in the benefits of speculation, but by a conviction of its immorality. Attempts by the state to regulate the joint-stock economy were worse than useless for they would merely encourage even more blind speculation. The only effective regulation that could be exerted was by the shareholders themselves, but only bitter experience could induce them to do this. Whether 1866 would have this effect, only the shareholders could decide: it was not a question for the state.

This crisis of 1866 posed a severe challenge to the framework of company law erected between 1855 and 1862. The principle of limited liability was thrust back onto centre stage: some thought it had encouraged the speculation which had led to the crisis; many believed that it should not be so freely available to businessmen and that limited companies should be more rigorously policed. Yet the principle never lost its support within parliament, which believed that the troubles were a result of the fact that earlier legislation had not gone far enough down the road of limited liability. By allowing companies to reduce their capitals and share denominations, legislators would complete the job begun in 1855. This was the totality of their ambition: they did not think it their role to regulate how the joint-stock economy operated beyond this. While popular and parliamentary views thus seemed to be dichotomous, there was an increasingly pervasive sense of the inevitability of the limited company which engendered more than a degree of fatalism. In 1872 Carlyle thought that limited liability was completely entrenched, and that the culture of what he called 'promoterism' was here to stay, gloomily predicting in his last work that it 'would cost any Ministry its life in a day' to attempt to repeal the limited liability laws.[137] Later, Spencer was to doubt the ability, or willingness, of parliament even to curb the power of directors:

> Three out of four of our legislators have seats on one or other board of directors: some of them seats on many boards. The reforms made by them in their capacity of legislators would restrict their powers in their capacity of directors. Any one who expects that they will thus sacrifice themselves takes a view of human nature altogether at variance with experience.[138]

By the late 1860s joint-stock companies had permeated the Victorian consciousness. Metaphors involving joint-stock companies were increasingly deployed to help make sense of political issues. For example, in 1866 a *Times*

---

136 Ibid. cxcvii. 992. The prosecution, privately financed, eventually went ahead, but the directors were acquitted.
137 T. Carlyle, *Last words of Thomas Carlyle – on trades-unions, promoterism and the signs of the times*, Edinburgh 1882, 22.
138 H. Spencer, 'The reform of company-law', in his *Facts and comments*, London 1902, 164–71 at p. 171.

leader on parliamentary reform likened the voting public to a body of share-holders, and wondered whether the new voters would be willing to pay off the huge national debt run up before they had a say in politics: 'We are changing the whole constituency – that is, the body politic. The firm is changing its members, and its identity may be questioned. Will all the burdens and obliga-tions of the old shareholders pass to the new?'[139] While the frequent spoofs of company prospectuses and other pastiches in the satirical magazines indi-cated contempt for the joint-stock system, they also suggest the arrival of joint-stock companies as fixtures of the nineteenth-century imagination, part of the Victorian mental furniture.

Company regulation was also successfully resisted because of the continued vitality of hostile conceptions of speculation and speculators. While David C. Itzkowitz admits that outbursts against speculation continued through Victoria's reign, he argues that such rhetoric 'seems to have carried less and less practical force as the century progressed'.[140] But these views were much more than merely a faint echo of the beliefs of an earlier age. In fact, a cynical view of the motives of shareholders and of the deleterious consequences of speculation continued to shape company law and government responses to corporate crime long into the second half of the century. This was perhaps the chief factor which legitimised the govern-ment's rejection of regulatory innovations in 1866–7. There may have been an instinctive desire in the aftermath of 'Black Friday' to tighten up the law to try to prevent similar calamities in the future, but these were easy to resist when everyone agreed that greedy speculators had precipitated the crisis. The question of company law reform was thus reduced to one of moral reform, and the legislation of 1855–62 stood intact.

[139] *The Times*, 19 Apr. 1866.
[140] Itzkowitz, 'Fair enterprise', 124.

Epilogue

William G. Roy has reminded us that 'there is no such thing as a "free" economy operating independent of the state. All economic systems involve specific rights, entitlements, and responsibilities enforced by some institutional mechanism embodied in political institutions.'[1] Today, companies in market economies across the globe are misleadingly conceived of as purely economic beings whose 'natural' state is one free of all political interference. For both left and right, the process of politics consists of determining the extent to which these free entities should be subjected to government regulation. This book has attempted to call into question such conceptualisations by drawing attention to the way in which the form of 'free market' capitalism existing today did not emerge organically and inevitably, but was the product of sustained government policy over a long period of time. Historians have tended to present the emergence of the joint-stock company in nineteenth-century Britain as a story of the removal of restrictions: companies emerged naturally once artificial obstacles preventing their formation were removed. This account instead argues that the joint-stock economy only emerged once a legal framework regulating the formation, existence and winding-up of companies, and rendering joint-stock property secure, was developed. It is an irony that the emergence of the limited company as the dominant, and in the twentieth century, practically the sole, form of business organisation, was an unintentional result of this policy.

The book has detailed three distinct phases of government regulation of joint-stock enterprise. The first phase, lasting until 1844, was posited on the need for the state to police company formation by withholding corporate privileges from all schemes bar those that could prove their public utility to parliament or the crown. This method of regulation became discredited by the early 1840s, not because joint-stock entrepreneurs had successfully made a case for extending access to corporate privileges, but because the system left too many firms outside the law where they could prey on the public with impunity, thus causing much economic instability. The solution reached was to bring all companies of more than twenty-five partners within the law by automatically incorporating them, replacing the government's traditional regulatory role with a system of regulation by public opinion. The government's role shrank to that of securing publicity of information about companies, allowing the public to make informed decisions as creditors, consumers

---

[1] Roy, *Socializing capital*, 285–6.

and investors. But access to limited liability continued to be restricted, partly because it was still closely associated with fraud and instability, and partly in an attempt to ensure that shareholders retained every incentive to perform their regulatory role.

This solution failed to stabilise the joint-stock system. The experience of the commercial crisis of 1847, and a series of insurance frauds, undermined claims that unlimited liability guarded against unsoundness. Creditors were using the unlimited liability of shareholders as an excuse to lend recklessly to unlimited companies. Shareholders were not using the information provided them by law to protect themselves; they regarded provisional registration as a guarantee of the *bona fide* of a concern; they accepted balance sheets as gospel, without realising that these were easily manipulated. The machinery established by the act had failed to make shareholders or creditors more vigilant or cautious, so fraud and mismanagement continued to plague the joint-stock economy.

Thus the system devised in 1844 was replaced in 1855–6 by general access to limited liability, and the removal of compulsory accounting and audit provisions. This was not, as is often assumed, the result of the development of 'modern' attitudes to companies and speculation. Many historians in the 1930s, and some more recently, presented the state's abandonment of a regulatory role as evidence that companies had finally managed to shake off the 'prejudices' and 'misconceptions' that had dogged their earlier existence. Others portray the legislation as the result of new, more recognisably 'modern', attitudes to growth and passive investment. Yet the state's aims in these years were broadly consistent with earlier policy: to stabilise what was still seen as an unstable sector of the economy, and to encourage shareholders to behave responsibly. Earlier efforts to make shareholders and creditors bear the regulatory burden had failed, but the changes of 1855–6 represented another attempt to make this work. With a system of limited liability, creditors would have to look to the assets of the company, not of the shareholders, for repayment. This, it was believed, would cut off the supply of unsound credit to bubble companies. Shareholders, though now enjoying limited liability, could no longer rely upon government provisions for their safety: they would have to negotiate with directors to secure the degree of access to information they required, and rely on their own efforts to police management. By placing the onus back on shareholders and creditors, the state was able to relieve itself altogether of responsibility for regulation. The commercial crisis of 1866 did nothing to shake confidence in these ideas which, in barely modified form, continued to form the basis of the state's policy through the rest of the century.

In the later years of the nineteenth century, companies and the speculation that sustained them both continued to enjoy at best a mixed profile. The left, which earlier in the century had seen the joint-stock principle as a force for the emancipation of the working classes, now held the rise of the company responsible for the 'degradation and wretchedness' of the lives of

working men and women.[2] The extent of dubious pre-allotment share dealings and the ease with which official quotations were granted on the Stock
Exchange led to a brace of parliamentary investigations into Stock Exchange
practice in the 1870s, either side of another on the joint-stock companies
acts.[3] Although these did not result in legislative action, the steady stream of
criticism of companies and speculation which had characterised the early
years of the century did not abate. In 1876 *Blackwood's* condemned 'the
extraordinary increase in the sheer unadulterated gambling which now goes
on in the Stock Exchange'.[4] For the late nineteenth-century novelist George
Gissing, speculation was 'the great legalised game of hazard', an 'odious vice'
which upset quiet, honest industry. It was an integral part of the whirlpool
which made up 'civilised' London life.[5] Others were a little more flippant, but
still betrayed the hold of traditional ideas: in Oscar Wilde's *The picture of
Dorian Gray*, the artist Basil Hallward remarks that with an evening coat and
a white tie, 'anybody, even a stock-broker, can gain a reputation for being
civilized'.[6] Lower down the social scale, opinion was little different: the Stock
Exchange was dubbed 'the thieves' kitchen' by London cabdrivers.[7] Investors
did not escape criticism. W. P. Frith's series of five paintings, 'The race for
wealth', dating from 1877, is a traditional representation of the course of a
speculation: a financier promotes a mining scheme which promises enormous
wealth, for a while he lives in high society, but then the inevitable crash
comes, and with it, the ruin of his duped investors, who include a clergyman
and his wife and daughters, a widow and her young son and a country
gentleman.[8] The financier is imprisoned, but the investors are punished with
the loss of their fortunes. The symmetry of the fates of the 'spider' and the
'flies' was intentional. In Frith's view, 'both those who, in their eagerness to
become rich, rush into rash speculation, and the man who cheats them,
should all be punished'.[9]

But how do we reconcile the continued expression of such views with the
realities of the expansion of joint-stock enterprise and the burgeoning market
for company shares? The 'Great Depression' beginning in the 1870s, and the
spectacular failure of the unlimited City of Glasgow Bank in 1878, created a

---

[2] *Freedom* iii (1889), 1.

[3] *Select committee on loans to foreign states*, PP 1875 xi; *Select committee on the companies
acts, 1862 and 1867*, PP 1877 viii; *Royal Commission on the Stock Exchange*, PP 1878 xix. See
also Robb, *White-collar crime*, 82–4.

[4] [A. I. Shand], 'Speculative investments', BEM cxx (Sept. 1876), 293–316 at p. 311. For
more tolerant views of the Stock Exchange see [R. G. C. Mowbray], 'Stock-jobbing and the
Stock Exchange', BEM cxxvi (Aug. 1879), 181–206.

[5] G. Gissing, *The whirlpool*, London 1997, 8, 164.

[6] O. Wilde, *The picture of Dorian Gray*, London 2000.

[7] E. V. Morgan and W. A. Thomas, *The Stock Exchange: its history and functions*, London
1969, 239.

[8] Three of the pictures are reproduced in J. Taylor, 'Greed: the way they lived then', BBC
History Magazine ii (Dec. 2001), 40–2.

[9] W. P. Frith, *My autobiography*, 2nd edn, London 1887, ii. 144.

Table 11
Nominal value of securities quoted on the Stock Exchange, 1853–83 (£)

Type of security	1 Jan. 1853	1 Jan. 1863	1 Jan. 1873	1 Jan. 1883
Government stock	923,300,000	1,073,300,000	1,345,400,000	1,896,700,000
% of whole	(76%)	(67%)	(59%)	(52%)
Company shares	291,800,000	531,100,000	924,600,000	1,744,700,000
% of whole	(24%)	(33%)	(41%)	(48%)
Total	1,215,100,000 (100%)	1,604,400,000 (100%)	2,270,000,000 (100%)	3,641,400,000 (100%)

Source: Adapted from Morgan and Thomas, *The Stock Exchange*, 282.

climate in which the minimisation of risk provided by limited liability seemed ever more attractive.[10] Consequently, the 1880s saw an upsurge in the numbers of companies registering with limited liability.[11] While many of these were 'private' companies, small concerns which availed themselves of corporate privileges but did not offer shares to the public, the opportunities to invest grew and whatever views may have been expressed, clearly large numbers were willing to invest in company securities.[12] One estimate of 1906 put the number of individuals holding marketable securities at 250,000.[13] Whereas the value of government stock traded on the Stock Exchange doubled between 1853 and 1883, the value of company shares increased six-fold in the same period, growing from less than a quarter of all the securities traded to almost one half (*see* table 11).

Itzkowitz argues that such levels of investment were made possible because speculation had been made respectable by a process of disassociation with gambling. When the arrival of 'bucket shops', establishments run by brokers outside the Stock Exchange, challenged this arrangement late in the nineteenth century, they were rigorously excluded from definitions of respectable speculation.[14] But this explanation underestimates the endurance of harsh feeling towards mainstream speculative activity through these years. Were the Victorians merely guilty of hypocrisy? Did they want to enjoy the economic benefits of the corporate economy, whilst retaining a spurious

[10] Ireland, 'Limited liability company', 248–9.
[11] For a worried contemporary reaction to the trend see [W. R. Lawson], 'A black year for investors', BEM cxxxvii (Feb. 1885), 269–84.
[12] For more on the increase in registrations, and the emergence of the private company see Ireland, 'Limited liability company', 245–9.
[13] *Financial Review of Reviews* (Feb. 1906).
[14] Itzkowitz, 'Fair enterprise'.

sense of moral superiority by every now and then condemning speculation and love of Mammon? The picture was in fact slightly more complex than this. Rather than the line being drawn between 'fair enterprise' on one hand and gambling and bucket shops on the other, the boundary late Victorians increasingly drew was between informed and uninformed speculation. Speculators who lost because they had not taken the trouble to research their investments were no better than casino fodder; they deserved to lose, for they turned investment into a game of chance. Speculation based on more than hunches or tips, however, had acquired a respectable status. This was largely a question of class: the respectable investor was conceptualised as a wealthy man of business, who moved in the same social and business circles as the directors he elected. As Josephine Maltby has pointed out, his access to information was superior to that of smaller investors. His channels of information were primarily informal, deriving from his personal links to directors; he did not need to rely solely on formal structures such as annual general meetings or the publication of accounts. He minimised risk by exploiting his business and personal networks to the full.[15] Allied to the class aspect was a geographical one: speculators who were based in London had much better access to information or gossip which they could turn to their advantage when making business decisions. Provincial investors would not be privy to this, and would thus be forced to make decisions based on insufficient knowledge. In the world of joint-stock finance, where appearances could so often be deceptive, these were important points. Facts which were common knowledge to City 'insiders' were unknown outside of these circles: one correspondent remarked that 'no Life Assurance secret will keep for twenty-four hours in London, and therefore within the charmed circle the condition of every office is approximately known and talked about, even though no accounts be published'.[16] Thus, the 'gentleman capitalists' of the metropolis could speculate with complete respectability, for their privileged position divorced their acts from the hapless speculations of retired colonels and country parsons. Gladstone would not have thought he was being inconsistent when he spoke out against the 'greed' of those who speculated 'in concerns of which they know nothing at all', while himself investing heavily in a number of risky prospects, ranging from Egyptian bonds to shares in the Metropolitan and District Railway.[17] The former yielded him a profit, partly because of his own political actions, the latter lost him £25,000. But, of course, his investments, no matter how hazardous, would be informed by knowledge and mature reflection rather than the manias which steered the masses to catastrophe.

These distinctions were marked in late nineteenth-century fiction. Bracebridge Hemyng's collection of short stories, *The stockbroker's wife and*

15 J. Maltby, 'UK joint stock companies legislation, 1844–1900: accounting publicity and "mercantile caution" ', *Accounting History* iii (1998), 9–32.
16 Anon., 'The Albert Life Assurance Company', *WR* xcii (Oct. 1869), 532–50 at p. 538.
17 *Hansard*, 3rd ser. cxcvii. 992 (1 July 1869); R. Jenkins, *Gladstone*, London 1996, 507.

other sensational tales of the Stock Exchange, contains the familiar elements of the genre: fraudulent promotions, guinea-pig directors and spectacular failures. Several stories detail how well-connected gentlemen stray into speculation. But unlike the stories of Evans and Meason a generation earlier, no moral opprobrium is attached to these acts. The men know what they are doing, and more often than not they succeed. Thus, in *The hypochondriac; or, a cure for the blues*, Sir William Benson is thrown into a decline after his niece marries a poor curate. But he is saved by Mr St Albans Smith, a stockbroker who introduces him to speculation. Benson is a changed man, spending all his time in the office, and becomes an expert speculator. The drama of the story centres on his dealings of Russian stock, which he is 'bearing'. The suspenseful way in which the speculation is presented encourages the reader to empathise with Benson as he watches the latest prices come through on the tape.

As he sat in his chair he read, 'Russian 89, 88, 87.'
St Albans Smith stood by his chair.
'Have you sold much?' He asked.
'100,000,' replied the old baronet, tremblingly.
'That is a heavy account.'
Tick, tick!
87, ½, 6.
There was a pause. . . .
Again the price of Russians dropped. Everybody seemed to be selling.
Tick, tick.
86, 85, 84.
Sir William could hear his heart beat.
Tick, tick.
Russians 83, 82, 81.
Another pause, longer than the preceding ones.
Tick, tick.
81, ½, ¼, 80.
Sir William gasped for breath. He had made £10,000.

He accumulates 'an enormous fortune' by playing the markets, and dies of indigestion after a Lord Mayor's dinner.[18]

For small, provincial, investors, it was another matter. Their ignorance of the realities of the joint-stock economy was dramatised in Mrs Riddell's best-selling 1860s novel, *George Geith of Fen Court*. Ambrose Molozane, a Hertfordshire squire, approaches Geith, a City accountant, to find out whether his large investment in a mining company, whose shares are at a heavy discount, will ruin him. Geith denies any expertise on the subject of mines: 'There is only one thing I do know, which is, that I should never

[18] B. Hemyng, *'The stockbroker's wife' and other sensational tales of the Stock Exchange*, London 1885, 155–6.

invest one sixpence in them.'[19] But it soon becomes clear that the accountant understands a lot more than the squire, who is entirely ignorant of his legal standing *vis-à-vis* the company. He asks Geith, 'Is a man liable to the extent of his shares?' The accountant tells him that he is, and that unless the mine is managed on the cost-book principle, he will be liable to the extent of the company's debts.[20] He asks the uninformed investor whether the company is managed in this way, and the duped squire replies, 'I am sure I cannot tell . . . I know nothing about it except that they told me I should never have to pay more than the first instalment unless I chose, and that I should be able at any time to sell at a hundred per cent profit.' His 100 fifty-pound shares, with twenty pounds paid up, are worse than worthless as they carry with them a huge liability, and Molozane is ruined. When Geith looks into the affair, he finds that the secretary of the concern was a man named Punt, a scoundrel infamous in business circles in the City, but unknown to provincials like Molozane. Those in the know could not possibly be duped by such men, but country-dwellers were without this knowledge and were incredibly vulnerable.[21] While there was sympathy for the motives of some cash-strapped provincials who were driven onto the stock market, readers were reminded that the moral of periodic financial panics was that

> wary investors should hold more closely than ever by the good old-fashioned maxim that great interest means bad security. If they are hesitating between low and high dividends they will do well to remember that although in the one case they may have to put up with disagreeable privations, in the other they may be inviting irremediable ruin.[22]

Thus, there was a marked difference between the needs of large, well-connected speculators, and small ones. Government legislation was largely irrelevant to the protection of the former: as one solicitor argued in 1895, shareholders who wanted reliable accounting information did not need balance sheets; they went straight to the directors to get it privately. Only small shareholders harassed directors for accounting information to be disclosed at general meetings, demands which were incompatible with the company's need for secrecy: 'Trading companies cannot give detailed information in general meeting, or even in private, with safety, except to large shareholders.'[23] Large shareholders did not need the legislature to insist on full disclosure in company prospectuses: if subscribers doubted the legitimacy of figures contained in the prospectus, it was up to them to ask the directors

---

19 Trafford, *George Geith*, 24.
20 The cost book system was a form of business organisation unique to mining: Harris, *Industrializing English law*, 190–2.
21 Trafford, *George Geith*, 25, 27.
22 [Shand], 'Speculative investments', 316.
23 H. Brown, *Report of the departmental committee appointed to inquire what amendments are necessary in the acts relating to joint stock companies*, PP 1895 lxxxviii. 75–6.

personally how the figures were arrived at. If no answer were given, or the answer were unsatisfactory, they need not buy the shares.[24]

There were, of course, other means to obtain information. The press had sometimes viewed itself as a potential regulator of joint-stock enterprise, helping shareholders to fill the regulatory void left by the government in 1855–6 by directing them to sound investments and warning them of dubious ones. On the enactment of the 1855 Limited Liability Act, for example, the *Morning Chronicle* stated that it was henceforth the journalist's duty 'to scrutinize on fitting occasions the mass of inchoate projects' and give readers his opinion on them, separating the good from the bad.[25] Poovey has argued that now 'some financial journalists began to serve as moral watchdogs as well as chroniclers of the City'. But she recognises the limited impact they had, noting: 'When journalists revealed that ethical transgressions existed in the financial world, they also betrayed their own inability to make companies moral.'[26] In addition, moral watchdogs were just as likely to warn the public away from joint-stock speculation altogether than attempt to function as investment advisers. Thus, the *Graphic* noted in 1879 that

> nearly every species of associated enterprise has been discredited by the thieves and scoundrels who have joined in such undertakings. What with rotten banks, sham mines, railways whose stock is merely a vehicle for gambling, and dishonest foreign loans, the would-be investor is forcibly reminded that as regards earthly treasure thieves break through and steal . . . just as much as they did eighteen hundred years ago.[27]

The *Graphic* did not attempt to guide its readers through this mass of undertakings. Rather, it urged the government to make consols accessible to small investors, permitting them to get 3 per cent rather than making do with the lower savings banks rates. Such advice, essentially the same as that given by Thomas Mortimer's *Everyman his own broker* over one hundred years earlier, was, of course, little use to budding stock market operators.[28]

The situation changed in the 1880s, however, with not only an increase in the numbers of popular investment guides published for the benefit of amateur investors, but also the arrival of the 'new financial journalism'. Influenced by the American financial press, it sought to convey financial informa-

---

[24] Bramwell expressed this view in *Twycross v. Grant, Clark, and Punchard* (1877), 36 LT 812. This case concerned the prominent financier Albert Grant's promotion of the Lisbon Steam Tramways Company, whose £309,000 capital included a hidden sum of £57,000 which was promotion costs for Grant and a business associate. The case was originally decided against Grant, and a split decision in the Court of Appeal meant that the original decision stood, despite Bramwell's efforts. But the questions raised during the appeal cast the responsibilities of promoters into serious doubt.

[25] *Morning Chronicle*, 14 Aug. 1855.

[26] Poovey, 'Writing about finance', 25, 29.

[27] *Graphic*, 3 May 1879.

[28] See chapter 2 above.

tion to investors in a lively fashion, often in the form of share 'tips', and was also geared towards exposing bad or fraudulent promotions. The mission of uncovering financial corruption carried echoes of earlier battles against the corruption of the state: Herman Hess, editor of the *Critic*, published his *Black book* which listed the names, addresses and business activities of hundreds of 'guinea pig' directors.[29] Yet the new journalism was severely compromised by conflicts of interest, for newspapers could be used to 'puff' the latest schemes of their editors or proprietors. In 1887, for example, Harry H. Marks used the *Financial News*, which he edited, and which was pledged to 'expose fraud wherever we find it', to urge the public to invest in the Rae-Transvaal Gold Mining Company, which he promoted. The company was a fraud, and was wound up before it found any gold, but Marks profited enormously from the affair.[30] Others doubted that corruption was endemic, but thought that 'the increasing tendency to sensational writing' in City columns meant that they conveyed more of the imaginations of the journalists that wrote them than the realities of the market, and were therefore useless as 'a safeguard for the ignorant or unwary'.[31] The extent to which the information provided by the press rivalled that obtainable by large London investors and enabled small shareholders to behave more 'rationally' in the financial markets must therefore be seriously doubted.

The recognition that small, uninformed shareholders were essentially gamblers did not condemn them in all eyes. Robert Palmer Harding, an accountant and a witness before the 1877 Select committee on the companies acts, proposed to institute regulations on minimum subscriptions prior to incorporation, and minimum shareholdings for directors, to ensure that the companies invested in by the ill-informed shareholder had at least some substance. Robert Lowe, chairman of the committee, and architect of the limited liability act of 1856, pressed him on the point:

Lowe: But if he likes to risk his money on that why should he not?
Harding: You prevent betting, and interfere in many ways with the freedom of the distribution of money.
Lowe: But that betting is gambling?
Harding: So is taking shares, in many instances, and nothing else.[32]

Others agreed that such speculator-gamblers needed protection. When Lowe suggested to Richard Malins that nothing could save shareholders or

---

[29] Hess claimed that he was offered a five-figure sum not to publish the work: H. Hess (ed.), *The Critic black book*, London 1901–2, i, p. vii. In 1819 the radical journalist John Wade published the immensely successful *Black book*, containing extensive information on government sinecures and other forms of corruption.
[30] Johnson, 'Civilizing mammon', 314–16. For more on Marks see D. Porter, ' "A trusted guide of the investing public": Harry Marks and the *Financial News*, 1884–1916', *BH* xxviii (1986), 1–17.
[31] [Shand], 'Speculative investments', 313–14.
[32] *Select committee on the companies acts*, PP 1877, 419.

customers who failed to take the trouble to look after their own interests, Malins retorted: 'If they were all as well informed as Mr. Lowe, or had been Chancellors of the Exchequer, it would be different; but a great many of them are as ignorant as gate-posts.' Malins thought that the legislature owed 'some degree of protection' to those clearly 'incapable of protecting themselves'.[33]

But this was by no means the majority view. As Frith's words had suggested, the sense remained that shareholders had a responsibility not only to themselves, but to the public, to regulate the behaviour of the companies in which they invested. Shareholders who neglected this responsibility were in effect destabilising the joint-stock economy by permitting their companies to behave irresponsibly whilst providing them with the capital with which they could cause considerable mischief. The state should do nothing to help these shareholders perform their regulatory role, since, as was thought to have been the case with the 1844 act, the faintest whiff of government approval could be regarded by investors as an official guarantee against loss, and thus an excuse for inaction.[34] Such views had not dimmed appreciably by the late nineteenth century. Cottrell claims that by 1877 Lowe had come 'to regret the radical nature of his 1856 bill', but there is little evidence of this.[35] His draft report as chair of the 1877 select committee showed him in typically robust form, claiming that without individual vigilance,

> so called safeguards are only means of creating undeserved confidence; if this course be followed they are unnecessary. All directions that particular things should be done in the course of business are in themselves mischievous, inasmuch as they tend to create a feeling of false security, and thus to enfeeble the motive for that thorough investigation which alone can make an investor safe.[36]

Later still, a bill of 1888 which would have provided for the standardisation of balance sheets met with fatal opposition, on the grounds that it would establish 'what the credulous would take for a sort of Government guarantee against fraud which in reality is nothing of the kind'.[37] Some politicians were explicit in arguing that the state had no responsibility to legislate for the 'unintelligent'.[38]

But it seemed that such views, based on a conception of shareholders as political actors in their 'little republics', were being thoroughly undermined

---

[33] Ibid.

[34] See chapter 4 above.

[35] Cottrell, *Industrial finance*, 52.

[36] *Select committee on the companies acts*, PP 1877, p. vii. Lowe's words were expunged from the final report, which recommended various amendments to the law, but these were ignored by parliament.

[37] *The Times*, 18 July 1888.

[38] Sir J. Goldsmid, *Hansard*, 4th ser. cccxlv. 710 (11 June 1890).

by the changing nature of joint-stock enterprise.[39] For, at a time when the lower ranks were slowly being brought within the pale of the constitution, small shareholders were being shunted to the margins of the joint-stock system. As companies grew in size and appealed for capital from greater numbers of people, the influence of individual shareholders declined. With shareholders geographically spread and unknown to one another, attending general meetings became more difficult for many, and it also became harder to marshal concerted action against boards. It is easy to see how this may have led to a degree of fatalism, with small shareholders reasoning that it was impossible to exert any influence in the running of a company, especially since directors could control proceedings with their proxy votes, and therefore not playing any part in governance at all. Although Marx had claimed that joint-stock companies were associations of capital, not individuals, in practice this was not exactly the case.[40] Most companies either placed caps on the number of votes individual shareholders could cast, or adopted graduated voting scales which diluted the voting power of large shareholders in an effort to ensure that the voices of small shareholders would be heard. From 1845 the default system provided by the government for companies which did not specify voting procedures in their articles of association was a graduated scale, which betrayed a view of the company as a collection of individuals as well as a collection of shares. But such voting arrangements became less common in the later years of the century, until legislation in 1906 adopted the one-share-one-vote system as the default, thus recognising it as the norm.[41] This seriously reduced the power smaller shareholders could wield in their companies. And with investors increasingly advised to keep diversified portfolios to minimise risk, the idea that they could regulate all the companies in which they had invested began to seem unrealistic.[42] Even larger shareholders faced the same problem.[43]

Other changes were taking place. The increasing fashion for fully paid up, freely transferable, shares meant that companies no longer took on the character of their shareholders in any meaningful sense. Freely transferable shares also meant that where shareholders were once owners of the assets of the company, they became merely owners of rights to the profits of the company, a subtle though important distinction which effectively 'externalised' share-

39 The phrase 'little republics' to describe joint-stock companies was used by Lowe in parliament in 1856: ibid. 3rd ser. cxl. 134 (1 Feb. 1856).

40 See chapter 1 above.

41 C. A. Dunlavy, 'From citizens to plutocrats: nineteenth-century shareholder voting rights and theories of the corporation', in K. Lipartito and D. B. Sicilia (eds), Constructing corporate America: history, politics and culture, Oxford 2004, 66–93 at p. 84.

42 Anon., 'Albert Life Assurance', 537; Anon., 'Limited liability', EdR clxiii (Jan. 1886), 71–87; A. Emden, 'The crying need for reforms in our company law', Nineteenth Century xxxv (June 1894), 1033–50; The Times, 28 Feb. 1899.

43 Maltby, 'UK joint stock companies legislation'.

holders from the companies in which they invested.[44] The company was now made up of its capital, not those who owned this capital: it had become an entity distinct from its shareholders. If the company had a human form, it was not the shareholders, but the board. The shareholders' will was not necessarily the company's will, their interests were not necessarily the company's interests. To release information to the shareholders at an annual general meeting was now considered to make it 'public'. Directors were therefore justified, in the interests of the company, in withholding information from the shareholders. As Ireland comments, a reified conception of the company was now emerging.[45]

By the century's end these changes were stretching to the limit traditional notions of shareholders as partners. That means existed for shareholders to gain the information and exert the influence necessary to safeguard their investments had for a long time been an integral element of the rationale of non-intervention by the state. So long as the mass of shareholders were viewed as 'the company', the arrangements they made between themselves were not the business of the state. But once shareholders had been purged from the political arena of joint-stock companies, once their political role within the company was sidelined, the argument that government intervention was necessary to protect them and the public gained legitimacy. As self-governing republics, companies had failed. Investment had been stripped of its political connotations; it was now a primarily economic act, in which the state had a responsibility to ensure that the dice were not loaded in favour of one party. Even *The Times* now recommended the implementation of safeguards to protect investors: 'The world is more educated than it was', it wrote in 1894, but 'the ordinary Englishman needs protection when he goes into the City to do business with the astute gentry who construct ephemeral companies.' Safeguards sufficient in 1862 now seemed 'ridiculously inadequate'.[46]

Governments were always more willing to regulate monopolies such as rail, gas, water or tram companies, not just in terms of publicity of accounts and compulsory audits, but also by controlling prices and profits.[47] But they could also be persuaded to introduce legislation in other sectors where the public interest seemed especially vulnerable such as insurance and banking. Following the Albert Life Assurance fraud of 1869, assurance companies were obliged to deposit their accounts annually with the Board of Trade.[48] After the City of Glasgow Bank failure of 1878, internal bank audits were rendered compulsory.[49] But each time the reforms were far less sweeping than many

---

[44] Ireland, 'Capitalism without the capitalist', 68–9.
[45] Ibid. 47.
[46] *The Times*, 20 Nov. 1894.
[47] Daunton, *Trusting leviathan*, 266–8.
[48] 33 & 34 Vict. c. 61, s. 10.
[49] 42 & 43 Vict. c. 76, s. 7.

wanted: calls for government audit of accounts were firmly rejected.[50] Progress with general company reform also seemed disappointing. Lord Salisbury's government announced its intention to introduce reforming legislation in 1888, but this only resulted in two relatively minor acts in 1890 relating to winding up and companies' memoranda of association. In 1894 the Board of Trade appointed a committee under Lord Davey to set out a programme of company law reform, but it was not until 1900 that the government succeeded in securing the passage of a new companies act.[51] This measure imposed new regulations as to the qualification of directors, the allotment of shares and the content of prospectuses, and stipulated that prospectuses be filed with the Registrar.[52] It also made the registration of mortgages and the appointment of auditors by shareholders compulsory, made it easier for shareholders to call special general meetings and established procedures regulating a company's first general meeting in order to make it more difficult for directors to conceal information from shareholders.[53] These amendments amounted to an acknowledgment by the state that, as one MP put it, the 'honest investing public . . . required protection'.[54] Indeed, the president of the Board of Trade, Charles Ritchie, asserted that while it was impossible to prevent shareholders 'being foolish in the investment of their capital', the law 'ought, *as far as possible*, to provide safeguards to protect the public against misleading or fraudulent devices or the fraudulent use of existing legal machinery'.[55]

But the 'as far as possible' revealed that Ritchie believed that the extent to which the state could protect the public was severely circumscribed. Governments refused to rethink in a more fundamental way their approach to the corporate economy even though the rationale for their policy since the 1840s had been proven to be faulty. The state had renounced its right to withhold corporate privileges, somewhat carelessly in 1844, enthusiastically in 1855–6, and now it could not conceive of claiming it back, for to do so would be an unwarranted interference in private enterprise. The conceptualisation of the joint-stock company as a privatised entity reigned supreme, and this placed narrow limits on the policies that could be envisaged. The members of the Davey Committee stressed that they had

> dismissed from their consideration every suggestion for a public inquiry by the
> registrar or other official authority into the soundness, good faith, and pros-

[50] For more on calls for greater government intervention see S. P. Walker, 'More sherry and sandwiches? Incrementalism and the regulation of late Victorian bank auditing', *Accounting History* iii (1998), 33–54 at p. 41.

[51] Cottrell, *Industrial finance*, 64–75.

[52] 63 & 64 Vict. c. 48, ss. 3–10. The 1844 act's requirement that prospectuses be registered had been repealed by an act of 1847: 10 & 11 Vict. c. 78, s. 4.

[53] 63 & 64 Vict. c. 48, ss. 13–18, 21–23.

[54] Sir R. Reid, *Hansard*, 4th ser. lxxxvii. 78 (30 July 1900).

[55] Ibid. lxxxiv. 1141 (26 June 1900). Emphasis added.

pects of the undertaking . . . It would be an attempt to throw what ought to be the responsibility of the individual on the shoulders of the State, and would give a fictitious and unreal sense of security to the investor, and might also lead to grave abuses.[56]

This stance received widespread backing. The *Quarterly Review* condemned 'the reactionary view that limited liability is a dangerous privilege which should be taken away from any person who is guilty of non-meritorious conduct'. That limited liability was a right was axiomatic: indeed, by the end of the century, the history of the process by which it was made a right was becoming a little hazy. The same journal referred to 'the discussions which preceded the passing of the Act of 1862 . . . The principle of limited liability was at one time on its trial; since 1862 its acceptance is *chose jugée*'.[57] Yet, of course, the principle was debated and accepted in 1855–6: the act of 1862 was a consolidating act.

The way was clear for the emergence in the twentieth century of the limited company as the 'normal' form of business organisation. Faith in the superiority of the unlimited partnership faded; limited companies were accepted as natural, inevitable and desirable features of a healthy economy, and the only means by which Britain's receding industrial and financial greatness could be prolonged. Their origin as creations of the state was forgotten; notions of their duty to serve the public became a distant memory: their sole function was to generate a profit. Calls to subject them to greater regulation could be resisted by citing the right of private enterprise to operate free of state interference. Of course, not everyone welcomed the hegemony of the company. Yet both left and right have subscribed to these myths of the origins and nature of the company, which has the effect of stunting the political debate on the role of big business in modern society. This debate would be enriched by recognising that by delegating political powers to businessmen, the state created political entities unchecked by any meaningful form of accountability, and, therefore, able to use their considerable powers despotically. Ultimately, it is only by recognising 'private enterprise' as nothing of the sort that companies can be made to serve the public interest.

---

[56] *Report on the acts relating to joint stock companies*, PP 1895 lxxxviii. xiv.7.
[57] [A. C. Clauson], 'The reform of company law', *QR* cxci (Apr. 1900), 373–92 at pp. 378, 377.

Bibliography

Unpublished primary sources

Birmingham, City Library
Birmingham Debating Society records

London, British Library
Aberdeen papers
Gladstone papers

London, Guildhall Library
Union Society of London records

London, National Archives
Board of Trade papers
Cardwell papers

Microfilm
English cartoons and satirical prints, 1320–1832, in the British Museum, microfilm,
    21 reels, Cambridge 1978

Published primary sources

Official documents and publications
Hansard's parliamentary debates, 1st–4th ser. (1803–1900)

Parliamentary papers

Bills
*A bill to alter and amend an act passed in the 6th year of the reign of King George the
    First . . . for the prevention of frauds in the establishment of joint stock companies*,
    PP 1825 i
*A bill to amend an act for better enabling Her Majesty to confer certain powers and
    immunities on trading and other companies*, PP 1837–8 vi
A bill to amend the Companies Act of 1862, PP 1866 ii

Committees and commissions
Select committee on private business of the House, PP 1824 vi
Select committee on the Arigna Mining Company, PP 1826–7 iii
Report on the law of partnership, PP 1837 xliv
Select committee on private business, PP 1837–8 xxiii

Select committee on private business, PP 1839 xxii

Select committee to inquire into the state of the laws respecting joint stock companies, PP 1844 vii

Select committee on private bills, PP 1846 xii

Select committee on railway acts enactments, PP 1846 xiv

Select committee on investments for the savings of the middle and working classes, PP 1850 xix

Select committee on the law of partnership, PP 1851 xviii

Royal Commission on the assimilation of mercantile laws in the UK and amendments in the law of partnership, as regards the question of limited or unlimited responsibility, PP 1854 xxvii

Royal Commission on amendments in the law of partnership, PP 1854 xxvii

Report from the select committee on income and property tax, PP 1861 vii

Select committee on the limited liability acts, PP 1867 x

Select committee on loans to foreign states, PP 1875 xi

Select committee on the companies acts, 1862 and 1867, PP 1877 viii

Royal Commission on the Stock Exchange, PP 1878 xix

Accounts and papers

Account showing the total number of petitions for private bills presented to the House of Commons, 1825–29, PP 1829 xxi

Copy of the minute of the Lords of the Committee of Privy Council for Trade, dated 4 November 1834, on granting letters patent, PP 1837 xxxix

Return relating to railway bills, PP 1840 xlv

Return of the number of railway bills brought into parliament in each year since 1839, PP 1843 xliv

Alphabetical list of the names, descriptions and places of abode of all persons subscribing to the amount of £2,000 and upwards to any railway subscription contract deposited in the private bill office during the present session of parliament, PP 1845 xl

Alphabetical list of the names, descriptions and places of abode of all persons subscribing for any sum less than £2,000 to any railway subscription contract deposited in the private bill office during the present session of parliament, PP 1845 xl

Return of joint stock companies registered under 7 & 8 Vict. c. 110, PP 1845 xlvii

Return of the number of private bills introduced, and of acts passed, since the year 1838, PP 1846 xxxiii

Petitions, orders in council, memorials and correspondence, with the Board of Trade on the grant of a Royal Charter of Incorporation to the London, Liverpool, and North American Screw Steam-Ship Co. PP 1852–3 xcv

Statement of names of permanent public officers who hold employment out of their office, as directors of life assurance, railway, banking or commercial companies in 1852, PP 1854 xxxix

Returns of all applications to the Board of Trade for grants of charters with limited liability, PP 1854 lxv

Report by the Registrar of Joint Stock Companies to the Committee of Privy Council for Trade, PP 1846 xliii; 1847 lix; 1847–8 li; 1849 l; 1850 lii; 1851 liii; 1852 li; 1852–3 xcix; 1854 lxv; 1854–5 l; 1856 lv

Report of the departmental committee appointed to inquire what amendments are necessary in the acts relating to joint stock companies, PP 1895 lxxxviii

Newspapers and periodicals

All the Year Round
Annual Register
Bentley's Miscellany
Blackwood's Edinburgh Magazine
Circular to Bankers
Cobbett's Weekly Register
Companion to the Almanac; or Year-Book of General Information
Course of the Exchange
Daily News
Diogenes
Economist
Edinburgh Review
Financial Review of Reviews
Fortnightly Review
Fraser's Magazine
Freedom
Fun
George Cruikshank's Table-Book
Graphic
Household Words
Illustrated London News
John Bull
Judy
Law Times
Lloyd's Weekly Newspaper
Manchester Guardian
Morning Advertiser
Morning Chronicle
Morning Herald
Morning Post
News of the World
Nineteenth Century
Observer
Punch
Quarterly Review
Railway Record
Saint Pauls Magazine
Standard
Temple Bar
The Times
Tomahawk
Weekly Dispatch
Westminster Review
Will-o'-the-Wisp

Contemporary books and articles

Anon., *An account of the South Sea Scheme and a number of other bubbles . . . with a few remarks upon some schemes which are now in agitation*, London 1806

———— ['Philopatris'], *Observations on public institutions, monopolies, joint stock companies, and deeds of trust: shewing the advantages the public derive from competition in trade*, London 1807

———— *Observations on the manner of conducting marine insurances in Great Britain; and on the report of the select committee of the House of Commons*, London 1810

———— *Observations on the establishment of new water works companies*, London 1824

———— *A list of joint-stock companies, the proposals for which are now, or have been lately, before the public. From 'The Monthly Repository of Theology and General Literature'*, London 1825

———— ['A Merchant'], *Letter to John Taylor, Esq respecting the conduct of the directors of the Real del Monte Company relative to the mines of Tlalpuxahua*, London 1825

———— *Remarks on joint stock companies by an old merchant*, London 1825

———— *The South Sea Bubble, and the numerous fraudulent projects to which it gave rise in 1720, historically detailed as a beacon to the unwary against modern schemes . . . equally visionary and nefarious*, London 1825

———— ['Investigator'], *Beware the bubbles!!! Remarks on proposed railways, more particularly on that between Birmingham and London*, London 1831

———— 'The Stock Exchange, no. I', FM iv (Dec. 1831), 577–85

———— 'The Stock Exchange, no. II', FM iv (Jan. 1832), 714–26

———— 'The Stock Exchange, no. III', FM v (Mar. 1832), 155–65

———— *The Real Del Monte mining concerns unmasked, and a few facts on stock jobbing schemes, with a view to prevent the public from becoming the dupes of self-interested speculators and adventurers*, London 1833

———— *Remarks on the objections to joint stock banks*, London 1833

———— ['G. H.'], *The American mines; shewing their importance, in a national point of view*, London 1834

———— *Observations on the Trading Companies Bill*, London 1834

———— ['Investigator'], *The Bank of England, and other banks*, London 1840

———— *A defence of joint-stock banks and country issues*, London 1840

———— *Speculation*, Oxford 1850

———— ['Dot'], *The Stock Exchange and its victims*, London 1851

———— 'Partnership with limited liability', WR lx (Oct. 1853), 375–416.

———— *Exposure of the Stock Exchange and bubble companies*, London 1854

———— ['A Shareholder'], *Mining & miners and diggers & priggers*, London 1854

———— ['A Manchester Man'], *The law of partnership: a reply to the speech of the right hon. E. P. Bouverie, MP*, London 1855

———— *Commercial morality; or, thoughts for the times*, London 1856

———— 'The poverty of wealth', TB vi (1862), 12–25

———— 'City intelligence', TB xi (1864), 491–500

———— 'The financial pressure and ten per cent', FM lxxiv (1866), 229–42

———— ['1915'], *Overend, Gurney, and Co., or the saddle on the right horse*, London 1866

———— ['A Barrister'], *Overend, Gurney, and Co., (Limited): a plain statement of the case*, London 1867

——— 'John Skeeme, the promoter', *AYR* xviii (1867), 342–6, 376–81

——— 'The Albert Life Assurance Company', *WR* xcii (Oct. 1869), 532–50

——— 'The Stock Exchange', *Saint Pauls Magazine* vi (1870), 605–18

——— 'Limited liability', *EdR* clxiii (Jan. 1886), 71–87

Archbold, J. F., *The law of limited liability, partnership, and joint-stock companies*, London 1855

Argyll, G. D. C., *The unseen foundations of society: an examination of the fallacies and failures of economic science due to neglected elements*, London 1893

[W. Aytoun], 'The champions of the rail', *BEM* lxx (Dec. 1851), 739–50

Bamford, F. and the duke of Wellington (eds), *The journal of Mrs Arbuthnot, 1820–1832*, London 1950

[J. Barrow], 'Canals and rail-roads', *QR* xxxi (Mar. 1825), 349–78

Bell, R., *The ladder of gold, an English story*, London 1850

Bernard, W. B., *Locomotion*, London 1842

Besant, W. and J. Rice, *The golden butterfly*, London n.d.

Boardman, H. A., *The Bible in the counting-house: a course of lectures to merchants*, London 1854

Boucicault, D., *The school for scheming*, London 1847

Bray, J. F., *Labour's wrongs and labour's remedy; or, the age of might and the age of right*, London 1968

Bulwer-Lytton, E., *The Caxtons: a family picture*, London n.d.

Burchell, J., *The Joint Stock Companies Registration Act*, London 1844

Byron, H. J., *A hundred thousand pounds*, London 1866

Callender, W. R., *The commercial crisis of 1857: its causes and results*, London 1858

Carlyle, T., *Last words of Thomas Carlyle – on trades-unions, promoterism and the signs of the times*, Edinburgh 1882

——— *Past and present*, London 1895

——— *Latter-day pamphlets*, London 1911

Claeys, G., *Selected works of Robert Owen*, London 1993

Clarke, C., 'How the balance came out: a tale of the Stock Exchange', *TB* xix (1866), 120–37

[Clauson, A. C.], 'The reform of company law', *QR* cxci (Apr. 1900), 373–92

Cobbe, F. P., 'What is progress, and are we progressing?', *Fortnightly Review* vii (1867), 357–70

Cobbett, W., *Advice to young men, and (incidentally) to young women, in the middle and higher ranks of life*, London 1906

Cockton, H., *George St George Julian, the prince*, London 1841

Colchester, Lord Charles (ed.), *The diary and correspondence of Charles Abbot, Lord Colchester*, London 1861

Collyer, J., *A practical treatise on the law of partnership*, London 1832

Combe, A., *The sphere for joint-stock companies: or, the way to increase the value of land, capital, and labour*, Edinburgh 1825, repr. in *Motherwell and Orbiston: the first Owenite attempts at cooperative communities, three pamphlets 1822–1825*, New York 1972

Costello, D., 'The joint-stock banker', *Bentley's Miscellany* xxxix (Apr. 1856), 346–65

———,'The joint-stock banker', *Bentley's Miscellany* xxxix (June 1856), 551–66

Cox, E. W., *The Joint Stock Companies Act 1856, for the regulation of companies with or without limited liability*, London 1856

———— *The new law and practice of joint stock companies, with and without limited liability*, London 1857

Crowquill, A., *How he reigned and how he mizzled: a railway raillery*, London 1849

Cumming, J.,'The age we live in', in *Young Men's Christian Association*, 308–36

Day, H., *Critical examination of such of the clauses of the act of 6th of George I as relates to unlawful and unwarrantable projects: demonstrating that the present joint stock companies are neither within the letter nor spirit of that act*, London 1808

———— *A defence of joint stock companies; being an attempt to shew their legality, expediency, and public benefit*, London 1808

Dickens, C., *Our mutual friend*, New York 1978

———— *Little Dorrit*, London 1992

———— *Martin Chuzzlewit*, Oxford 1994

———— *The life and adventures of Nicholas Nickleby*, Ware 1995

[Disraeli, B.], An *inquiry into the plans, progress, and policy of the American mining companies*, 3rd edn, London 1825

———— *Lawyers and legislators: or notes on the American mining companies*, London 1825

———— *The present state of Mexico*, London 1825

———— *Letters: 1815–1834*, Toronto 1982

[Eden, F.], *On the policy and expediency of granting insurance charters*, London 1806

Emden, A.,'The crying need for reforms in our company law', *Nineteenth Century* xxxv (June 1894), 1033–50

[Empson, W.], 'English corporations and endowments', *EdR* lxviii (Jan. 1834), 469–98.

English, H., *A general guide to the companies formed for working foreign mines*, London 1825

———— *A compendium of useful information relating to the companies formed for working British mines . . . with general observations on their progress*, London 1826

———— *A complete view of the joint stock companies formed during the years 1824 and 1825*, London 1827

English reports, London 1964–2001

[Evans, D. M.], *The City; or, the physiology of London business*, London 1845

———— *Facts, failures and frauds: revelations financial mercantile criminal*, New York 1968

———— *The commercial crisis, 1847–1848*, Newton Abbot 1969

———— *Speculative notes and notes on speculation ideal and real*, New York 1969

Farren, G., *A treatise on life assurance*, London 1823

———— *Hints, by way of warning, on the legal, practical, and mercantile difficulties attending the foundation and management of joint stock banks*, London 1833

Fawcett, H., 'To what extent is England prosperous?', *Fortnightly Review* xv (1871), 40–52

Field, E. W., *Observations of a solicitor on the right of the public to form limited liability partnerships, and on the theory, practice, and cost of commercial charters*, London 1854

Fisk, G., 'The moral influence of the commercial spirit of the day', in *Young Men's Christian Association*, 261–84

Frith, W. P., *My autobiography*, 2nd edn, London 1887

George, J., *A view of the existing law affecting unincorporated joint stock companies*, London 1825

Gilbart, J. W., *The moral and religious duties of public companies*, 2nd edn, London 1856

Gilbert, W. S., *The Savoy operas*, London 1963

Gissing, G., *The whirlpool*, London 1997

Gow, N., *A practical treatise on the law of partnership*, London 1823

[Greg. W. R.], 'Investments for the working classes', EdR xcv (Apr. 1852), 405–53

Hartnoll, J. H., *A letter to the right hon. E. Cardwell, M.P., president of the Board of Trade, on the inoperative character of the Joint Stock Companies Registration Act, as a means of preventing the formation of bubble assurance companies, or of regulating the action of those honourably and legitimately instituted*, 2nd edn, London 1853

Hawes, W., *Observations on unlimited and limited liability; and suggestions for the improvement of the law of partnership*, London 1854

Hemyng, B., 'The stockbroker's wife' and other sensational tales of the Stock Exchange, London 1885

Hess, H. (ed.), *The Critic black book*, London 1901–2

Hobart, Lord, *Remarks on the law of partnership liability*, London 1853

Hodgskin, T., *Popular political economy*, London 1827

Howard, Dr E., *True forgiveness: a drama in three acts (illustrating the commercial crisis of 1866)*, London 1870

Jerrold, W. (ed.), *The handbook of swindling, and other papers*, London n.d.

Lalor, J., *Money and morals: a book for the times*, London 1852

[Lardner, D.], 'Railways at home and abroad', EdR lxxxiv (Oct. 1846), 479–531

[Lawson, W. R.], 'A black year for investors', BEM cxxxvii (Feb. 1885), 269–84.

Lectures delivered before the Young Men's Christian Association, 1847–8, London 1848

Lever, C., *Davenport Dunn; or a man of our day*, London 1859

Lewes, G. H., *The game of speculation*, repr. in M. Booth (ed.), 'The lights o' London' and other Victorian plays, Oxford 1995

Lewis, G. H., *The liabilities incurred by the projectors, managers and shareholders of railway and other joint-stock companies considered: and also the rights and liabilities arising from transfers of shares*, London 1845

Lovett, W., *Manifesto of the general convention of the industrious classes*, London n.d.

Lowery, R., *Address to the fathers and mothers, sons and daughters, of the working classes, on the system of exclusive dealing, and the formation of joint stock provision companies, shewing how the people may free themselves from oppression*, Newcastle 1839

Lowndes, M. D., *Review of the joint stock bank acts, and of the law as to joint stock companies generally: with the practical suggestions of a solicitor for their amendment*, London 1840

—— *The Liverpool Stock Exchange considered; with suggestions for its re-constitution on a safe footing*, Liverpool 1845

[McCulloch, J. R.], 'Joint-stock banks and companies', EdR lxiii (July 1836), 419–41

—— *Considerations on partnerships with limited liability*, London 1856

MacFarlane, A., *Railway scrip; or, the evils of speculation: a tale of the railway mania*, London 1856

Mackay, C., *Memoirs of extraordinary popular delusions and the madness of crowds*, Ware 1995

Macpherson, D., *Annals of commerce, manufactures, fisheries, and navigation*, London 1805

Manchester Young Men's Christian Association, 1855–6, London n.d.

Martin, A. P. (ed.), *Life and letters of the right honourable Robert Lowe, Viscount Sherbrooke*, London 1893

Martineau, H., *Illustrations of political economy. No. XI: For each and for all*, London 1832

Marx, K., *Capital*, Harmondsworth 1981

—————— and F. Engels, *Collected works*, London 1975–2001

[Meason, M. L.], 'Promoters of companies', *AYR* xi (1864), 110–15

—————— 'The Bank of Patagonia (Ltd)', *AYR* xiii (1865), 485–90

—————— 'How the bank was wound up', *AYR* xiii (1865), 276–82

—————— 'Insurance and assurance', *AYR* xiii (1865), 437–42

—————— 'Finance, frauds, and failures', *TB* xvii (1866), 381–95

—————— 'Twenty per cent: a banking tale of the present time', *TB* xvii (July 1866), 473–92

Mill, J. S., 'Civilization', *London and Westminster Review* iii/xxv (Apr. 1836), repr. in his *Essays*, xviii. 119–47

—————— *Essays on politics and society, collected works*, Toronto 1977

—————— *Principles of political economy*, Harmondsworth 1985

Mineka, F. E. (ed.), *The earlier letters of John Stuart Mill*, Toronto 1963

—————— and D. N. Lindley (eds), *The later letters of J. S. Mill, 1849–73*, Toronto 1972

[Morley, H.], 'The penny saved; a blue-book catechism', *HW* ii (1850), 81–4

Morris, A. J., *Religion and business; or, spiritual life in one of its secular departments*, London 1853

Mortimer, T., *The nefarious practice of stock-jobbing unveiled*, London 1810

Moss, E., *Remarks on the act of parliament, 18 & 19 Vict. c. 133, for the formation of companies with limited liability*, London 1856

[Mowbray, R. G. C.], 'Stock-jobbing and the Stock Exchange', *BEM* cxxvi (Aug. 1879), 181–206

[Mundell, A.], *The principles which govern the value of paper currency, with reference to banking establishments*, Edinburgh 1823

—————— *The influence of interest and prejudice upon proceedings in parliament stated*, London 1825

O'Brien, D. P. (ed.), *The correspondence of Lord Overstone*, Cambridge 1971

Oliphant, L., *Piccadilly: a fragment of contemporary biography*, Edinburgh 1892

Owen, Revd J. B., *Business without Christianity*, London 1856

Owen, R., *A development of the principles and plans on which to establish self-supporting home colonies*, repr. in Claeys, *Selected works of Robert Owen*, ii. 355–415

Parsons, A., *The Limited Liability Act and its legal interpretations*, London 1855

Patterson, R. H., 'The panic in the City', *BEM* c (July 1866), 78–93

Peacock, T. L., *The works of Thomas Love Peacock*, New York 1967

Phillips, E., *Bank of England charter, currency, limited liability companies, and free trade*, London 1856

Political Economy Club, *Minutes of proceedings, 1899–1920, roll of members, and questions discussed, 1821–1920*, London 1921

Potter, E., *Practical opinions against partnership with limited liability, in a letter to a friend*, London 1855

[Pulling, A.], 'Private bill legislation', *EdR* cl (Jan. 1855), 151–91

Rawson, Sir W., *The present operations and future prospects of the Mexican mine associations analysed by the evidence of official documents, English and Mexican, and the national advantages expected from joint stock companies considered; in a letter to the right hon. George Canning*, 2nd edn, London 1825

Reade, C., *Hard cash: a matter-of-fact romance*, London 1894

Reid, J., *Manual of the Scottish stocks and British funds, with a list of the joint-stock companies in Scotland*, Edinburgh 1841

[Robinson, E.], *The gold-worshippers; or, the days we live in*, London 1858

St John-Stevas, N. (ed.), *The collected works of Walter Bagehot*, London 1965–86

[Sala, G.], 'The golden calf', *HW* x (1854), 437–41

[Shand, A. I.], 'Speculative investments', *BEM* cxx (Sept. 1876), 293–316

[Sidney, S.], 'Ruined by railways', *HW* xi (1855), 114–19

Sinclair, C., *Sir Edward Graham: or, railway speculators*, London 1849

Smiles, S., *Character*, London 1882

——— *Thrift*, London 1882

Smith, A., *An inquiry into the nature and causes of the wealth of nations*, Indianapolis 1981

Smith, A., *The bubble of the age; or, the fallacies of railway investments, railway accounts, and railway dividends*, 3rd edn, London 1848

Spencer, H., 'Railway morals and railway policy', *EdR* c (Oct. 1854), repr. in his *Essays*, ii. 1–311

——— 'The morals of trade', *WR* lxxi (Apr. 1859), repr. in his *Essays*, ii. 107–48

——— *Essays: scientific, political, and speculative*, London 1878–83

——— 'The reform of company-law', in his *Facts and comments*, 164–71

——— *Facts and comments*, London 1902

——— *An autobiography*, London 1904

Stirling, E., *The railway king! A laughable farce, in one act*, London 1845

Stowell, Revd C., *The Christian man in the business of life*, London 1856

Sweet, G., *The Limited Liability Act, 1855*, London 1855

[Symonds, A.], 'Law of partnership', *WR* xx (Jan. 1834), 58–73

Taylor, J., *Statements respecting the profits of mining in England considered in relation to the prospects of mining in Mexico: in a letter to Thomas Fowell Buxton, Esq. MP*, London 1825

Taylor, T., *Still waters run deep*, London n.d.

——— and A. W. Dubourg, *New men and old acres*, in M. R. Booth, *English plays of the nineteenth century*, Oxford 1969–76

Thackeray, W. M., *The history of Samuel Titmarsh and the great Hoggarty diamond*, in his *The Yellowplush correspondence*, London 1903

Tooke, T. and W. Newmarch, *A history of prices and of the state of the circulation from 1792 to 1856*, London 1928

Trafford, F. G., *City and suburb*, London 1861

——— *George Geith of Fen Court*, London 1865

Trollope, A., *The three clerks*, Oxford 1989

——— *The way we live now*, Harmondsworth 1994

Warner, E., *The impolicy of the partnership law*, London 1854
Wilde, O., *The picture of Dorian Gray*, London 2000
Wordsworth, C. F. F., *The law relating to railway, bank, insurance, mining, and other joint-stock companies*, London 1837

Works of reference

Blaug, M. and P. Sturges (eds), *Who's who in economics: a biographical dictionary of major economists, 1700–1981*, Brighton 1983
Cook, C. and B. Keith, *British historical facts, 1830–1900*, London 1975
Cook, C. and J. Stevenson, *British historical facts, 1760–1830*, Hamden 1980
George, M. D., *Catalogue of political and personal satires*, London 1978
Houghton, W. E. and J. H. Slingerland (eds), *The Wellesley index to Victorian periodicals, 1824–1900*, Toronto 1966–89
Jeremy, D. J. (ed.), *Dictionary of business biography: a biographical dictionary of business leaders active in Britain in the period 1860–1980*, London 1984–6
Judd, G. P., *Members of parliament, 1734–1832*, Hamden 1972
Sainty, J. C., *Officials of the Board of Trade, 1660–1870*, London 1974
Simmons, J. and G. Biddle (eds), *The Oxford companion to British railway history*, Oxford 1997
Stenton, M. (ed.), *Who's who of British members of parliament*, Hassocks 1976
Stephen, L. and S. Lee (eds), *Dictionary of national biography*, London 1908–12
Thorne, R. G., *The House of Commons, 1790–1820*, London 1986

Secondary sources

Alborn, T. L., 'The moral of the failed bank: professional plots in the Victorian money market', VS xxxviii (1995), 199–226
—— *Conceiving companies: joint-stock politics in Victorian England*, London 1998
Altick, R. D., *The English common reader*, Chicago 1963
—— *The presence of the present: topics of the day in the Victorian novel*, Columbus 1991
Anderson, G. M. and R. D. Tollison, 'The myth of the corporation as a creation of the state', *International Review of Law and Economics* iii (1983), 107–20
Anderson, O., *A liberal state at war: English politics and economics during the Crimean War*, New York 1967
Arnold, A. J. and S. McCartney, *George Hudson: the rise and fall of the railway king*, London 2004
Atiyah, P. S., *The rise and fall of freedom of contract*, Oxford 1979
Auerbach, J. H., *The Great Exhibition of 1851: a nation on display*, New Haven 1999
Ayerst, D., *Guardian: biography of a newspaper*, London 1971
Bagwell, P. S., *The transport revolution from 1770*, London 1974
Banks, J. A., 'The way they lived then: Anthony Trollope and the 1870s', VS xii (1968), 177–200
Beresford, M. W., *The Leeds chamber of commerce*, Leeds 1951

Biagini, E. F., *Liberty, retrenchment and reform: popular liberalism in the age of Glad-stone, 1860–1880*, Cambridge 1992

—— 'Liberalism and direct democracy: John Stuart Mill and the model of ancient Athens', in his *Citizenship and community*, 21–44.

—— (ed.), *Citizenship and community: Liberals, radicals and collective identities in the British Isles, 1865–1931*, Cambridge 1996

—— and A. J. Reid (eds), *Currents of radicalism: popular radicalism, organised labour, and party politics in Britain, 1850–1914*, Cambridge 1991

Black, I. S., 'Spaces of capital: bank office building in the City of London, 1830–1870', *Journal of Historical Geography* xxvi (2000), 351–75

Blake, R., *Disraeli*, London 1966

Blaug, M., *Great economists before Keynes*, Brighton 1986

Booth, M. R. (ed.), *English plays of the nineteenth century*, Oxford 1969–76

—— '*The lights o' London*' and other Victorian plays, Oxford 1995

—— *Theatre in the Victorian age*, Cambridge 1995

Broadbridge, S. A., 'The sources of railway share capital', in M. C. Reed (ed.), *Railways in the Victorian economy*, Newton Abbot 1969, 184–211

Brown, L., *The Board of Trade and the free-trade movement, 1830–42*, Oxford 1958

Bryer, R. A., 'Accounting for the "railway mania" of 1845: a great railway swindle?', *Accounting, Organisations and Society* xvi (1991), 439–86

—— 'The Mercantile Laws Commission of 1854 and the political economy of limited liability', *EcHR* l (1997), 37–56

Burt, R., 'The London mining exchange, 1850–1900', *BH* xiv (1972), 124–43

Butler, H. N., 'General incorporation in nineteenth-century England: interaction of common law and legislative processes', *International Review of Law and Economics* vi (1986), 169–87

Campbell, R. H., 'The law and the joint-stock company in Scotland', in Payne, *Studies in Scottish business history*, 136–51

Cannadine, D., *The decline and fall of the British aristocracy*, London 1996

Channon, G., 'Railways and English landed society', in his *Railways in Britain and the United States, 1830–1940*, Aldershot 2001

Chatterton, D. A., 'State control of public utilities in the nineteenth century: the London gas industry', *BH* xiv (1972), 166–78

Clark, P., *British clubs and societies, 1580–1800: the origins of an associational world*, Oxford 2002

Collini, S., 'The idea of "character" in Victorian political thought', *TRHS* 5th ser. xxxv (1985), 29–50

—— *Public moralists: political thought and intellectual life in Britain, 1850–1930*, Oxford 1993

Cooke, C. A., *Corporation, trust and company*, Manchester 1950

Cottrell, P. L., 'Railway finance and the crisis of 1866: contractors' bills of exchange and the finance companies', *Journal of Transport History* n.s. iii (1975), 20–40

—— *Industrial finance, 1830–1914*, London 1980

—— 'Sir Samuel Morton Peto', in Jeremy, *Dictionary of business biography*, iv. 644–53

Cunningham, H., *The challenge of democracy: Britain, 1832–1914*, Harlow 2001

Daunton, M. J., ' "Gentlemanly capitalism" and British industry, 1820–1914', *Past & Present* cxxii (1989), 119–58

―――― *Progress and poverty: an economic and social history of Britain, 1700–1850*, Oxford 1995

―――― *Trusting leviathan: the politics of taxation in Britain, 1799–1914*, Cambridge 2001

―――― *Just taxes: the politics of taxation in Britain, 1914–1979*, Cambridge 2002

Davidoff, L. and C. Hall, *Family fortunes: men and women of the English middle class, 1780–1850*, London 1992

Davies, P. N., *Sir Alfred Jones, shipping entrepreneur par excellence*, London 1978

Dodd, E. M., *American business corporations until 1860*, Cambridge, MA. 1954

DuBois, A. B., *The English business company after the Bubble Act, 1720–1800*, New York 1971

Duguid, C., *The Stock Exchange*, London 1904

Dunlavy, C. A., 'From citizens to plutocrats: nineteenth-century shareholder voting rights and theories of the corporation', in K. Lipartito and D. B. Sicilia (eds), *Constructing corporate America: history, politics and culture*, Oxford 2004, 66–93

Ellegard, A., *The readership of the periodical press in mid-Victorian Britain*, Goteborg 1957

Evans, G. H., *British corporation finance, 1775–1850: a study of preference shares*, Baltimore 1936

Everard, S., *The history of the Gas Light and Coke Company, 1812–1949*, London 1949

Falkus, M. E., 'The British gas industry before 1850', *EcHR* xx (1967), 494–508

Feltes, N. N., 'Community and the limits of liability in two mid-Victorian novels', *VS* xvii (1974), 355–69

Finn, M. C., *The character of credit: personal debt in English culture, 1740–1914*, Cambridge 2003

Flinn, M. W., 'The Poor Employment Act of 1817', *EcHR*, xiv (1961), 82–92.

Flint, K., *The Victorians and the visual imagination*, Cambridge 2000

Ford, P. and G. Ford, *A guide to parliamentary papers*, Oxford 1956

Freedeman, C. E., *Joint-stock enterprise in France, 1807–1867*, Chapel Hill 1979

―――― *The triumph of corporate capitalism in France, 1867–1914*, New York 1993

Freeman, M., *Railways and the Victorian imagination*, New Haven 1999

Freeman, M., R. Pearson and J. Taylor, ' "Different and better?": Scottish joint-stock companies and the law, c. 1720–1845', *EHR* cxxi (2006), forthcoming

French, E. A., 'The origin of general limited liability in the United Kingdom', *Accounting and Business Research* xxi (1990), 15–34

Fukuyama, F., *The end of history and the last man*, London 1992

Gambles, A., 'Rethinking the politics of protection: conservatism and the corn laws, 1830–1852', *EHR* cxiii (1998), 928–52

―――― *Protection and politics: Conservative economic discourse, 1815–1852*, Woodbridge 1999

Garnett, R. G., 'Robert Owen and the community experiments', in S. Pollard and J. Salt (eds), *Robert Owen, prophet of the poor*, London 1971, 39–64

Gray, D. J., 'A list of comic periodicals published in Great Britain, 1800–1900', *Victorian Periodicals Newsletter* xv (1972), 2–39

Harling, P., *The waning of "old corruption": the politics of economical reform in Britain, 1779–1846*, Oxford 1996

Harris, R., 'Political economy, interest groups, legal institutions, and the repeal of the Bubble Act in 1825', *EcHR* l (1997), 675–96

———— *Industrializing English law: entrepreneurship and business organization, 1720–1844*, Cambridge 2000

Hassan, J. A., 'The growth and impact of the British water industry in the nineteenth century', *EcHR* xxxviii (1985), 531–47

Henderson, J. P., 'Agency or alienation? Smith, Mill, and Marx on the joint-stock company', *History of Political Economy* xviii (1986), 111–31

[Hennell, T.], 'Railway finance', *QR* cxxii (Apr. 1867), 489–506.

Hilton, B., *Corn, cash, commerce: the economic policies of the Tory governments, 1815–1830*, Oxford 1977

———— *The age of atonement: the influence of evangelicalism on social and economic thought, 1785–1865*, Oxford 1988

Hodgkins, D., *The second railway king: the life and times of Sir Edward Watkin, 1819–1901*, Cardiff 2002

Hoppen, K. T., *The mid-Victorian generation, 1846–1886*, Oxford 1998

Hoppit, J., 'The myths of the South Sea Bubble', *TRHS* xii (2002), 141–65

Hughes, L. K. and M. Lund, *The Victorian serial*, Charlottesville 1991

Hunt, B. C., *The development of the business corporation in England, 1800–1867*, Cambridge, MA. 1936

Ireland, P. W., 'The rise of the limited liability company', *International Journal of the Sociology of Law* xii (1984), 239–60

———— 'Capitalism without the capitalist: the joint stock company share and the emergence of the modern doctrine of separate corporate personality', *Legal History* xvii (1996), 41–73

———— 'History, critical legal studies and the mysterious disappearance of capitalism', *Modern Law Review* lxv (2002), 120–40

Itzkowitz, D. C., 'Fair enterprise or extravagant speculation: investment, speculation, and gambling in Victorian England', *VS* xlv (2002), 121–47

James, L., *Fiction for the working man, 1830–50*, Harmondsworth 1974

Jefferys, J. B., 'The denomination and character of shares, 1855–85', *EcHR* xvi (1946), 45–55.

Jenkins, R., *Gladstone*, London 1996

Johnson, P., 'Civilizing mammon: laws, morals, and the City in nineteenth-century England', in P. Burke, B. Harrison and P. Slack (eds), *Civil histories*, Oxford 2000

Jones, A., *Powers of the press: newspapers, power and the public in nineteenth-century England*, Aldershot 1996

Jones, S. and M. Aiken, 'British companies legislation and social and political evolution during the nineteenth century', *British Accounting Review* xxvii (1995), 61–82

Killick, J. R. and W. A. Thomas, 'The provincial stock exchanges, 1830–1870', *EcHR* xxiii (1970), 96–111

Kostal, R. W., *Law and English railway capitalism, 1825–1875*, Oxford 1994

Kynaston, D., *The City of London: a world of its own, 1815–1890*, London 1995

Lenman, B., *An economic history of modern Scotland, 1660–1976*, London 1977

Lewin, H. G., *The railway mania and its aftermath, 1845–1852*, Newton Abbot 1968

Lobban, M., 'Corporate identity and limited liability in France and England, 1825–67', *Anglo-American Law Review* xxv (1996), 397–440

Loftus, D., 'Capital and community: limited liability and attempts to democratize the market in mid nineteenth-century England', *VS* xlv (2002), 93–120

Lohrl, A., *Household Words: a weekly journal, 1850–1859, conducted by Charles Dickens*, Toronto 1973

McKendrick, N., 'Literary luddism and the businessman', in P. N. Davies, *Sir Alfred Jones, shipping entrepreneur par excellence*, London 1978, pp. ix–lvi

——— ' "Gentlemen and players" revisited: the gentlemanly ideal, the business ideal and the professional ideal in English literary culture', in N. McKendrick and R. B. Outhwaite (eds), *Business life and public policy*, Cambridge 1986, 98–136

McVeagh, J., *Tradefull merchants: the portrayal of the capitalist in literature*, London 1981

Maier, P., 'The revolutionary origins of the American corporation', *William and Mary Quarterly*, 3rd ser. i (1993), 51–84

Maltby, J., 'UK joint stock companies legislation, 1844–1900: accounting publicity and "mercantile caution" ', *Accounting History* iii (1998), 9–32

Mathias, P., *The brewing industry in England, 1700–1830*, Cambridge 1959

——— *The first industrial nation*, London 1969

Michie, R. C., *Money, mania and markets: investment, company formation and the Stock Exchange in nineteenth-century Scotland*, Edinburgh 1981

Miller, A. H., 'Subjectivity Ltd: the discourse of liability in the Joint Stock Companies Act of 1856 and Gaskell's *Cranford*', *English Literary History* lxi (1994), 139–57

Millward, R., 'The political economy of urban utilities', in M. Daunton (ed.), *The Cambridge urban history of Britain*, III: *1840–1950*, Cambridge 2000, 315–50

Mirowski, P. 'The rise (and retreat) of a market: English joint-stock shares in the eighteenth century', *Journal of Economic History* xli (1981), 559–77

Monypenny, W. F., *The life of Benjamin Disraeli*, London 1929

Morgan, E. V. and W. A. Thomas, *The Stock Exchange: its history and functions*, London 1969

Morison S. (ed.), *The history of* The Times, London 1939

Muldrew, C., *The economy of obligation: the culture of credit and social relations in early modern England*, New York 1998

Munn, C. W., 'The development of joint-stock banking in Scotland, 1810–1845', in A. Slaven and D. H. Aldcroft (eds), *Business, banking and urban history: essays in honour of S. G. Checkland*, Edinburgh 1982, 112–28

——— 'The coming of joint-stock banking in Scotland and Ireland, c. 1820–1845', in T. M. Devine and D. Dickson (eds), *Ireland and Scotland, 1600–1850: parallels and contrasts and economic and social development*, Edinburgh 1983, 204–18

Napier, T. B., 'The history of joint stock and limited liability companies', in *A century of law reform: twelve lectures on the changes in the law of England during the nineteenth century*, South Hackensack 1972, 379–415

Neuburg, V. E., *Popular literature: a history and guide*, Harmondsworth 1977

Newsome, D., *The Victorian world picture: perceptions and introspections in an age of change*, London 1997

Nicoll, A., *A history of English drama, 1660–1900*, Cambridge 1952–9

Ó Gráda, C., *Ireland: a new economic history, 1780–1939*, Oxford 1995

Oppenlander, E. A., *Dickens's 'All the Year Round': descriptive index and contributor list*, Troy 1984

Parker, R. H., 'Regulating British corporate financial reporting in the late nineteenth century', *Accounting, Business and Financial History* i (1990), 51–71

Parris, H., *Government and the railways in nineteenth-century Britain*, London 1965

Payne, P. L., 'The emergence of the large-scale company in Great Britain', *EcHR* xx (1967), 519–42

―――― *The early Scottish limited companies, 1856–1895: an historical and analytical survey*, Edinburgh 1980

―――― (ed.), *Studies in Scottish business history*, London 1967

Peacock, A. J. and D. Joy, *George Hudson of York*, Clapham 1971

Pearson, R., 'Shareholder democracies? English stock companies and the politics of corporate governance during the industrial revolution', *EHR* cxvii (2002), 840–66

―――― *Insuring the industrial revolution: fire insurance in Great Britain, 1700–1850*, Aldershot 2004

Perkin, H., *Origins of modern English society*, London 1985

Pocock, J. G. A., *Virtue, commerce, and history*, Cambridge 1985

Pollard, S. and J. Salt (eds), *Robert Owen, prophet of the poor*, London 1971

Poovey, M., *Making a social body: British cultural formation, 1830–1864*, Chicago 1995

―――― 'Writing about finance in Victorian England: disclosure and secrecy in the culture of investment', *VS* xlv (2002), 17–41

―――― (ed.), *The financial system in nineteenth-century Britain*, Oxford 2003

Porter, D., ' "A trusted guide of the investing public": Harry Marks and the *Financial News*, 1884–1916', *BH* xxviii (1986), 1–17

Postan, M. M., 'Recent trends in the accumulation of capital', *EcHR* vi (1935), 1–12

Read, D., *The power of news: the history of Reuters, 1849–1989*, Oxford 1992

Redford, A., *Manchester merchants and foreign trade, 1794–1858*, Manchester 1934

Reed, J. A., 'A friend to mammon: speculation in Victorian literature', *VS* xxvii (1984), 179–202

Reed, M. C. (ed.), *Railways in the Victorian economy*, Newton Abbot 1969

Rendall, J., ' "A moral engine"? Feminism, liberalism and the *English Woman's Journal*', in J. Rendall (ed.), *Equal or different: women's politics, 1800–1914*, Oxford 1987, 112–38

Richards, P., 'R. A. Slaney, the industrial town, and early Victorian social policy', *Social History* iv (1979), 85–101

Ridley, J., *The young Disraeli*, London 1995

Robb, G., *White-collar crime in modern England: financial fraud and business morality, 1845–1929*, Cambridge 1992

Rose, N., *Powers of freedom: reframing political thought*, Cambridge 1999

Roy, W. G., *Socializing capital: the rise of the large industrial corporation in America*, Princeton 1997

Russell, N., *The novelist and mammon: literary responses to the world of commerce in the nineteenth century*, Oxford 1986

Saville, J., 'Sleeping partnership and limited liability, 1850–1856', *EcHR* viii (1956), 418–33

Scott, W. R., *The constitution and finance of English, Scottish and Irish joint-stock companies to 1720*, New York 1951

Searle, G. R., *Corruption in British politics, 1895–1930*, Oxford 1987

—— *Entrepreneurial politics in mid-Victorian Britain*, Oxford 1993

—— *Morality and the market in Victorian Britain*, Oxford 1998

Seavoy, R. E., *The origins of the American business corporation, 1784–1855*, Westport, CT 1982

Shannon, H. A., 'The coming of general limited liability', *Economic History* ii (1931), 267–91

—— 'The first five thousand limited companies and their duration', *Economic History* iii (1932), 396–424

Shattock, J. and M. Wolff (eds), *The Victorian periodical press: samplings and soundings*, Leicester 1982

Smart, W., *Economic annals of the nineteenth century*, New York 1964

Smith, G. and A. Smith., 'Dickens as a popular artist', *TD* lxvii (1971), 131–44

Steig, M., '*Dombey and Son* and the railway panic of 1845', *TD* lxvii (1971), 145–8

Sutherland, J., *The Stanford companion to Victorian fiction*, Stanford 1989

Taylor, J., 'Private property, public interest, and the role of the state in nineteenth-century Britain: the case of the lighthouses', *Historical Journal* xliv (2001), 749–71

—— 'Greed: the way they lived then', *BBC History Magazine* ii (Dec. 2001), 40–2

—— 'The joint stock company in politics', in M. J. Turner (ed.), *Reform and reformers in nineteenth-century Britain*, Sunderland 2004, 99–116

—— 'Commercial fraud and public men in Victorian Britain', *Historical Research* lxxvii (2005), 230–52

Thompson, N., *The real rights of man: political economies for the working class, 1775–1850*, London 1998

Todd, G., 'Some aspects of joint stock companies, 1844–1900', *EcHR* iv (1932), 46–71

Trela, D. J., 'Thomas Carlyle On *trades-unions, promoterism and the signs of the times*: an unknown and nearly unpublished manuscript', *Victorians Institute Journal* xxv (1997), 230–50

Trentmann, F. 'Political culture and political economy: interest, ideology and free trade', *Review of International Political Economy* v (1998), 217–51

—— 'National identity and consumer politics: free trade and tariff reform', in P. O'Brien and D. Winch (eds), *The political economy of British historical experience, 1688–1914*, Oxford 2002, 187–214

Walker, D. M., *A legal history of Scotland*, Edinburgh 1988–2001

Walker, S. P., '*Laissez-faire*, collectivism and companies legislation in nineteenth-century Britain', *British Accounting Review* xxviii (1996), 305–24

—— 'More sherry and sandwiches? Incrementalism and the regulation of late Victorian bank auditing', *Accounting History* iii (1998), 33–54

Weiss, B., *The hell of the English: bankruptcy and the Victorian novel*, Lewisburg 1986

Wiener, M. J., *English culture and the decline of the industrial spirit, 1850–1980*, Cambridge 1981

Williams, O. C., *The historical development of private bill procedure and standing orders in the House of Commons*, London 1948

Williams, T. I., *A history of the British gas industry*, Oxford 1981

Winter, J., *Robert Lowe*, Toronto 1976

Unpublished theses

Glick, D., 'The movement for partnership law reform, 1830–1907', PhD diss. Lancaster 1990

Harris, R., 'Industrialization without free incorporation: the legal framework of business organization in England, 1720–1844', PhD diss. Columbia 1994

Hudson, S. J., 'Attitudes to investment risk amongst West Midland canal and railway company investors, 1760–1850', PhD diss. Warwick 2001

Jefferys, J. B., 'Trends in business organisation in Great Britain since 1856', PhD diss. London 1938

Loftus, D., 'Social economy: cultures of work and community in mid-Victorian England', PhD diss. Southampton 1998

Taylor, J., 'Transport, *laissez-faire*, and government policy in Britain in the first half of the nineteenth century', MA diss. Kent 1999

Index